DogSmart

DogSmart

The Ultimate Guide for
Finding the Dog You Want and
Keeping the Dog You Find

Myrna Milani, D.V.M.

CB
CONTEMPORARY BOOKS

Library of Congress Cataloging-in-Publication Data

Milani, Myrna M.
    DogSmart : the ultimate guide for finding the dog you want and keeping the dog you find / Myrna Milani.
       p.   cm.
    Includes index.
    ISBN 0-8092-3150-6
    1. Dogs.   2. Dogs—Selection.   3. Dog breeds.   I. Title.
SF426.M55   1997
636.7—dc21
                                                                              97-10646
                                                                              CIP

Interior design by Mary Lockwood

To two of the brightest stars in the human-canine
bond constellation: William E. Campbell, behaviorist and
wonderful colleague, for sharing so much all these years,
and the late Job Michael Evans, trainer and most special friend

Contents

Introduction

When David and Jodi Hollinger get their new Dalmatian pup, Elmo, they vow to do everything right.

"Too many of our friends own dogs with behavioral or medical problems that arose because they didn't get off to a good start," Jodi explains. "They didn't realize it takes time and effort to do it right."

"And it takes money, too," David adds. "That's why Jodi and I saved up until we could buy Elmo the best of everything. Plus we intend to devote the entire summer to making him the perfect pup."

By taking advantage of their company's flexible workweek plan and their vacation time, the Hollingers rarely leave Elmo at home alone during the next three months. They hire the most famous trainer in the state to give their new pup private lessons; Elmo eats the highest-quality food and receives state-of-the-art medical care when needed. By the time the Hollingers resume their normal lifestyle in September, they feel convinced that their now five-month-old Dalmatian and they will become the envy of every dog owner they know. One week, two chewed books, three shredded plants, and four puddles of urine later they decide their beloved new pet has developed some rare form of canine brain disease. "What else could it be?" Jodi wails in distress. "We did everything right!"

When I first began working with problem dogs and their owners more than 20 years ago, it all seemed so simple. At the time, I thought designing a training, exercise, feeding, and health-care program that would meet the needs of increasingly busy dog owners would solve all of their problems. So did a lot of other trainers and behaviorists, and over the years a steady stream of books, videos, and even computer programs has analyzed every conceivable aspect of contemporary dog ownership.

However, in our quest to develop the right method to select a new puppy or dog as well as the right training, exercise, feeding, and health-care programs, we overlooked one crucial fact: not only does each owner, dog, and environment exhibit unique characteristics, they also form a unique unit that continually changes.

One of my favorite truisms states that if you don't know where you're going, any road will get you there. The Hollingers chose "the most expensive road" because it made the most sense to them. Other new owners pick what they consider the fastest road, or one recommended by four out of five movie stars or veterinarians or Lassie's mother. When it works, it does so because that particular method happens to meet that particular owner's and that particular dog's needs. When it doesn't, most likely it fails to address human and/or canine needs that the owners didn't even think about before. I know I certainly didn't give a whole lot of thought to any exceptions when I used to formulate my "one-size-fits-all" rules.

When I work with the owner of a problem dog now, I try to help that person understand what the dog communicates through its behavior (including its health), as well as what the owner communicates to the dog through his or her responses. I begin by couching this in terms of the sciences of the human-animal bond and ethology (animal behavior), then focus on the relationship between that one particular owner and one special dog in their unique environment. With this accomplished, I help the owner work out a program to solve the problem in a way that will meet his or her specific needs.

Over the years, more than a few people have asked, "Is there some book that tells me all this?" and I always answered, "No, because each owner and dog is different." A book describing a program that holds true for the Hollingers and Elmo might not hold true for another couple and their Dalmatian, or if the Hollingers had chosen a golden retriever instead, or even an adult Dalmatian or a female instead of a male pup. Further, any program I outline for them today might not work next month if David gets laid off, or if the couple suffers marital strife or trades in their downtown apartment for a home in suburbia.

Nonetheless, I've often asked myself: Would it be possible to write a book that would enable prospective or new dog owners to analyze all of the crucial variables for themselves, and then use that knowledge to select the best dog and the best programs to meet their and their new dog's specific needs from the ever-enlarging ocean of options?

Would it be possible for owners to construct a personalized knowledge base that could change and grow as they and their dogs change and grow?

It seemed to me it would be possible given the fulfillment of two conditions: an objective presentation of the material and a willingness on the reader's part to work through the most intimate as well as the most common aspects of dog ownership. That was the genesis of *DogSmart*.

In order to accomplish my goals for this book, I use anecdotes in each chapter that place a wide variety of owners in a broad range of situations with many different breeds. While some of these anecdotes represent specific owners and dogs I've known over the years (including myself and my own pets), others portray a composite of numerous pets and owners in order to illustrate a particular point more clearly.

If personal experience and input from owners and other professionals indicate that a particular approach deserves consideration in a particular situation—such as fast-paced training for fast-paced dogs, withholding food and water from a dog with diarrhea, or assembling a disaster kit—I mention it. Similarly, if personal experience and input from others indicate that one option will work better than another under certain circumstances, I point that out, too. For example, while the Hollingers' idea of investing more time in Elmo to provide him with a good beginning makes sense superficially, this approach runs so contrary to their regular schedule that they wind up training him twice—once to meet the artificial ideal they created for him during their first three months together, and the second time to meet their real needs. Consequently, and in spite of the soundness of the theory behind the first approach, the Hollingers would have fared much better had they chosen a program that they could incorporate into their existing lifestyle rather than changing their lifestyle to fit the program.

While I did strive for objectivity, sometimes I didn't succeed. Several times during the writing of this book, my agent, editor, and dear friend, Michael Snell, would ask me for more concrete "quick tips" and "how-tos" to speed new dog owners on their way. Sometimes I could do it, but other times, I couldn't. We reached a crisis in the chapters on training and training aids, two subjects near and dear to my heart.

As I tried to put some order into the mind-boggling array of available training methods and devices, and reconcile these with increased reports of canine aggression and my unshakable belief in the inextricable relationship between the canine mind and body, I couldn't shake my equally firm belief that quick fixes create or worsen far more problems than they cure. However, unlike nonveterinarians proposing or condoning such approaches who then can walk away from the owner and animal if the quick fix doesn't work, I feel professionally and morally obligated to euthanize those animals, if necessary, when the problem irreparably damages the human-canine relationship. That obligation, above all others, led me to scrutinize every quick fix or miracle cure, and to clearly define which ones will—and won't—work for what kinds of owners and dogs, when, where, how, and why.

As I mentioned, in addition to presenting the latest bond and behavioral data and the many options available to contemporary dog owners as objectively as possible, I believed a book like this would require that readers be willing to work through the most intimate as well as the most common aspects of dog ownership. Michael and I anguished over this, too. Would the length of the book and the work involved turn off some readers? My answer to that came when a trainer who loves my books sighed, "But Myrna Milani writes for people with brains. If only all my clients had brains." After I stopped laughing enough that I could think clearly again, I pondered that statement and came to some conclusions.

First, I don't write for the dog-owning intelligentsia, but I do write for people who want to stretch the limits of their relationships with their dogs. In fact, some of the greatest insights shared with me about such considerations as humans' orientations toward animals; owners' time, financial, emotional, and physical limits; the effects of the environment; and the owners' leadership style on the human-canine relationship come from people whose lives would strike many observers as less than optimal: single moms trying to create a quality life for kids, dogs, and themselves on a shoestring; owners with AIDS, chronic fatigue syndrome, or chronic depression; senior citizens with limited income and/or physical ability; and 10-year-olds desperately clinging to a beloved dog no one else in the household can stand. Although I don't mind writing for dog owners with brains, I like to think I write books for dog owners with hearts, too.

To help you get your brain and your heart on the right track, I divided the book into two parts. In Part I, "Finding the Dog

You Want," the first chapter helps you explore your orientation toward dogs, and any financial, time, emotional, or physical limits that may affect your relationship with your new pet. Although the Hollingers enjoy their new pup, they view him as a possession they hope will make their dog-owning friends envious. What advantages and disadvantages does this view offer over one in which we see our dogs as our fur-covered babies?

The next chapter attempts to put some order into the chaos of purebred dogs. Twenty years ago, I used to differentiate medical, behavioral, and bond problems. Now, thanks to the increased research on the bond and the mind-body effect, I realize that every canine medical problem contains both a behavioral and a bond component, and every canine behavioral problem takes its toll on the animal's health and its relationship with the owner. Consequently, we need to know what goes on in a prospective dream dog's mind as well as its body, so we can determine if its needs coincide with our own.

In the third chapter, you'll answer the question, "What makes my house a home for me and my new dog?" Because the Hollingers don't think about Elmo's environmental needs beyond getting him his own bed, they don't see their house from the pup's point of view: establishing and protecting his territory looms as his—and all dogs'—most powerful drive. Owners who fail to take this into account can inadvertently create pets who bark and chew at the table leg or themselves out of boredom or fear, or leave piles and puddles by the front and back doors— or even on the owner's bed.

In the last chapter of Part I, we explore the fascinating subject of human-canine pack structure. In my experience, more than 90 percent of all canine problems, and more than 99 percent of those involving aggression, result from a lack of human leadership in the human-canine pack. Are we really doing our dogs a favor by treating them as our best friends? We accept many dominant canine displays in the name of love, but do we do it because we really feel this way, or because we find it easier than accepting the responsibility that goes with true leadership?

In each of the four chapters, exercises give you the opportunity to apply the principles discussed to yourself and your particular situation. The more time you spend on these, the more specific information you'll gain about your own unique requirements. If you find yourself thinking you don't have time to complete the exercises, you might want to ask yourself how you'll ever find time to establish and maintain a quality relationship with a dog.

In Part II, "Keeping the Dog You Find," you'll apply everything you learned about yourself, your dream dog, your environment, and your leadership style to the selection of training, exercise, feeding, and health-care programs that will best meet your and your new dog's needs. Each of these chapters also suggests other sources of information you may find helpful and explores the advantages and disadvantages of the various options. The costs given in the financial discussion of each program reflect averages calculated from pet stores, wholesale and retail mail-order catalogs, pet superstores, veterinary clinics, feed stores, and department stores such as Wal-Mart and K mart. Although I believe that most discussions provide a fairly accurate picture, sometimes prices for an item varied so widely that I felt like the woman with her head in the freezer and feet in the oven whose average temperature was normal. Because of this, it definitely pays to comparison shop, and these chapters suggest what to look for when you do.

The exercises in Part II give you the chance to review the particular programs that appeal to you in light of what you learned about yourself and your dream dog in the first part of the book. The Hollingers send Elmo to the most expensive trainer in the state, oblivious to the fact that the trainer uses methods they could never use at home, given their orientation toward dogs and their lifestyle. Likewise, they pick a wonderfully nutritious, balanced diet for their new pup, but the long drive required to purchase the horrendously expensive food puts such a strain on their tight schedule and budget that the harm this feeding program does to their relationship far outweighs any good the diet might do to Elmo's body.

The book concludes with a description of an at-home physical, behavioral, and bond health checkup you can accomplish in two minutes with a little practice, one you can constantly update to meet your own and your dog's changing needs.

"Why didn't you put the two-minute check in the first chapter?" the frazzled Hollingers, eager for a quick fix to solve Elmo's present and future problems, want to know.

While we all desire instant gratification, I chose the placement specifically because the speed and accuracy with which you can conduct this examination depends on your understanding of all the concepts discussed earlier in the book. A recurrent theme throughout the pages ahead is that dog owners can't determine abnormal if they don't know normal first. Just as the Hollingers will miss the early signs of an ear, eye, or gum infection because they don't know what Elmo's healthy ears, eyes, and gums look like, they'll also miss early signs of problems in his behavior and their relationship if they don't understand the basics that underlie these, too.

Owners who experience less than optimal relationships with their dogs often make comments such as, "If only I'd known how much my dog's breed (my job, the kids, my boyfriend, the other dog, my landlord, my neighbors, my training and exercise programs, etc.) would affect everything, I never would have done what I did." In other words, if they'd known where they wanted to go—toward a lifelong rewarding relationship with a healthy, well-behaved animal within the context of their own busy lives—they would have chosen a different road to get there.

No book can cover all the roads available. However, the chapters ahead can help you construct a compass based on solid knowledge of yourself, your dream dog, your environment, and your leadership style, and define what a rewarding human-canine relationship means to you. Given that awareness, you can then chart a course and select the programs that not only will allow you to achieve this goal, but also enable you and your new dog to enjoy each other's company every step of the way.

DOGSMART

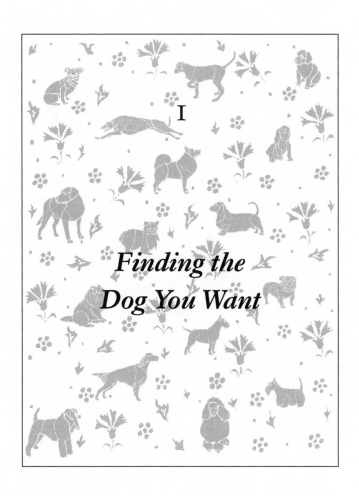

I

Finding the Dog You Want

I

In a Mirror Dimly

*How Our Orientations Toward Dogs
Influence Our Relationships with Them*

Terri Shackley, Bruce Graham, and Elaine Cowan all get their
rottweilers from the same breeder, a woman famous for
breeding intelligent animals with excellent temperaments.
Although all three owners tell the breeder they want a dog
primarily for companionship, each of them defines that word
differently. Terri, an unmarried social worker, wants an animal on
which she can lavish attention evenings and weekends; Bruce, a
medical technician who lives alone on the edge of an unsavory
neighborhood, wants a self-sufficient dog for protection; and
Elaine wants a pet to keep her latchkey kids company. By the time
the littermates' third birthdays roll around, Terri's now-obese pet,
Kemper, suffers from one ailment after another, and Bruce has
given his dog, Turbo, up to a rescue group after the dog menaced
his four-year-old nephew. Of the three animals, only Elaine's Barney
seems destined to enjoy a long and happy life with his owner.

Three quite similar pups, three different owners, and three
radically different outcomes. How did it happen? The answer
stems in part from the different orientations that people main-

tain toward dogs in our society. Every day another new training program, device, or drug adds to the already bewildering array of products promising to turn even the worst doggy demons into saints. New medical and surgical techniques rivaling those used in human medicine offer our canine best friends an increasingly good chance to enjoy a 15-year life span, while a mind-boggling assortment of diets and exercise programs help guarantee they'll spend those years fit and trim.

Against this rosy background, many owners and dogs play out a much grimmer reality. Euthanasia still ranks as a primary cause of canine death, with owners citing behavioral problems as the primary reason for getting rid of their pets. More and more insurers nationwide add a surcharge or deny home owner's insurance entirely to owners of pit bulls, rottweilers, Dobermans, German shepherd dogs, Akitas, chows, and other breeds with reputations—deserved or not—for aggression. Obesity and other nutritional problems continue to plague more than a third of our pets, in spite of all those wonderful new exercise and dietary options designed to meet every dog's needs. A 1994 study by Purdue veterinarians Gary Patronek and Larry Glickman estimates the mortality rate of dogs in the United States at 12.4 percent; that translates into an average canine life span of 8 years rather than the expected 15, in spite of some extraordinary advances in veterinary science and medicine.

How can this be?

To some extent, we can blame it on an embarrassment of riches for us and our canine companions. Various studies indicate that the average person can keep track of five to seven different objects or concepts simultaneously. For instance, given a minute to memorize a list of 20 names, most of us automatically focus our attention on five to seven of these and ignore the rest. The same phenomenon befalls Terri, Bruce, and Elaine when they walk into a bookstore: they see so many different books and videos on canine training and care that they don't know where to begin.

Our often hectic lifestyles further complicate this process. Like the person given one minute to memorize those 20 names, Bruce and Terri can steal only a few minutes from their lunch hours to leaf through all those books; Elaine tries to fit it in between a business meeting and picking up one of the kids at school for a dental appointment. Is it any wonder so many people wind up trying to shoehorn themselves and their dogs into programs that don't meet either their own or their pets' needs?

"Unless you can give me five extra hours in my day, I don't see how I can ever own a well-trained dog," Bruce says mournfully as he looks at old photos of himself with the dog he gave up.

"While you're at it," Terri adds, stuffing yet another pill down Kemper's throat, "I could use a little extra cash in my checking account to pay for all this state-of-the-art medical treatment, too."

Like Bruce and Terri, many owners blame their pets' problems on a lack of time or money. However, while treating problems can take a great deal of time and cost a great deal of money, *preventing* problems requires relatively little of either.

"I'm a single mom with a limited budget and not a lot of spare time who wanted a dog as much as my kids did," Elaine describes her not unusual situation. "I couldn't afford not to know how a dog would fit into our lives before I got one."

Elaine's observation and subsequent success with Barney underscore one of the most commonly overlooked truths about pet ownership: *The vast majority of problems people experience with their pets result from a lack of knowledge, not a lack of time, money, or love.*

In the pages ahead we're going to look at the four factors that form the cornerstones of every human-canine relationship:

- the owner
- the dog

- the environment
- the human-canine social structure

Then we'll apply this knowledge to the selection of the training, exercise, feeding, and medical programs that will best fit an owner's and animal's specific needs.

Throughout this process, I'll ask you to stop and consider these aspects of dog ownership as they specifically relate to you and your own household. If you do, by the time you finish the book you'll know exactly how to establish your own solid human-canine foundation and select the programs that are best for you and your new dog.

Let's begin with some "want lists."

Dream Dog Want List

Make a list of the qualities you envision in your perfect dog. Include categories such as breed, sex, age, temperament, and color. If you think a mixed breed could meet your needs, include qualities such as the animal's adult size and type of coat.

If you plan to get an older dog (more than four months of age), don't forget to note any preferences about sexual status. Because neutering both males and females before sexual maturity confers significant health and behavioral benefits, I strongly recommend that prospective owners get the complete medical and behavioral histories of any intact (unneutered) animals who capture their fancy before making a final decision. If you desire to breed your new dog, include complete medical and behavioral histories of the dream dog's parents on the want list, too.

For example, under "Training" Terri notes her strong dislike of the use of corporal punishment and a desire for a program she can accomplish at home. Make your lists as specific and detailed as possible because the more you know about what you want, the easier it will be to find an animal and programs to meet those needs.

Dream Program Want List

List the four basic programs—Training, Exercise, Feeding, Medical—that will exert the greatest influence over your relationship with your dog and record any characteristics you consider "must haves" in each category.

The Dog in the Mirror

Most people typically assume one of three orientations toward dogs:

- dogs viewed as people (anthropomorphic orientation)
- dogs viewed as objects (chattel orientation)
- dogs viewed as limited partners (integrated orientation)

Traditionally scientists accused people who related *any* animal behavior to any similar human behavior of anthropomorphism, which they viewed as the scientific equivalent of a mortal sin. A typical stereotype in the companion-animal arena depicted a middle-aged, overweight, frizzy-haired woman babbling baby talk to an aging, overweight, frizzy poodle. Notwithstanding such extremes, most of us treat our pets anthropomorphically from time to time. In fact, in a 1995 survey of pet owners conducted by the American Animal Hospital Association, 61 percent of the dog owners surveyed said they consider their pets "children." Moreover, it seems safe to say that *all* dog owners occasionally treat their animals anthropomorphically, depending on the dog's behavior.

"No way!" Bruce vigorously protests. "I like dogs that act like dogs, and that's how I treat them. You'll never see me with a dog wearing a sweater!"

That may be true, but let's ask Bruce why he didn't have Turbo neutered at six months as both the breeder and his veterinarian recommended.

"Well, geez, I can see neutering a female so she doesn't have pups, but what kind of a life would that be for a male? It would ruin him."

Bruce's highly anthropomorphic response doesn't strike him that way. Like most dog owners, he lacks a clear idea of what constitutes anthropomorphic behavior, primarily because many in the scientific community can't agree on it, either. But thanks to a decade of human-animal bond and ethology (animal behavior) studies, our view of anthropomorphism has changed dramatically. Historically, most scientists publicly (if not necessarily privately) supported the definition of animals as nonthinking, nonfeeling machines proposed by René Descartes in the seventeenth century. This view didn't rest on any scientific data, but rather represented these early scientists' attempts to keep the Church from interfering with science or, more specifically, the scientists themselves. Those who dared attribute human qualities to animals quickly earned their colleagues' wrath for the simple reason that doing so could cost them all their jobs, if not their lives.

Given this dual censure by the Church as well as the scientific community, we can appreciate how the ban against anthropomorphism became so firmly entrenched. Now, however, an increasing number of studies in the field of animal consciousness by reputable scientists have slowly but surely undermined this view. At the same time, human-animal bond studies continually add to the list of physical and psychological effects animals can produce in humans, and vice versa. In the 1980s, research proved that the presence of a dog could lower human blood pressure and increase the survival rate of some heart-attack victims. Almost daily, new studies demonstrate how pets can positively affect a wide spectrum of human conditions from cholesterol and triglyceride levels to the development of social skills and concern for others of all species.

As the line between what it means to be human and what it means to be animal becomes fuzzier, so does the definition of anthropomorphism. More and more scientists insist that there's nothing wrong with using human terms to explain animal behaviors that resemble human ones. Nonetheless, problems can and do arise when humans project their own beliefs onto animals without any regard to the source of those beliefs.

Let's consider what happens to Terri Shackley and her dog, Kemper.

"Ouch, that really hurt!" Terri yelps in surprise and pain when she slams the door on her finger. When Terri accidentally slams the door on Kemper's paw and he howls, she believes he experiences the identical feelings.

In this situation, the connection Terri makes between her own response and her dog's strikes most of us as reasonable, even if some scientists might condemn it as anthropomorphic. However, let's take a look at what happens next.

"Those pills the doctor gave me for my finger made it feel a lot better, so I'm going to give you one of them, too," Terri tells Kemper as she hunts through the medicine chest for the container of prescription painkiller. "Then we'll go pick up the pizza."

Although dogs and humans can take some of the same medications, Terri's belief that what works safely for her will automatically also benefit her pet backfires. Instead of making Kemper more comfortable, the drug causes him to vomit explosively, and Terri winds up rushing him to the emergency clinic instead of the pizza parlor.

Another example of how Terri's anthropomorphic views can create problems occurs when Kemper's limp persists three days after the door-slamming incident.

"I know you're just limping to make me feel guilty about hurting you," Terri chides the dog.

This particular anthropomorphic evaluation of Kemper's behavior may or may not be accurate. Because dogs, like people, respond to conditioning, if Terri babied Kemper and gave him special treats whenever he limped (yelped, looked at her a certain way, sighed, trembled during his veterinary examination), the dog would quickly learn to exhibit those behaviors whenever he wanted attention. If Terri used this technique to get a little sympathy herself, her belief that her dog limps merely to get her attention would make even more sense to her.

However, suppose that, even though Terri sustained only a minor injury when she slammed the door on herself, she broke several bones in Kemper's paw when she did the same thing to him. Under those circumstances, Terri's anthropomorphic view would cause her pet to suffer needlessly and possibly end up with a truly serious problem.

"Great!" groans Terri. "How can I tell whether my views reflect good or bad anthropomorphism?"

The answer to that brings us back to *knowledge*. Some ethologists use the term *empathy* or *accurate empathy* to describe the intimate awareness of an animal's behavior that's necessary to legitimately equate it to that of a human under similar circumstances. In order to know whether what we attribute to an animal represents an accurate evaluation of its true state or a projection of our own beliefs, we need to know everything we can about that species and that individual. If Terri knows little or nothing about dogs in general, rottweilers in particular, and especially Kemper, she doesn't treat him like a person out of love; she treats him like a person out of ignorance.

The dog itself can serve as the best indicator of the quality of any anthropomorphic views imposed upon it. Owners who share empathic relationships with their dogs also share stable relationships with them. Although this alone doesn't guarantee either a healthy or a well-behaved dog, it does help guarantee that the dog will act in a way that the owner finds acceptable.

Consider obese animal-owner combinations, for instance. If Terri accepts her own extra pounds, she would need a compelling reason not to accept Kemper's. As a veterinarian who has encountered this situation in both medical and behavioral practice, I can report that even the fact that the situation poses a threat to the dog's life often won't induce some owners to change their beliefs. In terms of the human-canine bond, the dog's condition validates the owner's: those who correct their animal's bad habits often rightfully fear that they'll lose their validation for their own. Naturally, the ideal, most trouble-free relationship pairs an owner whose anthropomorphic responses toward dogs arise from knowledge, with an animal whose breed and temperament enable it to meet those human expectations.

Anthropomorphic Analysis

Note any of the items on your dream dog and program lists that carry a strong positive or negative emotional charge. Study these carefully and determine which ones result from your knowledge of dogs; label these "KA" for "knowledge-based anthropomorphism." Place an "EA" for "emotion-based anthropomorphism" beside those that arise from feelings based only on your own human experience.

If Terri believes female dogs make better pets because she read up on this subject and discussed it with owners or breeders of the kinds of dogs she likes, then she would put a "KA" beside this preference. However, if she wants a female because she finds it easier to get along with the women than the men with whom she works, that same entry would rate an "EA."

Bear in mind that this isn't a test with right and wrong answers. Think of it as a do-it-yourself self-evaluation to help you develop a clear understanding of how you relate to dogs, and of the advantages and disadvantages of that orientation for any existing or future relationship with any pet you may own.

Dogs as Objects

Most dog lovers find the idea of treating animals as objects or chattel totally unacceptable because they equate this approach with inhumane treatment and abuse. However, much abuse actually results from anthropomorphism because abusive owners project their anger and frustration about their own human inadequacies onto their animals. Those who treat dogs as chattel, on the other hand, display little, if any, emotion toward the animal.

Consider the case of Bruce Graham, who went to a first-rate breeder and paid top dollar for a rottweiler after he read an article that listed the breed among those most likely to deter burglars and other criminals. He went about the purchase of a dog with the same cool detachment that characterized the replacement of the furnace in his newly gentrified home mere blocks from a high-crime area. Based on the article, Bruce chose the biggest male in the litter, then named the dog Turbo five days later when a co-worker asked him the dog's name and he said the first thing that came to mind rather than admit he'd never given it a thought. Turbo received all his vaccinations on schedule, attended and did well in obedience class, and ate the highest-quality food. However, even though Bruce gave his dog the best of everything that money could buy, he treated the dog like an animated piece of furniture.

"That's terrible!" exclaims Terri, voicing a sentiment shared by many dog lovers who consider such an attitude callous and inhumane.

Nonetheless, even the best owners succumb to this orientation occasionally. When a high fever of unknown origin puts Terri's mother in the hospital, Terri doesn't even think about her pet until her mother's condition stabilizes two days later. Other owners tell tales of coming home with a splitting headache after a grueling day at work only to encounter a letter from the Internal Revenue Service. They can barely remember if they fed the dog at all, let alone what they fed it and when.

Do situations arise in which the chattel orientation could benefit the dog as well as the owner? Many dog lovers would rush to insist that no circumstances could *ever* warrant such a human response. However, let's ask that same question using slightly different terminology: Can you imagine a situation in which your dog would benefit if you viewed it *objectively*?

"Oh, absolutely," Bruce volunteers immediately. "Once when I was visiting my sister, her dog got hit by a car. She totally freaked out, and that so frightened the dog he wouldn't hold still, and all that movement made his injuries even worse. I finally had to send her into the house so I could calm the dog down and get him to the vet's."

But what about Bruce's orientation toward his own dog? How did he feel when it caused him to give his pet up?

"I know now that the way I related to Turbo did contribute to his problems, but I think it was definitely to his advantage that I could view the situation objectively when he snapped at my nephew. Otherwise I might have enrolled him in some training program I wasn't committed to because I felt guilty. Worse, I might have given in to my sister's demands that I put him down," Bruce frankly admits. "But because I could put my emotions on hold, I could give him up to people who can give him what he needs and find him a good home."

Bruce's story contains an interesting paradox about human orientations toward animals. When the going really gets rough, sometimes the greater the owners' emotional involvement, the less beneficial the support they can give the animal just when it needs it the most. Thus, as we saw with the anthropomorphic orientation, the success of the chattel orientation depends on the owner's knowledge. When Bruce was faced with an injured animal, his medical knowledge enabled him to respond with cool objectivity and save the animal's life. However, when he routinely assumed that orientation toward Turbo, his ignorance of the human-canine bond and its effects precipitated a relationship-shattering disaster for himself and his pet.

Once again we see how an orientation that may superficially appear black or white in reality offers owners a wide range of options—provided they possess the knowledge to recognize and use these options properly.

Chattel Check

Take another look at your descriptions of the ideal dog and its training and other programs. This time put a "KC" next to those qualities you believe represent a chattel orientation based on knowledge, and an "EC" next to those that reflect a desire to distance yourself from that particular aspect of pet ownership.

For example, if you indicated that you don't particularly care about the breed because you've spent a great deal of time around dogs and find many breeds and mixes acceptable, put "KC" after that response. However, if you don't care because you're getting a dog only because the kids want one, put "EC" beside that entry.

"Isn't an 'emotional chattel' view an oxymoron?" Bruce wants to know.

In a way, yes. But it also springs from a feeling that no need exists to learn more about this particular subject, and that should serve as a warning flag.

Again, bear in mind that no right or wrong answers exist. Given that more than 50 million dogs populate this country's households, it seems safe to say there's a dog to meet just about any prospective owner's needs—provided that person has a clear idea of what those needs are.

The Integrated Human-Canine Partnership

When I first began writing about human-canine relationships, I referred to the third human orientation toward dogs as the "bonded orientation" and both naively and romantically presented it as *the* way to relate to a dog. I've since renamed it the *integrated orientation* for several reasons. First, referring to an orientation as "bonded" implies that people who relate to animals in any other way don't form bonds with them. However, if *any* kind of a relationship exists, then some kind of bond exists. So, all relationships are bonded ones to some degree, and some bonds may be more stable and beneficial than others.

Second, you may count me among those trainers and veterinarians who at one time naively believed we could *create* a solid bond between an owner and an animal simply by making or keeping that animal well behaved and healthy. That illusion lasted until surveys of owners indicated that we experts had it backwards: the presence of a solid bond between owner and pet leads owners to seek help when problems with the pets arise, not vice versa. While improving an animal's health and behavior may enhance a relationship, it can't create a bond if one doesn't exist. Even more confounding, a solid and stable bond can actually cause owners to accept even the worst behavior or medical problems in their pets. Put another way, love can make us as blind to our dogs' faults as it does to those of the people we love.

I opted to use the term *integrated* to describe the orientation because people who adopt this as their primary orientation integrate an awareness of their own and their dogs' limits into the relationship. Although all owners place limits on their relationships with their dogs, those who use this orientation acknowledge that such limits exist, and they consciously set ones that best meet their own and their dogs' needs. Unlike proponents of the anthropomorphic and chattel orientations, people who adopt this approach seek to define the boundaries of the relationship rather than increase or decrease their emotional involvement with the animal.

What kinds of limits do owners who use this approach impose? Most fall into one of four broad categories:

- financial
- time
- emotional
- physical

As with the other two orientations, the integrated orientation has the potential to either undermine or enhance a given relationship. And once again knowledge of ourselves, our dogs, and the orientation plays a critical role in the outcome.

To see how this works, let's observe what happens to Terri and Kemper when she unwittingly establishes a limit that runs counter to her reality.

"I don't care how much it costs to find the cause," Terri insists, dismissing her veterinarian's efforts to discuss the costs involved when Kemper experiences periodic bouts of diarrhea. "The sky's the limit when it comes to my dog's health."

Three weeks later when Terri receives the final results of an extensive battery of tests along with the bill for these services, the shock just about sends her into orbit herself.

"There goes my vacation!" she wails.

Terri made her sky's-the-limit decision based on two anthropomorphic beliefs:

- She would want everything done for herself in a similar situation.
- Cost is no object because her employer provides excellent medical insurance coverage.

A third, even more rarely acknowledged, belief also comes into play:

- Though Terri thought she wanted state-of-the-art medical treatment for her dog, she didn't realize that her veterinarian had access to—and would utilize—many of the same highly sophisticated and expensive options available in human medicine.

I can still recall the shock of clients touring the medical practice where I worked when they discovered we used gas anesthesia on the majority of our patients because it offered greater safety and shorter recovery time compared with (less-expensive) injectable anesthetics. They would have felt much more shocked had I told them we used one particularly safe anesthetic gas rarely used in human hospitals because it was too expensive!

Like my clients, Terri didn't realize just how high the veterinary sky could be when she set it as her limit. When her veterinarian tried to tell her about the more than 120 known causes of canine diarrhea and that the tests for some of the rarer ones would cost a small fortune, Terri refused to listen. Nor did she want to hear that keeping a record of what Kemper ate for a few weeks might help prove that her habit of feeding him scraps from her own plate, rather than any disease, was causing the problem. However, when all the tests came back negative along with that huge bill, Terri wished she hadn't given in to her emotions when she established her limits.

Now let's revisit Bruce and Turbo to see how a desire not to become emotionally involved with an animal also can affect our limits.

"I breed my dogs to perform a wide range of functions," the breeder boasts as Bruce writes out the check for his new pup. "All my breeding stock have championships in obedience and agility, and they routinely visit local nursing homes and hospitals."

"That's nice," Bruce replies politely. "How much bigger will this pup get?"

This brief exchange offers telling evidence that the breeder and Bruce maintain very different ideas regarding the limits of this dog and any relationship with it. The breeder's boast clearly defines Turbo as a dog with both great intelligence and a strong sense of function. For the pet owner, this should translate, "If you don't give this dog something to do with all that potential, he'll find something himself." Meanwhile, Bruce sees the pup almost strictly in terms of its ability to scare off criminals. He trains Turbo to the point at which he can trust the dog not to destroy the house in his absence, and he provides the rottweiler with quality food and medical care. However, he does all this to protect his investment—in both his home and the dog—and not because he cares about the animal.

In both of these situations, a lack of knowledge assaults the owners on four fronts:

- They don't clearly understand their own orientations toward dogs.
- They don't recognize the limits they place on their relationship with the dog.
- They don't recognize their dog's limits.
- They don't recognize how their own and their dog's limits combine to form the matrix that holds the relationship together.

To keep this from happening to you and your dog, let's examine the human limits that exert the greatest influence in the human-canine relationship.

The Money Trap

If 61 percent of us think of our dogs as family members, that immediately puts us in a bind relative to any financial limits we might place on the relationship. After all, surely only the most despicable parents would put a dollar value on their kids and their care. Moreover, all too many professionals in the animal care industry strongly reinforce this notion, albeit more often for bottom-line than "family values" reasons. Nonetheless, according to the *U.S. Pet Ownership & Demographics Sourcebook* (American Veterinary Medical Association, 1993) more than a third of households with annual incomes between $12,500 and $60,000 include a dog. In addition, young, middle-aged, and older parents own more dogs than any other life-stage group, which means that many of those incomes must meet the needs of children as well as pets. So, even though most dog owners would like to say that money is no object when it comes to their pets, when push comes to shove, it is.

Given that reality, we can approach this aspect of dog ownership in one of three ways:

- We can deny any financial limits and hope it never becomes an issue.
- We can react emotionally.
- We can critically analyze our finances in terms of how much we can reasonably spend on a dog and its upkeep.

Does this mean you need to incorporate your dog into your monthly budget? Not necessarily, although some pet owners find that approach does work well for them. More commonly, however, owners maintain a rough idea of how much they can reasonably afford to spend on a dog. Whether that idea pans out or not depends on the quality of the data that goes into the estimate.

For example, when single parent Elaine Cowan and her two youngsters decide they want to add a dog to their household, like most prospective owners, they first ask, "What kind of a dog?"

After falling in love with her uncle's rottweiler, hearing many good things about a local rottweiler breeder, and seeing a litter of her pups, they decide they want a rottweiler too. However, like too few prospective owners, Elaine tallies up the cost of the pup, the routine puppy vaccinations, worming, heartworm preventative, and neutering to see if she can work it into her budget that first year. Luckily, the veterinarian she chose offers a puppy payment plan that would enable her to pay for these services in 12 monthly installments during that period, which further simplifies these calculations.

"C'mon, Mom," the eleven-year-old Cowan twins urge their mother once she decides she can cover the expenses. "Let's go get a puppy!"

"Not so fast," Elaine says, handing them tablets and pencils. "Don't forget we'll need to buy dog food, a leash, and probably at least two or three collars. Plus I insist that we go to puppy kindergarten and obedience classes so *all* of us will be able to handle a dog who could weigh over a hundred pounds."

Most of us would agree that Elaine appears to have a pretty firm grip on the financial obligations inherent in puppy parenthood and whether or not she can afford them. Then she makes a statement familiar to many dog owners.

"Once we get through that first year, it'll just be routine stuff after that," she tells the twins.

It's tempting not to ruin this sunny scenario of responsible pet ownership with any grim predictions. However, more than a few human-canine relationships come to a dismal end or become irreparably damaged when owners fail to evaluate their financial limits throughout the dog's life.

"What's to consider?" Terri Shackley asks. "You either treat any problems that arise or you don't. Right?"

Not necessarily. Recall how Terri's failure to consider her own limits caused her to dismiss the other, lower-cost options that her veterinarian tried to propose. Granted some practitioners might not so readily volunteer such information, but most do respect their clients' financial limits and try to work within them. If the veterinarian doesn't offer alternatives, there's absolutely nothing uncaring about an owner saying "I'm sorry I can't afford that. Is there something less expensive we could try?" Nor is it at all callous to admit, "I really want to do that for my dog, but I can only do it if I can arrange some kind of time payment plan."

To be sure, it takes courage to express financial concerns openly. Most of us can summon a vision of a veterinarian, vet tech, or relative who will insinuate that we don't love our dogs because we raise the issue of money. However, owners who address the issue up-front fare much better than those who don't. By doing so, they establish open lines of communication with their veterinarians, a quality that will benefit all aspects of the animal's treatment. On the other hand, owners who evade the issue and take on financial obligations they can't meet come to resent both those providing the service and their dogs whom they see as the cause of their problems.

For example, suppose Barney develops a seasonal dry-skin problem and Elaine allows her veterinarian to talk her into switching him to an expensive premium dog food she really can't afford. Rather than feeling grateful when the veterinarian pronounces the dog's coat greatly improved six months later, she wonders if the veterinarian cares more about her money than her dog's health. When a neighbor mentions that he treats a similar problem by adding oil to his dog's regular kibble, Elaine's negative feelings intensify.

"Why did I ever get that darned dog in the first place?" she grouses when she tallies up the cost of Barney's special diet. "I could've taken the twins to visit my folks for the holidays with all the money I've spent on dog food this past year."

Because money does loom as a real issue for most pet owners, it makes sense to recognize any limits and then select a dog and related programs we can fulfill within those limits. Remember, *preventing* medical and behavioral problems costs much less than treating them. Some of the healthiest and best-behaved dogs I know belong to people on limited budgets. Because they know they can't afford costly treatments, they do everything in their power to avoid problems. While some people might say money rather than love motivates this behavior, I disagree. I see these owners' willingness to recognize their financial limits as a far more loving than mercenary response.

Canine Finances

Examine your checkbook entries or bank statements from the past year: How much can you reasonably afford to pay for your dream dog? How much can you comfortably spend for its upkeep?

As one who views her monthly bank statements with as much enthusiasm as a letter bomb, I realize that determining this amount may appear to require superhuman effort. On the other hand, I also know of more than a few human-canine relationships that soured when owners lost their hearts to an expensive pup in a pet shop, then couldn't afford to care for it properly.

If you bite the bullet and determine that value now, it will keep you from living beyond your canine financial limits.

Time Marches On

A former employer of mine claimed that only two kinds of veterinarians practice medicine: those with time and no money, and those with money and no time. However, a lot of veterinarians, like a lot of dog owners, would place themselves in a third category: those with neither time nor money. The fact that it takes time to build and maintain a mutually rewarding relationship with a dog leads some breeders and animal shelters to prohibit people who work outside the home from buying or adopting their animals. Although we reasonably could apply such a rule to certain human-canine combinations, most contemporary dog owners do fall into this forbidden category at one time or another.

Therefore, it makes sense for prospective owners to recognize just how much time they can invest in a relationship with a pet.

Let's look in on Elaine and the twins again. Before they bring Barney home, Elaine and the children work out a schedule of dog-related activities and post it on the refrigerator door. The first schedule they devise incorporates the breeder's recommendations of 20-minute walks each morning and evening, plus after each of the pup's three feedings. It also includes a training program's recommendation of two 10-minute training sessions a day.

Although theoretically sound, this schedule fails miserably when the Cowans try to put it into practice. One day Barney gets one 20-minute walk and two 5-minute ones. The next, he misses one walk altogether, but the twins take him for an extra-long walk that evening to make up for it. When soccer practice begins, the walks consist of little more than taking the pup outside long enough to relieve himself. Barney's training sessions succumb to the same erratic fate. Because Elaine knows that consistency serves as the cornerstone of housebreaking and other training programs, she soon realizes that this plan could do more harm than good.

"All right, let's forget about that schedule," she announces to the twins. "Let's figure out the minimum amount of time each of us can *guarantee* to spend with Barney every single day. Then we'll come up with a plan that fits that."

At this point, some dog lovers might feel sorely tempted to protest that those who don't have the time shouldn't own a dog. I disagree for two reasons. First, we know from bond research that the more complex the life, the more those involved in that life may need the special companionship a pet can provide. Second, even though it may take people with a hectic lifestyle a little longer to teach a pup the basics, owners committed to five-minute sessions once or twice a day can train a dog every bit as well as those who can spend several hours daily working with the animals.

Moreover, nothing says busy owners need to set aside separate times to exercise *and* feed *and* train the dog. One holistic training philosophy proposes dividing the animal's daily ration of dry kibble into several portions. The dog eats one of these out of its bowl as usual; the owner spreads another portion about the yard and lets the dog forage for it, an excellent form of mental and physical exercise, and a third portion gets hidden, once again providing the dog with an opportunity to exercise mind and body as it hunts for its meal. Making the dog sit or lie down while you prepare its meal also combines training and feeding programs.

Similarly, the daily walk easily lends itself to training. Instead of just walking Barney to the park and back, the Cowans make him come, sit, stay, walk, run, do figure eights, and reverse direction quickly to teach him to heel during this same interval. While Elaine watches her favorite television show, she holds Barney in the down position to teach him the "long down." When she works at her desk, she attaches his leash, allows him just enough slack to lie down on the floor next to her, and sits on the rest of it. At first he tries to get her attention, but she ignores him, and in no time he learns to lie quietly beside her while she works.

Canine Time Limits

Divide a sheet of paper into seven columns, one for each day of the week, and then divide each column into 24 one-hour blocks. Mark off any blocks already committed to other activities such as work, school, sleep, soccer games, or choir practice. The open areas define the time you or your family have available to spend with your dog.

Once again, the more you put into this exercise, the more you'll get out of it. The goal isn't to determine *if* you can fit a well-behaved and healthy pet into your hectic lifestyle, but *how* to do it the best way.

Emotional Roller Coasters

In addition to the emotions or lack of emotion inherent in the anthropomorphic and chattel orientations, people establish other emotional limits that can affect their relationships with their pets. Do you envision a relationship with your dog filled with exciting new challenges? Or do you see your pet as a calming influence in your life? Do you consider yourself an extrovert or an introvert? Do certain odors bother you? What about certain colors? How do you feel about dogs who drool or blow bubbles when they snore? What about dogs with high-pitched voices: do you think they sound cute, or does the sound send shivers up your spine like fingernails on a blackboard? Do you think of yourself as a patient person, or would you qualify as a member of the audience of the "Short Attention Span Theater"? Are you afraid of big dogs? Little dogs?

Your answers to these and similar questions that explore the emotional aspects of dogs and dog ownership can tell you a lot about the breed and individual dog that will best suit your needs.

"Why in the world do you want a rottweiler?" Elaine's best friend asks. "Why not a nice little dog that's easier to handle?"

"Forget it!" Elaine exclaims. "I was raised with a Chihuahua no one could touch with a 10-foot pole. There's no way I'd trust one of those little killers around my kids!"

Of course, such strong feelings about a particular breed may stem from little beyond one bad—or good—experience. None-theless, they can exert a potent influence on a relationship. Suppose, for example, that Elaine allows her friend to talk her into giving up her "silly prejudices" and getting a Chihuahua. Given the magnitude of Elaine's negative feelings and all of the other limits inherent in her busy lifestyle, only a truly extraordinary animal could please her. A less-saintly animal who might make a fine companion for an owner who feels at least neutral, if not positive, about the breed would wind up waging a constant battle to prove its worthiness to Elaine. Although the dog may eventually change her mind, Elaine's feelings might also lead her to consciously or subconsciously relate to the animal in a way that undermines its behavior.

Compare that relationship with what she experiences with Barney, a member of a breed she adores because her favorite uncle owns one and because she loves the way rottweilers grin. Where she wants Barney to succeed, she expects the Chihuahua to fail.

Let's look at another example of how human emotional limits can affect canine behavior. When I was a veterinary student, part of my training involved providing medical treatment to dogs being trained as guide dogs for the blind. After we students finished our work, quite a surprise awaited us. We were blindfolded and given a lunch consisting of spaghetti and a tossed salad, foods specifically chosen to remind us how much we depended on our sight to accomplish even the most simple tasks. By the time we finished battling with our food, even the cockiest among us felt less than confident. Then we were led outside one by one and given a dog trained to negotiate the complex city environment.

"I'll be about 10 feet behind you all the way," promised the trainer after issuing a few instructions about how the dog would behave and how I should respond to her.

Then he vanished into the blackness with everything else.

I stood there paralyzed with the sound of the traffic and a nearby construction site roaring around me. Only sheer willpower led me to utter that tentative command: "Walk."

All my beliefs about dogs as our best friends and trusting them with our lives coalesced in a few, what seemed like endlessly long, minutes. At first the dog literally dragged me along, even prompting me at intersections to reach out with my foot and test the height of the curb when fear made me forget to do so. However, eventually I reached the point where I could either make the necessary leap of faith to function as a unit with this dog (a critical concept we'll discuss in more detail later) or hang on to my fear. No doubt exhaustion rather than courage made me opt for the former. Then it all magically came together. As soon as I relaxed, I could feel the dog's entire demeanor change. It was as if suddenly she could enjoy her work.

While attributing the change in the dog's behavior to my own emotions may strike some doubters as doggy voodoo, scientific evidence supports such effects. Recall those studies of the human-animal bond that demonstrate how animals affect humans physiology and behavior. The bulk of this data began appearing in the 1970s, but even earlier studies proved the converse, that humans can affect animals, too. In addition to making hungry dogs drool when he rang a bell, Ivan Pavlov's experiments in the early 1920s demonstrated what he called the "Effect of Person," the ability of a person to significantly alter a dog's heart rate merely by being there, and often with no external changes in the dog's appearance.

In another experiment, Pavlov injected dogs with morphine and discovered an even more intriguing aspect of the human-animal bond and its effect on the canine mind-body. Although he intended to study the physiological effects of the drug, which causes dogs to vomit almost immediately and then sedates them, he became sidetracked by the psychological effects produced by the experiment itself. After he'd injected the dogs several times, he noticed they would automatically vomit and fall asleep when they saw him pick up the syringe and bottle of morphine!

Given such data, does it seem foolish that our feelings about a particular dog could affect its physiology and behavior as much as the dog might ours? Doesn't it make sense to evaluate any emotional limits we place on dogs and our relationships with them so that we don't violate these limits and make ourselves and our pets miserable? If Elaine allows the twins to coax her into getting a dog whose breed, color, personality, or activity level bothers her, the dog will know.

I've always maintained that our pets function as four-legged, fur-covered mirrors of ourselves. Put in terms of emotional limits: if you want a calm, happy dog, you may need to become a calm, happy owner first.

Dog Owner Psychoanalysis

List any canine physical or behavioral characteristics that elicit strong positive or negative emotions from you. Then evaluate these in terms of your own personality. Do you expect your dog to come immediately when called? How would you feel if your dog growled at you? Do you consider yourself a mellow or an intense person? Can you take criticism? Do you lose patience easily?

Nobody knows your emotional limits better than you. Although dogs can adapt to a wide range of human emotional responses, the more you know about your particular emotional hot spots and those of any other members of your household, the easier you'll find it to select a pet and complementary programs that won't trigger these hot spots.

Customized Canine Training

As a rookie veterinarian more than 20 years ago, I was knocked flat one day by a big mush of a golden retriever who then proceeded to sit on me.

"Bet you can't bench-press that dog," chortled one of the technicians.

That challenge ignited my feminist neurons, and I did succeed in elevating the dog enough to make him decide to sit somewhere else. However, that was then, and this is now. Although I still feel comfortable around large dogs, I also realize that, as a small, middle-aged woman, brute strength probably won't see me through if I encounter a male Doberman with an attitude. In other words, I know my physical limits.

When we look at the bond data on the positive effects of animal companionship, it's easy to adopt a "love-conquers-all" view of dog ownership. Even though some elitists still cling to the view that only those with the time, money, and emotional and physical wherewithal to treat a dog properly (according to their definition of that word, of course) should be allowed to own dogs, bond research contends the opposite. That research indicates that the people who benefit most from animal companionship belong to groups that society classifies as physically, emotionally, or socially impaired. However, rather than proving that *anyone* can own a dog, these studies point out the critical role that knowledge of human limits plays in the success of these very special human-canine relationships.

Most of us would probably define ourselves as physically capable of handling a dog. In reality, however, most of us couldn't do this without the dog's cooperation. Instead, we knowingly or unknowingly interact with the dog in such a way that we need little or no physical control over it under normal circumstances— what I call an "invisible leash." This works so well that most of us don't even think about any physical limits—until the dog spies something particularly enticing on the other side of the street, then ignores our commands and drags us through rush-hour traffic to check it out.

Although the belief that he couldn't handle Turbo if the dog attacked an innocent person led Bruce to give up his dog, Terri and the Cowans harbor no such fears about their ability to control their pets. How come? All three dogs came from the same litter and belong to a long line of animals known for their excellent temperament as well as their strength. Shouldn't all owners worry as much (or as little) about their ability to control such an animal?

The reason Bruce worried and Terri and the Cowans don't takes us back to human beliefs and knowledge. First, although Bruce had grown up with several mongrels, he'd never owned a purebred dog before. Like more than a few people with this background, he thought that the more he paid for a dog, the more perfect an animal he'd get. However, a dog's breeding, no matter how good or bad, functions more as potential than guaranteed fact. The dog's relationship with the owner and the environment and the methods the owner chooses to fulfil the animal's physical and psychological needs determine how that potential will manifest in that particular relationship.

Because Bruce chose to distance himself from Turbo, he never developed the kind of strong bond that serves as an invisible leash. Because he lacked that, the 165-pound man rightfully concluded that his influence over the dog boiled down to physical control, a control he didn't feel confident he could achieve given his dog's size and strength.

Considering the avoidable and correctable nature of Bruce's problems, you might want to chastise him for bailing out of the relationship. Before doing that, however, consider how Terri views her physical relationship with Kemper:

"Kemper's such a baby, he wouldn't hurt a flea," she says gaily as the dog charges across the park to greet her best friend. "He just loves everyone."

In other words, Terri ignores the issue entirely. Whether that works or not depends on how well she can control all the other factors that determine the quality of the relationship. Imagine the obese, babied rottweiler cutting his footpad on a piece of glass during his evening walk in the park, sustaining a bloody but not life-threatening injury. In this situation, not only does Terri's anthropomorphic relationship with her dog lower his pain tolerance, her distress over his injury upsets him even more. When a concerned passerby attempts to help Terri restrain the dog to get a better look at the injury, Kemper knocks his owner flat and lunges at the stranger.

Now let's look in on the Cowans to see how owners who integrate their physical limits into the relationship deal with a large dog.

"When the kids and I decided we wanted a rottie, I knew right from the start that none of us could physically restrain a 100-pound dog if he wanted to do something we didn't want him to do," Elaine Cowan readily admits. "That's why I was determined to get a pup from someone who bred for temperament as well as looks, and why I budgeted for some kind of formal training for all of us for at least a year."

Although we don't often think of it that way, getting a pup rather than an older dog provides us with the safest opportunity to establish and test our physical limits with a pet, and then develop the confidence in the dog and ourselves necessary to switch over to nonphysical methods of control. The Cowan twins and their petite mother don't hesitate to play with their new pup, look in his ears and mouth, and hold his feet. If Barney resists handling, they don't back off but rather meet his actions with others that communicate their leadership. By doing so, they learn that they can trust him even as he learns that he can trust them. By the time the dog weighs almost as much as Elaine, she and the twins feel completely comfortable with him.

"Don't you think that's a little foolhardy?" asks Bruce. "After all, that dog could rip them to shreds."

Indeed he could, but so could all but the smallest dogs, given the right conditions. Knowing our physical limits and making a conscious choice to assert dominion via some other, nonphysical means depends on the development of that ephemeral quality known as *presence*. Think of the serenity and sense of playfulness radiated by martial artists whose black belts represent their mastery of the mental and spiritual, as well as the physical, aspects of their discipline. In the same sense, dog owners' presence doesn't result just from the ability to control our dogs physically; it also comes from the knowledge of ourselves and our pets that gives us the confidence to relate to them in a manner that guarantees we won't ever need to resort to force.

I emphasize the relationship between the owner's physical limits and the dogs' behavior because a failure to appreciate this connection leads to the most serious behavior and bond problems. It still amazes me how many people own dogs, supposedly for protection, that scare the pants off of them. The problem, moreover, isn't limited to certain breeds: for every owner who fears his or her own Doberman, German shepherd dog, or pit bull, we can find others whose toy poodles, Chihuahuas, or Yorkshire terriers intimidate them.

Although owners typically say they became fearful after the dog threatened them, in reality their fear preceded it and even *caused* the dog's behavior. That's why it's imperative for owners to evaluate their physical limits regarding any existing or prospective pet, and then to select an animal and/or a training program that will enable them to enjoy a solid relationship within those limits.

Naturally an owner's physical limits should come into play when selecting a diet, exercise, and medical program for the dog, too. However, sometimes the nature of the human-canine bond makes this a counterproductive strategy. For example, Terri Shackley considers herself the ultimate couch potato.

"If you had my job, you wouldn't want to do anything when you got home from work either," explains the supervisor of an overcrowded, poorly funded program for troubled kids as she munches Cheetos and periodically flips one to her dog.

It comes as no surprise that Terri and Kemper soon resemble couches more than potatoes and begin to experience the various ailments associated with carrying all that extra weight around. One evening Kemper slips on the ice as he trundles toward the house after relieving himself, falls, and can't get up. Although lifting the obese animal would prove daunting to even the most physically fit owner, Terri can't even budge him because of the problems caused by her own diet and lack of exercise. Instead, she must leave her beloved pet lying in the freezing rain while she scours the neighborhood for someone to help her.

The moral of this story? Owners who impose their own limits on their dogs should prepare themselves to deal with the consequences if these limits yield less than optimum results. A chattel-oriented scientist would say this means that the ideal dog for an overweight, anthropomorphic owner such as Terri who likes junk food and hates exercise would be a tiny, hyperactive "teacup" poodle with an iron stomach. Such a pet more likely could cope with the inappropriate diet and burn off those extra calories. Even if it became sickly and obese, Terri could pick it up and carry it if it got into trouble. While we may shudder at this solution when so many other, more beneficial ones exist for owner and animal alike, we can't deny its logic. Unfortunately, such is the nature of the problems that result when we impose our limits on our pets without working them through within ourselves first.

Dog Owner Calisthenics

Review the qualities you said you want in a dog and your relationship with it in light of any physical limits. Do you consider yourself a jock or a couch potato? How do these limits affect your own life? How would they affect your dog? How might they affect your relationship? Which limits would you willingly change for your dog? Which ones do you consider inviolate?

Again, even though I deliberately chose some extreme examples to demonstrate the kinds of problems owners may encounter, no right or wrong answers exist. Far more often than not, owners don't get into trouble because they set the wrong limits. They get into trouble because they don't acknowledge their limits and how these may affect the relationship.

Polishing the Mirror

In the preceding pages we considered the human factors that exert the most influences over people's selection of and relationship with a dog. At the conclusion of the discussion of each human orientation, I asked you to evaluate yourself in light of that information, not with the idea of judging yourself, but to gain a better view of your beliefs about dogs. In the final step of this process, you combine all of this information to give you a clearer view of how you contribute to the relationship.

As noted previously, all dog owners may adopt any one of the three orientations at one time or another. Elaine makes no apologies for her unabashedly anthropomorphic view that Barney enjoys the twins' favorite video as much as they do. On the other hand, if Barney were to develop a medical or behavioral problem that threatened the health or safety of her children, she wouldn't hesitate to get rid of him (i.e., treat him more like an object than a furry humanoid). However, in most situations she takes an integrated approach and sets limits, such as allowing Barney on the couch in the family room but not on the beds.

In addition to recognizing what situations elicit each of these three orientations, we need to acknowledge that we and our dogs form a dynamic relationship, and that means today's beliefs and responses might change tomorrow. For the most part, Elaine consistently enforces her rule regarding what furniture Barney can claim. When one of her kids comes down with the flu and she needs to leave him alone for a few hours, though, that limit yields to the belief that allowing Barney to sleep with her son will make the child feel better. One day she comes home from work and sees the pup up on the couch—and covered with mud:

"Barney, you get off there, this instant!" she yells, even though she thinks of that couch as "Barney's couch." Later, when Barney becomes a beloved canine senior citizen, she bans him from the previously on-limits couch because she fears he might fall trying to get up on it when no one's home. However, even her strict rule about no dogs on the beds vanishes whenever one of the now grown twins comes home for a visit.

Although inconsistency can and does wreak havoc in a relationship under conditions we'll discuss in the following chapters, *knowledge* remains the key. No matter how simple or complex the problem, we can't begin to resolve it until we acknowledge its presence and the best of the many solutions available to us and our dogs.

Once we gain a clear view of our expectations and needs relative to a canine companion, the obvious question arises: What kind of dog will best suit me, and where can I find it?

To find a compatible canine companion, we need to understand the dog's expectations and needs as well as our own.

2

Form, Function, and Selection

*How Our Knowledge of the Canine Past
Can Help Us Select a Pet with a Rosy Future*

When I toss her bright blue rubber bone for my Welsh corgi, Violet, and watch her ecstatically dash after it, I try to imagine what goes on in her furry little head. When we play the game outdoors, she positions herself about 20 feet in front of me, presses her sausage-shaped body low to the ground, and never takes her eyes off me and the bone. When I throw it over her head, she pivots and races to catch it before it hits the ground. If I turn and throw the toy away from her, she charges toward it—and me—her fat little feet pounding the turf like a dwarf wildebeest on the rampage. If she overshoots her toy in her enthusiasm, she snarls at it as she snatches it up. Then she trots back to me grinning, holding her prize high for everyone to see. I suspect she'd play the game forever, but my throwing arm grows weary, and work calls.

"Violet," I call out as I throw the bone toward the front of the house rather than into the yard, "time to go in."

For the briefest instant I think I see disappointment in her eyes. Then she charges after her toy one last time, waits for me at the door, then curls up on the couch for a nap while I work.

———————

Based on what I've learned about the extraordinary sensory and mental world in which my dog lives, I know that her performance transcends a mindless dash to retrieve a silly toy. In 1954 neurobiologist James Olds provided a possible clue to what does go on in her head during these joyous intervals when he discovered the nonaddictive pleasure center in the brain. Olds observed that rats permitted to stimulate this area would do so continuously, showing no interest in food, water, or rest. However, no matter how much the animals enjoyed the sensation, when he disconnected them from the stimulator, they tried only a few more times to summon the pleasurable response before turning to other activities.

Similar experiments on other animals, including dogs and humans, yielded similar results. In that typically dry way of science, this intriguing phenomenon earned itself a less than intriguing name—Intracranial Self-Stimulation (or ICSS)—and eventual dismissal because it lacked the necessary pathological pizazz to spur further research.

However, even though most scientists may care little that our brains come hardwired to experience such nonaddictive pleasure, any dog owner who *enjoys* standing in subzero weather throwing a toy or stick to an equally joyous dog should find Old's discovery reassuring.

Lewis Thomas, a playfully brilliant scientist who did take time for fun, speculated in his book *The Fragile Species* (Scribners, 1992) that the ICSS serves to trigger the sensation of something no more or less scientific than the simple joy of being. Based on this insight, I suspect that a blue rubber bone flying through the air triggers the release of neurochemical substances that allow Violet to experience and relish her relationship with me, as well as her breed's history as herding dogs whose Flemish ancestors (and their owners) Henry I invited to settle in Wales in 1077, and her roots as a wild canid (the group that includes foxes, wolves, and wild dogs). For sure, she'd participate in this euphoric celebration 100 times a day if I could muster the energy to keep picking up and throwing the toy she drops so eagerly at my feet. Amazingly, though, for as much as she adores the game, a simple "No" will cause her to take a nap or seek amusement elsewhere.

Even though Violet doesn't compulsively insist on playing with the toy, she invariably treats it as if it holds great meaning for her. Practically every evening she takes it upstairs to the bedroom for safekeeping as soon as I turn in for the night. In the winter, she carefully places it on my pillow; in warmer weather, she puts it under the bed. She does this even though she may not stay in the room with me then, or even later that night. When she gets up in the morning, she takes her treasure back downstairs so she can grab it the instant an opportunity arises for play.

For whatever reason, playing with a toy of that particular size and shape apparently enables this particular dog to experience the joy of being. The game gives meaning to her life with me and other humans and links us in a way no other object or activity can.

Although the idea that this seemingly insignificant object should wield such power appears almost mystical, I'm equally captivated by the fact that her physiological and behavioral evolution have exquisitely programmed her to fulfill her needs in such an enchanting way.

As with all dogs, Violet's heritage forms a kind of three-layered physical and behavioral cake. The first layer consists of her primitive wild roots, the second of the effects of domestication, and the third of her specific breeding for form and function. Let's briefly consider the ingredients that go into each of these layers to see how each contributes to the overall makeup of a particular dog. That way we can better understand if and how a particular dog and person can fulfill each other's needs.

Tracing Canine Roots

Just as with all other living creatures, a combination of genetic and environmental factors makes every dog unique. Also as in all living creatures, early experience can exert profound effects on what occurs in the dog's life later, especially the development of the human-canine bond. Because of this, let's first consider those lingering genetic influences of the past that can exert potent effects on the health and behavior of even the most civilized modern canine.

One of the most fascinating glimpses into this subject comes from experiments conducted on silver foxes by Soviet biologist Dmitry Belyaev and his colleagues. Because foxes don't respond well to training, Belyaev systematically bred only the tamest foxes in hopes of creating a more manageable animal. However, in a mere 20 years of genetic manipulation for this behavior, he literally created a whole new creature. Not only did this "new" fox readily approach people and greet them with the tail-wagging, face-sniffing, and hand-licking behaviors of a lovable family dog, but it also *looked* different. Floppy ears replaced erect ones; softer, multicolored coats replaced the coarser, silver ones; the annual heat cycle gave way to a semiannual one characteristic of domestic dogs.

Clearly, these changes revealed something, but what?

A telling clue to the nature of the changes produced by domestication came from the sounds Belyaev's foxes made. Unlike wild canids of all species whose adults rarely bark, these animals barked and yapped like pups throughout their lives. In the process of breeding only for tameness—a behavioral quality of young animals—Belyaev's team automatically wound up with the immature physical characteristics that went with that trait. Based on these results, the scientists concluded that domestication somehow freezes animals in both physiological and psychological states of immaturity.

According to this theory, the modern dog's behavior reflects two quite different heritages. First, it claims a legacy from those strong, relatively quiet adult wild ancestors whose traits enabled them to survive long enough to mate and raise their young. And second, it inherits a more vocal, immature bequest thanks to human selection for tameness, the primary quality necessary for an animal to survive and multiply in human society.

Put another way, our dogs represent a paradoxical behavioral hybrid. On the most primitive level, they retain the instincts that enabled only the most mature, quietest wild animals to survive. At the same time, however, domestication perpetuates behaviors—such as noisiness—that are associated with immaturity.

How does the dog's domestic heritage affect its sense of its own identity? Recall the old adage, "Birds of a feather flock together." Doves stick with other doves; wolves stick with other wolves. A tame or domesticated animal, however, accepts members of another species—specifically *Homo sapiens*—into its flock or pack. In essence, the process of domestication reduces an animal's sense of species identity: Belyaev's new foxes freely interacted with humans because they didn't view people as sufficiently different from themselves to pose a threat.

What a curveball this paradoxical mature and immature heritage can throw into the modern dog's thought processes! A clap of thunder startles Pansy as she waits for her owners to come home from work. Her mind immediately activates her survival instincts.

"Uh, oh. What's that?"

But does Pansy curl up and sleep out the storm like a solitary adult wild canid? Or does she whimper like a wild pup in hopes of summoning a companion?

It depends. If Pansy has a strong breed history, it might provide her with yet another option. Although the criteria of contemporary breed purity tend to focus primarily on physical appearance, all early breeds shared one psychological trait: a strong sense of function or purpose, and the brains and temperament to go with it. Whether bred to hunt, herd, or sit on her ladyship's lap, the animal's ability to perform its function took precedence over its appearance. An attractive dog lacking the desire and stamina to herd didn't impress a shepherd any more than a nasty lapdog impressed her ladyship. To borrow a phrase from architecture, the dog's form followed its function, just as Belyaev's foxes took on an immature appearance when bred for tameness. A particular dog's breeding, then, can imbue it with a strong sense of function and a set of specific behavioral patterns in addition to a specific coat or eye color.

What does that mean to Pansy, a beagle, and her owner? Consider these three breed-related facts:

- Beagles locate their prey by following its scent.
- They howl to alert the hunter to their location.
- They howl when they locate the prey.

Does it come as any surprise, then, that Pansy might let loose with a "hound dog howl" when the storm rages around her rather than whimper like a wild pup or sleep quietly like a wild adult?

Functional Foul-Ups

Even though a particular breed's appearance originally evolved to complement a function that in turn complemented its owner's needs and lifestyle, many prospective dog owners fall in love with a canine look, with no idea about any canine function that might go with it, let alone how they will fulfill it given their lifestyles and environments. Further complicating the issue, contemporary breeding practices yield dogs that span the functional spectrum from animals with a weak or distorted sense of self and function as a result of form-over-function breeding to those with strong functional roots who live in environments where they can't fulfill those functions.

For example, although boxers can claim a genetic heritage of bull-baiting working dogs, the modern version carries only the palest shadows of this functional breeding. Furthermore, because breeding programs traditionally focus more on physical characteristics, the breed also lacks the human-companion function bred into lapdog breeds. This in no way means that boxers can't make wonderful companions—they can and do—but rather that they typically lack the strong genetic programming for this characteristic built into Yorkshire terriers and King Charles spaniels.

At the opposite end of the function spectrum, we find breeds such as the Bernese mountain dog, a relatively new kid on the suburban canine block. Not only does the Bernese mountain dog possess a much stronger sense of function by virtue of its relatively recent introduction into the pet population, it also represents one of the few working breeds whose function—pulling carts—automatically brought it in close contact with humans. Compare this function with that of hunting and herding dogs whose tasks require that they focus on other animals as well as their owners.

We could bemoan the existence of breeding programs that ignore the strong role function plays in canine health and behavior, but the fact remains that both functional extremes exist in the canine spectrum, as does everything in between. Because of this, prospective owners need to understand a particular dog's position on the functional spectrum so they can determine whether they can provide the physical, psychological, and environmental support necessary to establish and maintain a rewarding relationship with that animal.

Though the domestic dog's physical form originally reflected a function desired by humans, two other human practices also significantly influenced the makeup of contemporary canines. First, while individual breeders may wax ecstatic about the superior intelligence and wonderful temperaments of a particular breed, show standards barely pay lip service to these qualities. Depending on the breed, a dog can earn more than 90 percent of its championship points by excelling in such body-part categories as size, head, body, legs and feet, tail, coat, and color and markings—hardly much of an incentive for a breeder to focus on temperament! Moreover, of those few points allotted to temperament, some standards may include rather nebulous qualities such as expression, awarding points for those deemed suitably "inquisitive" or "noble."

If Belyaev could greatly alter physical appearance by selectively breeding only for behavior, it seems logical that the opposite also holds true: breeding for physical qualities could result in concurrent behavioral changes. However, if breeders and judges don't consider the mental attributes of a purebred dog because they aren't part of the standard, they may simply ignore this possibility.

All of this would pose no problem for the average dog lover seeking a pet—except for one widespread misconception. Whether judges and breeders take temperament into account or not, most people associate a specific temperament with a specific breed, and they see that temperament comprising at least 50 percent of the canine package rather than the 10 percent or less required by the breed standard. Pair a few high-function Dobermans, rottweilers, or pit bulls with owners who can't meet those animals' needs, and soon the entire breed gets labeled "dangerous" and blackballed by the insurance industry. While I don't agree with the insurance industry's approach at all, if it compels those in the dog fancy to pay as much attention to function as form, such blatant discrimination may actually be a blessing in disguise.

More and more breeders who primarily sell pets to the general public recognize the need to focus on temperament as well as appearance. Unfortunately, some of these folks lack all but the most superficial knowledge of canine behavior. If the dog displays all the right physical characteristics, loves to play fetch, and knocks everyone down and licks them, it must be a perfect black Lab.

However, even though new dog owners may wind up with pets whose temperaments and brains don't match their beauty, we can't blame all functional foul-ups on judges and breeders. Owner lifestyle can deal contemporary dogs another devastating blow. It's all well and good to demand that rottweiler breeders aim for the physical soundness, temperament, and intelligence the animals needed to perform their original drover/guard dog function, but what exactly do we expect those dogs to *do* with all that fabulous potential in a three-bedroom ranch in suburbia, especially when their owners go off to work every day?

This dilemma afflicts not only the many working breeds that have captured the fancy of dog lovers worldwide, but also breeds such as Yorkshire terriers and King Charles spaniels. These animals can't fulfill their inherent companionship function when their owners leave them alone, either.

The astonishment on the face of a friend, a breeder and trainer, when I pointed out this contradiction may be a typical first reaction.

"Good Lord," he roared, "you think we should breed *dumber* dogs?"

No, I don't. But I do think every new owner should evaluate a dog in terms of its breeding—or lack of it—for function as well as form, and determine if and how that animal will fit with that particular owner in his or her environment.

Canine Reality Check

If a particular breed or mix of breeds appeals to you, do all you can to learn about its history and function. Note any inbred functions that might either complement or complicate your lifestyle.

In addition to talking to breeders and people who own the kind of dog you like, books such as Michelle Lowell's *Your Pure-bred Puppy: A Buyer's Guide* (Henry Holt & Company, 1990) or Benjamin Hart's *Perfect Puppy* (W. H. Freeman, 1996) can provide valuable insights. If you prefer videos you can see your favorite breeds in action in Handler's *Choosing the Perfect Puppy* and *Dogs! Dogs! Dogs!*

The Canine Identity Crisis Clinic

To see how form and function can affect an individual dog and its relationship with people, let's consider the case of ardent golden retriever lovers Ron and Bobbi McKelvey. Both Ron and Bobbi grew up with field goldens possessing great stamina and intelligence who would hunt all day, then patiently and good-naturedly endure the attention of boisterous children in the evening. When Ron and Bobbi married, they knew their lives wouldn't be complete without a golden.

The McKelveys bought their first ball of fluff, Penelope, from a co-worker of Ron's who had bred her "really sweet" female to her brother-in-law's "wicked mellow" male. The result was an enchanting creature, the sweetest, most laid-back golden retriever either Ron or Bobbi had ever known. Unfortunately, Penelope also suffered from severe hip dysplasia, a degenerative hip disease. Although replacement of one hip offered the dog temporary relief, the other hip eventually gave out and didn't respond to treatment. After all their emotional and financial investment, the McKelveys ended up having their beloved pet euthanized—a sad but not uncommon result when owners and breeders place more emphasis on temperament than physiological soundness.

Still determined to own a golden but not about to make the same mistake twice, the McKelveys then purchased a pup who was certified free of hip dysplasia and other physical defects from a top breeder of show animals. By the time Jason reached his first birthday, Ron and Bobbi wished he weren't quite so healthy. The idea of spending the next decade with a handsome but humorless animal who didn't hesitate to growl when irritated didn't thrill either of them. When Jason pins the plumber to the wall, the McKelveys give him up to a golden rescue organization.

In this second scenario, the pendulum has swung too far in the form direction. Although Jason's physical appearance is in keeping with the highest breed standard, he lacks the personality to go with it. Rather than the tractability of the wild pup or the patience and softly gripping velvet mouth of the field dog, he displays the aloofness and clamping hard-mouthed bite more characteristic of his mature wild dog ancestors.

The saga continues . . .

While at the rescue center, the McKelveys notice a dog quietly studying them from a nearby run. When they inquire about her, they learn she came from hunting stock.

"Diana's a trained field dog and requires a very special owner and environment." reports the volunteer.

The dog nuzzles Ron's hand, then gently licks Bobbi's fingertips.

"At last," they agree, "we've found our perfect dog!"

In their excitement, they don't remember a word the rescue rep tells them about Diana and her needs.

At this point the McKelveys' journey through the dog owner's equivalent of Dante's Inferno could follow one of four equally unrewarding paths for dog and owners alike. First, they could take Diana home that Saturday morning and spend the most wonderful weekend, only to arrive home Monday after work to find a note from their neighbor about their "#@%*& dog yapping and whining all day."

Given the dog's social nature (more on this in Chapter 4), it comes as no surprise that isolation creates stress. Nor should it surprise us that stressed animals display whatever behaviors they think will best relieve the stress. In Diana's case that means zipping through her quiet field dog breed behavioral repertoire in favor of the vocalizations of the wild pup in her effort to dissipate her anxiety. In the wild, these cries would attract other members of the pack and automatically solve the isolation problem. In suburbia, they more often bring nasty notes from neighbors or a summons from the animal control officer.

In a second variation on the mismatched field dog–working owner theme, the McKelveys come home and discover that Diana spent most of her day trying to chew through a window frame or the front door. No one would expect such hard-mouthed behavior from a working, velvet-mouthed bird dog. However, once again we see how stress can drive a dog beyond typical breed responses, this time to those more characteristic of a threatened adult wild animal capable of chewing its foot off if necessary to escape a trap.

In a third variation, a more introverted Diana relieves the tension by digging at and chewing herself rather than the window frame or door, a behavior that may result in chronic ear and/or skin problems. If the tension manifests in Diana's gastrointestinal tract instead, diarrhea (perhaps explosive and bloody) may occur. Sometimes these physical problems remain strictly emotion-based phenomena, but other times secondary infections, thyroid deficiencies, and other medical problems may further complicate the situation.

The fourth possibility hasn't been formally studied, but it happens often enough to warrant mention. In this situation, Diana plays a mind game instead of an environmental or body game; she experiences seizures. All subsequent tests come back negative, and the veterinarian diagnoses the problem as idiopathic epilepsy (seizures of unknown origin).

As a group, animals suffering from this condition tend to be highly intelligent creatures who possess a strong sense of function but lack self-confidence. They also tend to be well behaved, very attached to their owners and their territories, and relatively free of other medical problems. Where other animals relieve stress externally, these animals internalize everything. Instead of their brains sending a message to their bodies to do something— *"Bark!"* *"Chew the rug!"* *"Scratch your ears!"*—these dogs worry, increasing rather than alleviating the tension.

Sweet, quiet Diana paces from room to room and window to window in the McKelveys' home, her motion-sensitive vision, acute hearing, and strong sense of smell assaulting her with data. But there's too much of it. No sooner does the meter reader leave than the letter carrier arrives. Then the next-door neighbor yells at his cat, the street sweeper rumbles by, school lets out two blocks away, and a volunteer collecting for a charity pounds on the door.

All of these events assault the gentle, older dog, and there's no way she can get outdoors to determine the exact nature of these violations: Are they friend or foe? At the same time that her most primitive roots urge her, *"Protect your territory!"* her human interactions warn, *"Don't you dare make a mess in the house!"* *"Don't you even think about scratching!"*

If we accept that every thought precipitates electrochemical "firings," and that a seizure represents a misfire that precipitates a mental firestorm, we can assume that putting a dog with Diana's temperament and intelligence in this particular environment greatly increases the probability that she'll experience a misfire and subsequent convulsion.

Note that the McKelveys' rescued field dog differs from their first two goldens. Diana's breeding as well as her previous training and lifestyle made her strongly function oriented, and she now lives in an environment that doesn't meet her needs. She can't hunt any more than could the lame Penelope or hard-mouthed Jason.

"There aren't any birds in here," thinks Diana. *"What am I supposed to do all day?"*

As different as Diana's four possible negative responses may appear on the surface, each results from the fact that she couldn't fulfill her function in the McKelveys' environment.

Ralph Waldo Emerson noted that a man's work is his lengthening shadow. In the canine world, function is the shadow of the dog's identity. When we breed a function into a dog and then place it in an environment where it can't fulfill that function, it loses its identity. It doesn't matter if that function means sitting in someone's lap, herding sheep, or retrieving birds. Whether as a result of conscious human effort or accident, each dog comes to us equipped with an individual, breed, species, and wild ancestral database that can greatly affect the formation of the human-animal bond.

In any given situation, Pansy the beagle calls up what she considers the relevant data, sorting through it to determine the proper response. When a visiting toddler corners her in her single owner's bedroom, the old beagle first summons the most recent addition to her behavioral repertoire, her unique Human-Animal Bond Program:

"Did my owner teach me anything about little kids? Nope, nothing there. I'll try the Beagle Program. Hmmmm, lots about rabbits and smells. Guess I'll sniff the little critter."

Pansy approaches the newcomer tentatively.

"Yowl, he pulled my ear! Wow, that really hurt! I'm scared! I'm calling up the Basic Survival Program. 'Freeze, fight, or flee,' it says. Well, I can't run 'cause the kid's between me and the door. And I'm not gonna freeze 'cause he's making a grab for my ear again."

Snap!

"Take that, kid!"

Needless to say, canine identity crises have the potential to precipitate human crises, too!

Although we'll never know whether this bit of fancy represents true DogThink or not, owners who appreciate dogs as bearers of an imprint of wildness, the domestic canine species, and a specific breed or combination of breeds, as well as that of a unique individual, can do much to create a relationship and environment that enhances rather than antagonizes or denies their pet's sense of self and function.

Canine Function Check

Imagine your dream dog in your home. What do you envision your new pet doing in your presence? In your absence? Note whether these ideas result from any anthropomorphic or chattel views, and from either knowledge or emotion.

Image Dogs and the Killer Marshmallow Syndrome

How people perceive dogs of specific breeds is a final factor that may affect the canine sense of self and function. Some people raise, sell, purchase, or adopt a particular animal because they believe doing so confers a special mystique upon them. For example, some breeders pray that a member of their breed *won't* win best-of-show at the nation's premier dog show, the Westminster Dog Show, because they know such recognition attracts buyers more interested in owning a "winner" than a dog. Other people may select the biggest, smallest, ugliest, rarest, most elegant, or even the most fragile and unhealthiest dogs because of the attention these animals generate for the owner.

"Is it wrong to like the way a dog looks?" Ron asks thoughtfully. "I think goldens are the most beautiful dogs in the world."

Certainly an appreciation of a dog's physical appearance plays an important role in the owner's relationship with it. However, owners also should appreciate the intelligence, temperament, and functional needs of the animal that goes with the look. Image Dog owners care far more about any real or imagined messages they believe the animal conveys about them than they do about the dog's needs.

An offshoot of the Image Dog Syndrome, the Killer Marshmallow Syndrome involves members of breeds that elicit opposite and extreme human emotional responses as part of their mystique. Among the most common Killer Marshmallow breeds are Dobermans, German shepherd dogs, rottweilers, pit bulls, malamutes, and huskies, some of the same breeds currently targeted by the insurance industry as well as by promoters of so-called dangerous-dog legislation.

Like Image Dog owners, owners of Killer Marshmallows use their pets as advertisements for their personal beliefs about the kind of people who own these animals. However, they also project their beliefs about how dogs of that particular breed should act onto their dogs. Unfortunately, this combination yields results that make the breed appear decidedly schizophrenic. For every owner determined to prove his or her Doberman, rottweiler, or pit bull a vicious killer, we find one equally determined to prove another dog of that same breed a marshmallow. Every time one of the killers gets out of line and an outraged public labels the whole breed "dangerous," marshmallow owners flock to the media with pictures of their dogs sleeping with the baby.

Although we may wonder what goes through the minds of the killer- and marshmallow-makers, we can't deny the effect of these human orientations on the dog. All of the breeds involved in this human struggle represent intelligent animals with a strong sense of function, and neither the owner-assigned killer nor marshmallow role takes these behavioral traits and needs into account.

In addition to fuzzing the dog's sense of self and function, the Killer Marshmallow Syndrome affects how other people relate to the animal. Although owners who create killers or marshmallows may feel superior when other people shy away from their pets, neither type of dog elicits a stable, emotionally neutral human response, let alone a positive one.

Our dogs live in a human-centered world. When the primary species in their world routinely recoils at the sight of them, these animals hardly receive validation of a sense of self that reinforces strong domestic roots. The killer interprets this human response as submission and summons other dominant, usually aggressive wild canid displays which the owner (we hope) aborts. This "training" gives rise to an animal whose interactions with most humans result in a kind of *behavior interruptus* performed for the owner's gratification.

On the other hand, the marshmallow whose owner makes every effort to create a loving and gentle creature must deal with its confusion when people recoil: *"Why doesn't this person like me?"*

In this situation, the animal must overcome the person's fear before it can manifest its true friendly nature. While the owner enjoys seeing other people's amazed reactions to the marshmallow, the dog must cope with all the stresses imposed by the initially negative human response.

In a particularly naive variation of this theme, the killer owners believe the dog will threaten only people whom the owners don't like and will assume the marshmallow role with everyone else. When these animals bite an innocent person, the owners express horror that this happened, often insisting, "The meter reader (delivery person, neighbor, guest, cousin) must have done something to upset the dog." The fact that insurance companies have paid sufficient claims to victims bitten by these animals to blackball the entire breed strongly suggests that those who witnessed the incidents, treated the victim's wounds, or heard the evidence in court didn't agree.

Dream Dog Form Check

Review your description of your ideal dog, the ideal programs to go with it, and any limits you place on the relationship in terms of what you consider the ideal canine body type. Note which preferences reflect solid knowledge of that particular dog and its needs and which arise from emotion. Based on your new knowledge of the role the animal's form plays in its health and behavior, note any inconsistencies in your lists.

For example, if you love the look of a collie or Samoyed, can you free up the time to comb and brush such a dog or the money to pay someone else to do it for you? How do you feel about dog hairs on your clothing and furniture? If you opted for a poodle because they don't shed, did you allow for the time and expense involved in clipping the dog?

Dream Dog Function Check

Consider your dream dog in terms of its breed function and any time, emotional, or physical limits you noted previously. Note any areas of potential conflict as well as those in which your dream dog's function complements your lifestyle.

If you chose a black Lab, for instance, will your time limits permit you to train and exercise such a high-function animal's mind as well as body? What about your preferences for human-canine exercise programs? It may require a special effort to find the individual dog whose needs you can fulfill if you want only to jog around the block with your pet once a day.

Multiple-Dog Functions

What if you already own a dog and want to get another one? If that's the case, you should keep all of the previous points plus a few others in mind. Chapter 4 discusses in detail the critical role that the human-canine pack structure plays in the dog's sense of well-being, a role that becomes even more crucial in a multiple-dog household. At this point, however, suffice it to say that anyone thinking about adding another dog also must consider the pack dynamics that invariably will occur between any two dogs.

Two dogs may behave quite differently together from the way they behave alone because two dogs form a canine pack which plays by its own unique rules.

In general, the less alike the dogs, the more quickly they'll establish a stable pack. To understand how this works, let's suppose the McKelveys get a male golden pup and then adopt a two-year-old male golden when their pup reaches that same age. Then let's compare that experience with what happens when they add a female poodle pup to their household instead.

In the first case, the two dogs are so similar that it takes them a long time to work out which dog will lead their canine pack, and a fair amount of tension exists between the animals until they do. The longer the McKelveys try to run interference between the two goldens, the greater the tension between the dogs, and between the dogs and their owners. What should have been a few minor scuffles to determine pack order gives way to increasingly serious daily skirmishes. The well-meaning but naive owners aggravate the situation by punishing the animals or separating them with orders to "Be nice" whenever the dogs try to resolve this fundamental issue. Regardless of how lofty the philosophy that leads the McKelveys to take this approach, it completely ignores their dogs' most critical need.

In the second situation, the male golden so obviously dominates the much smaller female poodle pup that she considers all his dominant posturing a great game and cheerfully accepts it.

When adding a dog to your human-animal household, always remember that dogs *need* a pack structure in order to relax and feel comfortable. This doesn't necessarily mean that owners must mix and match dogs if they don't want to. Same-breed pairs can work very well, especially when owners see fulfilling any breed function as one of the most enjoyable aspects of dog ownership. One owner of two black Labs finds throwing sticks into the lake for his dogs for hours at a time great fun and exercise for all concerned. Another owner of two Shetland sheepdogs discovered that adding a second sheltie revealed never-before-recognized functional roots in the first.

"The day I got the second dog, I thought my first dog was so upset he'd had a stroke!" she recounted with a laugh. "He just kept circling the new dog again and again. But the longer I watched him, the more I realized he was trying to herd her. Now the two of them amuse themselves for hours herding each other around the yard."

In these situations, the combinations work because the owners recognized their dogs' needs as members of a certain breed, as individuals, and as members of both canine and human-canine packs.

The Search Begins

"Well, that's just great!" huffs Ron McKelvey. "Given all this form and function stuff we have to worry about, I guess if we want a good dog, we might as well build a shrine and pray for one."

Not exactly. Granted more than a few owners feel that locating a good dog borders on a religious experience, and many harried owners of sickly or unruly dogs consider a healthy, well-behaved animal nothing short of a miracle. However, this usually occurs when people lack a clear idea of what kind of a dog they want in terms of both its form and function and how these will complement their own needs and lifestyle. Lacking this knowledge, they pick a pup or dog based strictly on their emotions. For every doting pet owner who proudly proclaims, "I didn't pick Ralphie; he picked me!" we see a hundred more for whom this approach led to disaster.

Prospective owners who know what they're looking for don't stand in front of a litter in a box or a row of cages in a pet store or shelter while their feelings scramble their brains and they opt for the "est" animal (biggest, smallest, saddest) instead of the

best. Because they know what they're looking for and can critically analyze each animal in terms of its and their own needs,
they can find their ideal dogs in any number of places.

The most common sources include:

- casual breeders (such as friends and neighbors)
- professional breeders
- pet stores
- animal shelters
- breed rescue organizations

Let's consider how each of these sources may affect the
development of an animal's sense of self and function and subsequent compatibility with a particular owner and environment.

Homegrown Treasures

Although some people might disagree—and disagree strongly!—
good purebred and mixed-breed dogs can and do result from
planned and unplanned backyard liaisons. It doesn't lie completely in the realm of fantasy that the McKelveys could discover
a knowledgeable couple with a lifestyle similar to their own who
breed their goldens because they consider them such ideal pets,
which they perceive of as far more important than any breed
standard. Of course, these animals may not fulfill all the show
standards, and finding these rare gems takes time. Veterinarians
and their staffs, groomers, even personnel of breed rescue groups
and animal shelters may serve as reliable sources of information
regarding such breeders, although the latter two groups may prefer to place their own animals first.

The advantages of getting a pup from such a source include
seeing the pup in the environment in which it was raised and
comparing that environment with your own. The pup whelped
in a box in the family room where the owners and their children
spend much of their time gains a set of early experiences quite
different from those gained by the pup raised with five litter-

mates and six adult dogs in the spotless kennel owned by the single woman who works at home, or the one raised in a barn by the man who works a swing shift. Although all three environments could produce pups that make ideal companions, the more a pup's early experience mimics your own home environment and lifestyle, the more quickly it will adapt to its new surroundings.

In these settings you also can see how the adult dog—at least the pup's mother, and maybe its father, too—responds to its environment. Observe how the animals interact with their owners and other family members, as well as with you and members of your family. The former provides valuable clues to the animals' sense of self relative to humans, while the latter additionally shows how they react to novel stimuli such as visitors handling the pups. Beware of statements such as, "She's a wonderful dog, but she gets a little uptight when she has pups (sees strangers, children, beards, etc.)." If you have children, be sure to take them along. If you don't have children, borrow some kids for the occasion. It makes more sense to pick a pup who likes kids than to try to fit a kid-shy one into a singles lifestyle where kids may occasionally show up.

Check out the floor area around the pups for signs of good husbandry—clean bedding, fresh water, lack of odor. Although your heart may go out to that pup or dog stuck in the filthy box or kennel, exposure to such conditions can make these animals much more difficult to house-train, in addition to exposing them to parasites and disease. Let your eyes roam and take in any evidence of adult dog destruction, or barricades within the house that might hint at such destructive tendencies. A shredded couch, chewed woodwork, and urine-soaked rug should make you think twice about bringing that sweet little puffball into your meticulously renovated colonial home.

Many people list lower cost as a reason to purchase a purebred pup from a casual breeder. It's one thing to get a casually bred pet for less because the breeder likes the animal and wants it to go to a good home, or because the animal doesn't meet show or field standards. It's quite another to get such a deal because the breeder made the minimum investment in the dog's care, or knows of some hidden flaw in the animal and wants to get rid of it as quickly as possible. Whatever the circumstances, always keep one inviolate rule of dog ownership in mind: *There's no such thing as a free dog.*

The main disadvantage of getting a pup or dog from a casual breeder plagues all other sources as well: all pups reflect not only their parentage but also the knowledge of the people who bred and raised them. So, if you have any doubts about a potential pet, ask for the names of the veterinarian who tends the animals and people who purchased animals from this breeder in the past. Then call these sources and discuss the animals and breeder in question. Breeders who take good care of their animals and want their pups to go to the best homes won't hesitate to provide these names, and they'll even encourage you to contact these people for further information.

Going First Class

Professional breeders who show their animals remain the best source of pups for people who wish to do likewise, or for those who want an animal that meets strict breed standards. For those who want a pet as well as a show animal or just a pet with show qualities, the previously described process to evaluate the environment applies. Particularly note if the animals live in the household or in separate kennels. Although the amount and quality of human-canine interaction a prospective pet experienced always deserves consideration, this holds especially true for older animals.

Sometimes breeders will keep a pup until 8 or 9 months of age, or even older, in hopes it will develop some necessary show quality. If it doesn't, they sell it—often at a reduced price—or even give it away. If these animals live in a separate kennel except for brief trips into the house, and/or spend most of their time with dogs rather than people, their sense of self and function may develop quite differently from those who experience more consistent human companionship. This lack of early, varied, human-centered experience may result in a dog who finds the wide-open spaces terrifying or the comings and goings in a busy household more than it can handle. Dogs raised in restricted but complex environments may display very short attention spans, while those who spend most of their time with other dogs may not recognize human authority; a dog raised with 15 other dogs who goes inside the breeder's home for 10 minutes of "quality time" each morning, but spends the rest of the day in a kennel watching a hectic world of dogs and busy people go by, may wind up more frazzled than "socialized" by this experience. All of these developmental problems can foil the attempts of even the most loving owner armed with the best intentions and training program.

A more controversial issue related to show dogs is the use of surgical procedures and/or drugs to correct defects. Some breeders won't hesitate to do whatever it takes to show a dog, breed it, get a litter, and raise those pups. In addition to manipulating or enhancing the dog's basic physiology to achieve these goals, they now can add psychotherapeutic drugs to their repertoires: if Champion Rex of Runnymede owes his unflappable temperament to the little white pill he swallows twice a day, how well will he or his offspring fit into a hectic suburban environment?

However, it's one thing for a breeder to correct Coquette's overbite or drug Rex to quiet his preshow jitters and later sell these animals as pets on the condition that the new owner has them neutered. It's quite another for the breeder to present the dogs as perfect breeding specimens.

Whether you agree with these approaches or not, it behooves you to know and understand the complete physical and behavioral history of parents and pup, as well as any breeder expectations about the handling and treatment of your new dog. More than one busy owner who only wanted a good pet has wound up spending countless hours and dollars trying to track down some exotic dietary supplement, or to breed the animal in order to produce the litter necessary to fulfill an obligation to the breeder.

Read up on your dream breed. Ask questions. If you sense any hesitation on the breeder's part to answer your questions, back off. Recall what was said in Chapter 1 about how the dog's and owner's physiology and behavior affect each other for good or ill. Owners who believe their dogs reflect human behavior they find offensive—be these breeding practices, previous abusive treatment, or impositions placed upon the owner—relate to those animals differently from those who perceive their pets as ideal.

Fortunately, many excellent breeders offer many fine dogs, which raises another question: Should you let the breeder (or any expert) pick the pup or dog for you? The best answer to that remains a definite "Maybe."

The ideal situation matches a prospective owner who has general knowledge of dogs, specific knowledge of that breed—even if only from books—and a clear sense of the canine personality he or she wants and feels qualified to handle, with a knowledgeable breeder willing to do everything possible to provide the best animal to meet that owner's needs. Prospective owners who lack this awareness should choose knowledgeable breeders also capable of interviewing and evaluating potential buyers in terms of personality, lifestyle, and environment, and matching them with the animal that will best meet their needs.

"But what about the bond?" challenges Bobbi McKelvey. "What if I don't *like* the dog someone else picks for me?"

A valid point. If you truly dislike a certain dog, you shouldn't take it. This rarely happens, though. More commonly we feel ambivalent, a troublesome response to an encounter we've envi-

sioned as a most joyous event. Bobbi imagines a ball of fluff bur-
rowing into her parka for comfort, while Ron pictures a wiggly
fireball jumping up and licking his nose. They can't help but look
suspiciously at the self-contained creature the breeder recommends, the pup who eyes them curiously, then sniffs their shoes
carefully before falling asleep in a contented heap on Ron's
sneaker.

Anyone who works with problem dogs and their owners
knows that the sneaker-sleeper will fit the McKelveys' hectic
lifestyle far better than either of the two animals that fired their
imaginations. Unfortunately, and like many of us, the McKelveys
find the extremes—the most dominant or submissive animals—
more alluring than those behavioral middle-of-the-roaders. However, people who pick the extremes invariably experience the
majority of the problems with their pets. Nonetheless, the desire
for novelty looms as such a strong human trait that sometimes
it takes an almost heroic effort not to succumb to it.

Consider this telling, true story. After living with a series of
medical and behavioral rejects, I decided to buy a purebred dog
and do all the things I told my clients to do. I read up on various breeds and evaluated their merits in terms of my preferences
and lifestyle. After deciding on a Welsh corgi, I searched for a
litter meeting my criteria, then tested the litter at six weeks of
age using the recommended techniques. No doubt about it: that
female with the dark smudge on her head was my dream dog.

As I turned to leave the pups, a little male charged me
gleefully and practically climbed up my leg in his desire to lick
me. How could anyone resist such an obvious plea of *"I love you!
I want to go home with you!"*?

Then I noticed the runt of the litter huddled in the corner.

"Poor little thing," I said. "Surely someone with my exper-
tise could transform that pathetic creature into a wonderful pet!"

Only with the greatest effort did I resist these pups and stick
with my first choice. Doubts plagued me for the next two weeks.

"What if I made a mistake?" I wondered and, even worse, "What will happen to those other pups?"

When I returned to pick up my new pup, I thanked my lucky stars that the other two were already gone. Intellectually I knew I'd made the right decision, but . . .

During the first weeks with Violet, I felt completely disoriented. The pup rarely barked; she slept quietly in her carrier; she quickly mastered the basics of house-training; she adored playing with, and chewed only on, her toys. Troubling thoughts kept nagging me.

"There's something *wrong* with this pup. She's much too good. I bet she has a brain tumor."

Then suddenly the truth dawned.

"This is what it's like to own a stable dog!"

Violet had imbued the relationship with a serene quality I had never before experienced.

The moral? Give every newly acquired animal a chance. Just as love differs from lust, so those highly charged feelings we experience when we first meet a new animal may reflect our human emotions far more than any fact. Sometimes it takes a little time for us to get past our own mirrored reflections to see the real dog.

For anyone desiring more information on the selection of a purebred pup, Larry Shook's *Puppy Report* (Lyons and Burford, 1992) which offers insights into reckless breeding practices and how to avoid people who practice them, and Kempe's *Learn How to Choose the Right Dog* (Sandy Kempe, 1994), a guide to the purebred puppy decision-making process, both serve as valuable resources.

Buying a Pup in a Poke

In days of old, unscrupulous farmers would put cats instead of suckling pigs in burlap sacks or "pokes," and take them to the local market for sale. People foolish enough to buy "a pig in a poke" without opening it got an animal quite different from the one they thought they'd bought. Those who looked before they bought invariably "let the cat out of the bag."

Getting dogs from pet stores, animal shelters, and rescue groups can pose similar problems for the unwary buyer. We go in looking for one thing—maybe not even a dog!—and come out with something not at all like what we had in mind. In no way does this mean that these organizations deliberately attempt to snooker potential owners. However, the very nature of these sources makes it difficult to determine the animal's true history. Moreover, they often elicit the common human emotional response—"How much is that cute (sad, scared) puppy in the window!"—that may further undermine the selection process. By recognizing this phenomenon and how it affects the process, we can keep ourselves from getting a dog we don't want, or getting one we do want for the wrong reasons.

When the McKelveys fall in love with the golden puffball in the mall pet store, what concerns should pop into their minds about that animal's sense of self and function? Can they address those concerns? If not, they most likely won't have access to any firsthand information about the pup's parents to help them out.

Bear in mind that many of these animals come from puppy farms that supply pet stores all over the country, and most pet store personnel can offer few, if any, details about the pup's background. In addition, these pups may log quite a few miles and experience all sorts of travel-related stress as they make their way from farm, to distributor, to pet store. Moreover, they make this transition during that critical period when negative experiences can exert long-lasting effects. Ironically, this does tend to weed out the lines that lack the physical and tempera-mental soundness to survive all that stress, and those that do sur-vive can be remarkably stable.

That's the good news. The bad news is that inexperienced pet store personnel and potential buyers may excuse negative behavior—shyness, aggression—and any medical problems as a natural consequence of the pup's previous experience. But as noted, just the opposite should hold true: because the pup goes through so much *before* it reaches the pet store, it should take what happens in that new environment in stride. Bear in mind that most pet stores charge as much as, and often much more than, most breeders, and most guarantee only the animal's physical health. You usually can't return the pup if it acts even more apprehensive or aggressive in your home than it did in the cage.

Also, beware of those bargain pups on sale "this week only for half price," a common ploy used to sell older animals. Although some of these animals may make fine pets, recall our discussion of the effects of continuous kenneling during puppyhood and the resultant stunted world view. Such early puppyhood experience hardly bodes well for owners who envision a dog happily accompanying them on their brisk walks along crowded city streets.

So, before you start looking at those doggies in the window, put your emotions on hold. Before you fall head over heels in love with a pup who looks so sad it breaks your heart, ask yourself this critical question: *Do I possess the knowledge and time needed to correct any problems this pup might have, or the resources to hire someone to do it for me if I don't?*

Don't join the ranks of those worst-case-scenario owners who paid top dollar for a genetically shy or aggressive pup because they felt sorry for it, then made excuses for the behavior rather than seeking ways to alleviate it because they erroneously chalked it up to early abuse. Such owners wind up paying for little more than the privilege of making themselves and their pets miserable, often for years.

Second-Chance Solutions

Like animals from pet stores, pups and dogs from animal shelters often come with little history. While we do know what most pups go through before they wind up in pet stores, we can only guess what many of those shelter residents experienced: Did they come from litters whelped in loving homes or in abandoned junkyard cars? We do know that many adult dogs wind up in shelters because of their problems, sometimes medical but more often behavioral. People with healthy, well-behaved animals rarely give them up, and those who do usually place the animals personally.

In light of all this, shelter animals create a moral dilemma for the busy dog lover with a complex lifestyle. Let's put the McKelveys on the spot again. Suppose they want to own a dog and strongly support the concept of providing a good home for an animal who may have suffered in the past. They visit their local shelter and ask about goldens.

"I just know you're going to love this dog," the volunteer gushes as she leads Ron and Bobbi to "Luckless," a three-year-old, flop-eared, unneutered, gold-colored dog leaping and cavorting in a run.

When the McKelveys inquire about the dog's history, they learn that his owners abandoned him on the beach and that he survived by scavenging for three months until the animal control officer finally caught him. The volunteer recounts this tale of woe, all the while petting the contented dog leaning against her leg.

The McKelveys look at the gangly hulk, think of their new condominium and fussbudget neighbor, and just begin to murmur their regrets when the volunteer sighs, "If nobody takes him today, we'll have to put him down."

We can't blame often overworked and underpaid shelter personnel for resorting to emotional blackmail to place animals. However, it does no good to place a dog with people who lack the knowledge and skill to correct its problems. Fortunately, more and more shelters routinely screen owners and perform behavioral as well as physical evaluations of their charges, discuss any problems openly with prospective owners, and offer full support for any problem's resolution. In addition, many permit trial periods to help ensure that the animal will fit into the new environment and that the owners can cope with any problems that may arise. In these situations, the shelter places more emphasis on establishing solid, long-term relationships than on the numbers of animals placed.

If you decide to get a dog from a shelter, once again do yourself and the dog a favor by leaving your emotions at home. Don't accept the gory details of the previous owner's irresponsible behavior or the dog's imminent demise as substitutes for solid information about the animal's health and behavior, or for a staff committed to help you successfully integrate the animal into your household. In the worst-case shelter scenario, the McKelveys adopt Luckless in the spirit of Saint Francis, convinced that their desire to save his life will somehow magically cure all of his problems. When the dog chews up their rugs or kills the fussbudget neighbor's prized Persian, they feel trapped. How can they possibly give up the dog after they put their hearts and souls on the line? Surely Saint Francis would stick it out.

Dog Lovers to the Rescue

Recall that when the McKelveys' hard-mouthed golden proved too much for them to handle given their lifestyle, they chose to give him up to a golden retriever rescue group rather than an animal shelter.

"The people who run it love goldens as much as we do," Bobbi explained. "We knew they'd do everything to find Jason a good home."

Breed rescue groups operate essentially as breed-specific shelters and, like pet stores and shelters, may vary wildly in the quality of animals and support they offer. Some do an excellent job of screening animals and accept only those whose problem(s) they consider treatable. Most of these groups don't accept aggressive animals, and some initiate training programs to correct other problem behavior before placing a dog. Many also use foster care to evaluate animals for any medical or behavioral problems in a more natural home environment. This can provide a more realistic picture of an animal's personality, but any evaluation and remedial action depends solely on the knowledge and skill of the caretaker. Still other groups accept all dogs of a particular breed, regardless of any problems, and do everything in their power to place them, with or without trying to correct any problems.

Many times people think that obtaining a purebred animal from a rescue organization automatically confers two benefits: they save an animal, and it costs them much less than buying one from a breeder. However, remember those words emblazoned in the sky: *There's no such thing as a free dog.*

The groups that do the best jobs incur the most expenses and ask the highest fees, both from those who give up the animals and from those who adopt them. Nonetheless, they provide a valuable service for busy owners who want a purebred pet. The staffs get adequate histories from the previous owners and accept only those animals likely to succeed in other homes. They fill any gaps in the animal's history with their own observations and experience, and that of trained foster caretakers.

Like good breeders and shelter workers, quality rescue reps quiz any potential owner about lifestyle and ability to deal with any problems the dog may have. Above all, they don't pressure prospective owners to take a dog and, in fact, even may treat potential owners with a healthy dose of skepticism. Like those shelters committed to placing animals in homes where they can enjoy long and rewarding relationships, good rescue groups dedicate themselves not only to their breed, but also to the placement of animals in environments where they can succeed.

Information regarding specific breed rescue organizations is available from veterinarians, the American Kennel Club, local kennel clubs, shelters, and breed clubs as well as that emerging mother lode of dog information, the Internet. Bob Christiansen's *Choosing a Shelter Dog* (Canine Learning, 1995) is another good resource, showing readers how to evaluate prospective shelter or rescue dogs—including temperament testing.

Dream Dog Source Check

Make a list of points to notice and questions to ask before you buy, accept, or adopt an animal from anyone.

- Do all the animals here look healthy?

- Do the animals look happy and well behaved?

- How do these animals relate to me, and to other strange adults and children?

- Is this place clean?

- Are there any signs of destructive adult dog behaviors?

- How closely does the dog's physical environment resemble my own household?

- Is this person knowledgeable about this breed and this particular animal?

- Does this breeder breed for temperament as well as for physical soundness?

- Is this person willing to provide the name of the veterinarian who cared for the dog?

- Is this person willing to provide the names of people who have purchased or adopted animals from this source?

- Are there any strings attached to the purchase or adoption of this animal? What are they?

- How much time did this person spend with this animal? Doing what?

- What, if any, special needs does this animal have?

- Will this person be available to help if I run into problems integrating the animal into my household?

- Will this breeder, shelter, or rescue group take the animal back if it doesn't work out in my home?

Add any other questions that relate specifically to your own orientation toward dogs and any personal limits you may have. Don't be shy or embarrassed about asking these questions. The more you know about yourself and a particular pup or dog before you get it, the greater the likelihood you'll experience a long and rewarding relationship with that animal. Any breeder, pet store, animal shelter, or rescue group employee too busy or unable to answer these questions probably cares more about selling or getting rid of his or her charges than placing them in good homes. Although that doesn't rule out the possibility that you'll find a good dog from such a source, it should make you scrutinize these places and any animal residents with particular care.

Now that you know where you and your dog are coming from, we need to take a closer look at the environment where you're going to live together.

3

Inner and Outer Spaces

How the Human and Canine Senses of Place Influence Our Relationships

Merilee Roth surveys her living room critically.

"Gee, I don't know, Honey, I think the sofa should go by the window." She shakes her head. "No, wait. It might be drafty by that window. Better put it in the corner."

"I still think we should've gotten the blue one," grumbles her husband, Whit Naylor, as he moves the colonial wing-backed sofa for the third time that morning.

"Don't be silly!" Merilee retorts. "Then it wouldn't match the other things."

"I can see why you want it to match the chair," Whit agrees. "But why does it have to match the hammock in the kitchen? They're not even in the same room."

"I know that," Merilee admits as she nudges the blue wing-backed chair closer to the lamp with her foot. "But I want all our new pup's furniture to match so she'll know what's hers and what's ours."

——————

While the idea of buying dog furniture that matches the owner's decor may strike some as odd, practically every pet products catalog devotes space to such items, and such human-canine color-coordinated homes do exist. However, most dog owners dwell somewhere between these folks and those who gesture toward the shepherd chained to the doghouse and say, "I like dogs who know their place." We do maintain certain rules regarding a dog's place in our homes, drawing the line, for instance, at a collie sitting on the dinner table with her tail in the salad or leaping onto the bed during intimate interludes.

However, even though we may maintain strong ideas about a dog's sense of place, these ideas often arise haphazardly. Merilee feels terribly proud when she teaches her new border collie, Callie, to jump onto the utility table for grooming. And neither she nor Whit ever consider the possibility of their furry best friend sleeping anywhere but at the foot of their king-sized bed. Only when Callie comes to the perfectly logical canine conclusion that one table looks pretty much like another, and that her bed's her bed no matter what her owners might be doing in it, do they realize that they have set some rules, even if they never bothered to share these with their dog.

Like many other owners, Merilee and Whit bought all that expensive dog furniture for Callie without fully understanding their own and their dog's sense of place. Although few of us give much thought to all the details that go into making a living space a home, many architects, interior designers, decorators, psychologists, and philosophers, among others, have devoted much time to this subject. Recently, the topic of creating living spaces that meet both human and canine needs also got a major nudge toward respectability when a national magazine featured a home specifically designed and decorated to meet those dual needs. And cleaning expert Dan Aslett endeared himself to many dog owners when he devoted an entire book, *Pet Clean-Up Made Easy* (Writer's Digest Books, 1988), to this important environmental issue. Most certainly, creating a happy home for a new pet depends on critically evaluating our environments with both of our needs in mind, and doing so rests on that basic principle of dog ownership: It's much easier and less expensive to *prevent* problems than to correct them once they occur.

Even though we humans rarely acknowledge that we possess a territorial nature, animal behaviorists recognize establishing and protecting a territory as an animal's strongest drive.

"What does that mean?" Whit asks as he looks at the expensive dog bed in which Callie refuses to sleep.

It means that most animals won't eat or drink, let alone think about reproducing, if they don't feel comfortable in their space. Although the neutered status of the majority of our companion animals renders the latter consideration of little consequence, the relationship between eating and drinking and an animal's sense of place can create problems for owners and dogs alike. Just ask those owners who spend a significant portion of their vacations agonizing over whether the dog will starve to death at the kennel or won't eat for the house sitter. I can cite more than a few cases of vacations—and even one honeymoon—cut short for this very reason.

Similarly, the fact that dogs naturally mark their territories with their stool and urine creates problems for them in human society. When we house-train our dogs, we teach them to claim a space outdoors, and the location of that space can affect canine behaviors as diverse as protecting our homes and car-chasing. Animals who relieve themselves in the immediate vicinity of their homes focus their protective instincts on that space. Those whose owners take them to remote areas to eliminate may bolt out the door whenever the opportunity arises because they feel pressured to protect that space in the park more than their homes. Dogs who eliminate on both sides of the street may claim it as part of their territory and feel compelled to defend it against any trucks, cars, joggers, or bicycles that violate that space. Shy or older animals may eliminate inside the house because they feel overwhelmed by the thought of protecting house *and* yard in the owner's absence.

At the other extreme, some animals will refuse to eliminate in spaces they consider threatening for any reason. You can probably pull into any rest stop along a heavily traveled interstate and find at least one dog owner pleading with a pet to relieve itself. Kenneled or hospitalized animals also may refuse to urinate or defecate for territorial reasons, a behavioral decision that can lead to or complicate existing medical problems.

Finally, people who introduce a second dog into their homes may discover that the old or the new pet will begin to soil in the house to mark its territory. Other times, the new dog won't soil in the house, but it won't relieve itself in the yard or area around the house, either, because the old dog already claimed this space. In my situation, the established corgi immediately urinates wherever the new hound does, but the dogs tend to defecate in separate areas.

From these examples, we can see that our homes don't function merely as a backdrop to our interactions with our dogs like some set in a play. Instead, the space we share plays a major role in our interactions, providing subtle and not so subtle input that can greatly influence the quality of our relationships. To avoid winding up with a dog and an environment that have all the compatibility of an old sneaker and an evening gown, new owners need to answer three critical environment-related questions:

- What human needs must the environment meet?
- What canine needs must it meet?
- How can I best meet both types of needs within this setting?

Additionally, our homes must meet our and our dog's needs on three levels:

- physical
- mental
- emotional

To see how our existing or planned environments stack up, let's explore these different characteristics from both the human and canine points of view.

The Human-Canine Environmental Foundation

When Merilee and Whit decided to buy their first house, their want list looked like this:

- cost no more than $72,000
- structurally sound
- no more than an hour's drive from work
- large lot
- a minimum of three bedrooms
- two bathrooms
- modern kitchen

The couple's list naturally reflected their personal priorities. A perfect house in the perfect setting that costs more than they could afford doesn't interest them any more than the perfect house at a great price located too far from work. However, while Merilee and Whit both had wanted a modern kitchen, they forgot all about it the minute they saw the large, private, well-landscaped lot surrounding the older home they finally bought.

"Merilee and I do both enjoy cooking," explains Whit while watching the sun set from the deck, "but we work in crowded, fast-paced offices, and owning a place where we can enjoy some peace and quiet means a lot more."

"And we wanted to get a dog," Merilee adds, rubbing Callie's ears.

Once we buy or rent a house, condominium, or apartment, what attributes do we look for or add to make that physical space a *personal* space?

First of all, most of us consciously or subconsciously carve out a private space for ourselves within this larger one. Whit immediately sets up a "workshop" in one corner of the family room, even though all of his tools fit in a very small toolbox and his idea of fixing something amounts to calling a repairman. Merilee decides she needs a "little office" although she adamantly adheres to her vow not to bring her work home with her, and she claims another corner of that same room.

As soon as we claim our private territories, we typically set about furnishing them in a way that appeals to us. Whit and Merilee decorate the rest of their home in a uniformly coordinated colonial style, but Whit's corner of the family room boasts an old leather chair that perfectly fits his large frame, a traditional brass reading lamp, and a very high-tech large-screen television. Merilee helps him refinish an old oak table and matching chair which he uses as a desk.

Merilee then falls in love with a chrome-and-glass table which she pairs with a Victorian chair in her space. She stacks her favorite books on one end of the table where she can easily reach them from her "wickedly comfortable" recliner, an object she would never dream of putting in one of the other rooms because "it wouldn't fit."

Over time, the couple's personal spaces become even more personalized. Whit hangs a print of his alma mater and photos of treasured friends and events on the walls of his nook, and he keeps his current book and favorite magazines beside his chair on a small table he inherited from his grandfather. Merilee also decorates her space with personal memorabilia, automatically filing any letters, cards, or other "important" items she doesn't want to lose in the assortment of wooden boxes she keeps on her table.

Without necessarily realizing it, both of these people claimed a territory and marked it as theirs. Perhaps Merilee didn't deliberately stake out that particular corner of the family room, and she certainly never told Whit that he couldn't use it, but within a matter of months after they move in, Whit as well as their friends and family refer to the nook as "Merilee's office." Similarly, even though theoretically Merilee could sit in any chair in her home, she automatically thinks of that worn leather one as "Whit's chair."

Like Whit and Merilee, each of us claims and marks out a "territory," and how we do that affects our animals.

Personal Space Checklist

Think about your home in terms of your personal space and that belonging to any other members of your household. Imagine your dog sharing that space with you.

- What areas and furnishings, if any, are off-limits?

- How do you intend to enforce this rule?

- What would you do if your dog destroyed a treasured object?

- What do you plan to do to prevent this from happening?

Callie's Physical Space

Let's leave Merilee and Whit and their special chairs for a moment and observe how their border collie's physical space evolved. Shortly after Whit and Merilee moved in, they visited Whit's parents and instantly fell in love with Callie when they saw her snuggled among her seven littermates in the big cardboard box beside the woodstove in the kitchen. Although they knew Callie's mother adored herding sheep and working the farm with Whit's father, Whit and Merilee envisioned a much different life for their new pup: they wanted the same high-quality physical surroundings for her as they did for themselves.

Unfortunately, however, the young couple used the same human definition of "high-quality" that led them to purchase all that coordinated living room furniture they never use. The high-quality dog chair and sofa do blend right in, but their new pup never uses them, either. She does occasionally lie in the hammock in the kitchen, but only when her owners share that same space. When Whit and Merilee relax in their personal spaces in the family room, Callie tries to jump into their laps and sit with them in their chairs. When they won't allow her to do this, she lies mournfully on the floor at their feet.

Although most of us probably wouldn't provide our pets with such a lavish collection of dog furniture, many of us do take a "Field of Dreams" approach to our pet's physical space: if we provide it, they will use it. However, recall all the effort Whit and Merilee devote to personalizing their own spaces even though they don't acknowledge their territorial natures. Does it seem reasonable to assume that a dog with a strong territorial sense, like Callie, will just plop down anywhere?

Of course, it doesn't. In fact, most dogs won't settle down until they can claim a space in which they feel "personally" comfortable.

Consider Callie's wing-backed dog sofa and matching chair in her owner's carefully decorated living room. Compared with that cardboard box next to the woodstove, neither one of these stands a canine chance. Although some of us might retreat to private spaces in a far corner of the attic or basement to get away from the hustle of a busy household, dogs— and especially pups—are social animals. They want to be with others, and no piece of dog furniture in the world will entice the typical dog to accept it in place of companionship.

"I don't understand what's wrong with that dog." Whit shakes his head sadly when Callie immediately jumps off her dog couch and follows him back to the family room for the 10th time since they brought her home. "We got her the best of everything, and she won't use it."

Luckily for Callie, Whit and Merilee eventually give up and move the dog sofa into the family room with them. Callie immediately embraces this change because the new, more intimate setting provides a sense of security the living room didn't. Now that she has her space, she sets about personalizing it, too.

"Hey, cut that out! Stop digging at your sofa!" Whit shouts at the pup when she starts doing a little "remodeling" of her own.

Granted it smacks of anthropomorphism to try to imagine what runs through Callie's mind as Whit sits in his comfortable old chair with its curves and depressions that perfectly fit the contours of his body and yells at her for commencing exactly such a customizing process. However, we can't overlook either the correlation between the human and canine desires to claim the space intimately, or the inconsistency of Whit's condemning his dog for displaying behaviors so similar to his own.

Once Callie claims her special space and stomps one end of her dog couch to make it fit her more comfortably, she, too, accessorizes her home. Soon a collection of toys makes the space more intimately hers. A favorite stuffed toy occupies the other corner of the couch; a nylon bone, a squeaky toy, a fuzzy ball, and the cardboard tubes from a roll of paper towels and toilet tissue accent the floor space immediately around her sofa. Although we classify them all as toys, they serve the same intimate function as her owners' photos and memorabilia.

Not surprising to any dog lover, but fascinating to those who study the human sense of place, these pet toys also become part of the treasured "furnishings" of the owner's space, too. Whit keeps Callie's leash on the table next to his chair, and

Merilee keeps the dog's brush and comb in one of the boxes on her desk. Although Merilee and Whit would never consider throwing trash on the floor, they automatically crumple any sheets of paper they plan to discard into tight balls and toss them to Callie to play with because she always enjoys the game. The pup also loves to tear up cardboard tubes, and she'll gnaw at and play with a carrot for hours. Needless to say, a non-dog-owning visitor who saw the collection of paper balls, chewed cardboard, half-eaten carrot, and other "garbage" strewn about the floor of the couple's family room might seriously consider declining their invitation to stay for dinner!

Canine Personal Space Checklist

- Where will your new dog sleep at night?

- Where will it sleep during the day?

- What area or furnishings can the dog claim as its personal space?

If you intend to add another dog, don't automatically assume the dogs will sleep side-by-side on the oversized dog bed or on the couch. Although they may both share the owner's bed, they'll each most likely claim a personal space somewhere else in the home, too. In some situations, though, the existing dog may claim the owner's bed as its own and fight with any newcomer rather than share this choice piece of real estate.

Inner Space Furnishings

As we and our dogs customize our homes by manipulating various physical elements, we satisfy nonphysical as well as physical needs. While Whit and Merilee see their perfectly appointed living room as an ideal space in which to formally entertain guests, they interact with their closest friends in the family room. Another home may reflect the old saying, "No matter where I serve my guests, they always like my kitchen best." Although "food preparation" correctly describes the kitchen's physical function and "food consumption" that of the dining room, other nonphysical factors may give these spaces a potent emotional charge.

Consider the tale of Whit's chair. During his freshman year in college, Whit purchased his beloved chair for $25 from a senior who had purchased it from a retiring faculty member who had found it at a yard sale. The chair became a standing joke with friends and family because Whit insisted on taking it every time he moved to new quarters. Although he'd likely need to pay a junk dealer to haul it away, he wouldn't sell it for all the money in the world.

According to the experts who study how we relate to our personal spaces mentally and emotionally, we desire places that serve as quality sources of:

- shelter and security
- a sense of identity
- social contact
- stimulation
- memories

Let's see how each of these applies to us and our dogs, too.

Home, Safe Home

Above all, we humans treasure a space in which we feel safe and secure. The largest, most exquisitely decorated contemporary house holds no appeal if all that glass makes us feel exposed rather than at one with nature, or if we view all those expensive furnishings as dust catchers or burglar bait. However, if we feel safe and secure in our homes, we can sense the tension leaving our bodies the instant we cross the threshold after a hectic day.

The same holds even more true for our dogs, but many animals achieve this blissful state during only a small fraction of the time they spend in our sanctum sanctorums.

"How come?" asks Merilee, who sees her home as the ideal canine haven.

Because a dog views establishing and protecting a territory as its reason for living, the more attached it becomes to its owners and their belongings, the more responsible it feels for protecting their home in their absence. Although Whit and Merilee covet the thought of staying home all day like their dog, when they go off to work, Callie must go to work, too. While protecting a house with large expanses of glass may make her feel under siege (as it might some people), a home that allows her little access to a view of the outdoors may frustrate her even more. Imagine what happens when Callie hears a sound outside.

"What's that?" she wonders.

Immediately she tries to determine if the sound emanates from a friend or foe. If she can't, she might get as close as she can or dares and deposit a puddle of urine or pile of stool by the front or back door, her way of saying, "Keep out! This space belongs to me!" Or suppose by standing on her hind legs with her front paws on the windowsill she can see some rascally rabbit in the yard. In this situation, she might gnaw on the sill or dig at the rug to relieve her frustration.

Or consider what happens when Merilee takes the pup to visit her family. Merilee's younger brother presents Callie with the pup's favorite toy, a soft, squeaky, fuzzy ball. To everyone's surprise, the pup barely acknowledges the gift because all the new sounds, sights, and smells of this place—to say nothing of its human, canine, and feline occupants—so overwhelm her senses. However, once back in the shelter and security of her own home, she investigates her new toy in minute detail and soon plays happily with it.

Identity-Conferring Spaces

How do our environments affect our sense of identity? Do we feel differently about ourselves in our homes from the way we feel in other settings?

"Absolutely!" Whit volunteers as he drops into his old leather chair after returning home from a business trip. "I travel a lot, and even though I like the predictability of the chain hotels, they also make me appreciate how unique this place is."

Does Callie share this view?

You bet. When Callie returns home after an overnight stay at the veterinarian's following spaying, she immediately goes to the family room and sniffs all of her toys, paying particular attention to the new balls of paper her owners scattered around for her. The contented look on her face and the deep sleep that envelops her the instant she curls up on her own bed surely strikes a responsive chord in anyone who relishes that special joy of being back among one's own things after an absence. Nor do we need to return home from a trip around the world to appreciate this feeling.

On the other hand, if our environments don't meet our needs for some reason, then instead of identifying with them, we'll feel uncomfortable and even alienated in those surroundings. A friend of mine with excellent taste decided she wanted *the* perfect living room in her new house. After consulting a well-known decorator, she created an exquisite space filled with antiques, elegant white upholstered furniture, oriental rugs, and accessories.

"It's gorgeous!" I gasped when I saw it.

"I *hate* it," she announced, catching her Siamese cat in mid-leap over the white couch while her husband tackled one of the two schnauzers in hot pursuit of the cat. "When I'm gone, I spend all my time worrying about what the pets are doing to it."

Although my friend harbored an image of herself as the kind of person who would fit well in a beautiful setting, she overlooked the fact that, for as much as she loves and appreciates beautiful things, she loves her animals more. Given the open floor plan of her home and a lifestyle that negates closing off the special room or training all the pets to stay out of it, she ended up longing to replace the lovely furnishings with something that fit her—and her pets'—identities better.

Our dogs, too, can suffer identity crises in certain environments. After a month of having their every move scrutinized in the new room, my friend's dogs opted to slink quickly through the space, and only when necessary. They found the kitchen and her husband's den much more inviting. Although some of us may maintain images of elegant borzois gliding through French provincial boudoirs, Irish wolfhounds lounging in front of ancient stone fireplaces, or toy poodles nestled on frilly pillows, if these settings don't complement the animal's sense of self for whatever reason, they'll undermine rather than enhance the relationship.

A final variation of the identity theme brings us back to Merilee and her view of Whit's chair. Even though Merilee wouldn't normally sit in that chair because she finds the "lovable eyesore" lumpy and uncomfortable, when Whit goes away on business she finds herself drawn toward it. Similarly, when Merilee's work takes her away from home, Whit may sit at her desk to sort through the day's mail. In these situations, a personal space that so embodies its owner's identity will cause others to feel closer to that person simply by being there.

Our dogs elicit similar responses in their owners and experience a similar phenomenon. The night Callie spends at the veterinary hospital, Merilee automatically strokes her pet's favorite fuzzy ball when she thinks about her. Normally Whit barely notices Callie's leash on the table next to his chair, but that particular night his eyes repeatedly return to it.

For her part, Callie spends much of her nap time alone in her owners' home sleeping in the bedroom; she could sleep anywhere, but she identifies this room most strongly with her human companions. When she spends the night at the veterinary hospital, she rests easier in her strange surroundings because Whit leaves one of his old sweaters for her to sleep on.

The Human-Canine Meeting Place

Our homes provide a place for social contact not only because we can interact with others there, but also because we feel we can *control* interactions that occur in a familiar setting better. Ethologists refer to this as the *bourgeois effect*, a phenomenon sports enthusiasts call the "home team advantage." As any military commander involved in a long, frustrating war on enemy turf can attest, intimately knowing a space confers such a physical and psychological advantage to its inhabitants that they can easily resist assaults from outsiders with far better training and equipment.

Granted few dinner parties break out in warfare, but all social interactions do create a certain amount of stress even under the best circumstances. Where would you rather receive bad news: in a bustling hospital corridor or in your own home surrounded by familiar people, pets, and belongings? Where would you prefer to meet someone you don't know?

"That depends," Merilee answers thoughtfully. "I always try to meet one of my co-workers away from home because I can't get rid of her when she comes to the house."

"But what about Joe?" Whit asks, referring to Merilee's dominant and aggressive father.

"I'd much rather see him here at the house," she readily admits, "because I feel more confident dealing with his pushiness when I know Whit and Callie are in the other room."

Like most of us, Merilee maintains two views of her home as a haven, each of which elicits a different response. People she thinks might violate her sense of her home as a secure and comfortable shelter, she opts to meet somewhere else. However, she meets anyone she considers a personal threat in her home, where her familiarity with the environment makes her feel more confident and capable of controlling the situation.

Note that these phenomena refer to quality spaces, those with which the person experiences a bond that transcends that space's physical characteristics. If Merilee felt embarrassed about her home, her relationship with Whit, or her pup's behavior, the setting would contribute to rather than alleviate any stress associated with meeting her father.

How do our dogs feel about social contacts that occur in their home territories? Much of the canine response depends on the animal's personality, its relationship to its owner, and the quality of the environment. As pointed out in the previous chapter, dominant and submissive animals may relate to people quite differently, as will shy and reserved ones. A more timid animal who perceives its owner as dominant may hide behind that person when strangers arrive. However, if that same animal perceives itself as dominant to the owner, it may adopt the fear-fight mode and menace any visitors.

Social Contact Checklist

- How often do you entertain guests?

- Do both adults and children visit?

- Do dogs and other animals visit?

- Do others come into your home in your absence?

- How do you want your dog to act around your friends in your home?

- How do you want your dog to act around strangers in your home?

Many owners prefer veterinarians who make house calls because their pets love anyone who comes to the house. However, those same animals might go to pieces if their owners took them to a veterinary clinic for an examination. Other dogs react exactly the opposite, seeing the house-call veterinarian as a territorial violation and reason to resist any handling. Put those same dogs in an examination room on the veterinarian's turf, though, and they react neutrally or even positively to that same person.

The physical makeup of the environment also can affect an animal's response to visitors. Although Callie adores putzing around the cluttered spare bedroom with Whit, when a stranger comes upon her there, she finds the cramped quarters confining and acts leery in that social situation. Other dogs may respond the same way to an environment that they perceive as too open because they can't keep track of all that space at once.

Finally, how the dog reacts to other people in the owners' absence may differ markedly from how it acts in their presence. When Merilee cheerfully greets the letter carrier, Callie grins up at him, too. However, when he comes in her owners' absence, Callie greets him with "Keep away!" barks.

Stimulating Spaces

Quality spaces also stimulate us to grow. In his private nook Whit indulges a secret desire to write poetry, while Merilee dons one of Whit's old T-shirts and uses her exercise machine in the bedroom as she reads about South American birds, activities neither of them could comfortably pursue elsewhere. And who can put a price on the confidences we share with each other—or even aloud to our pets or ourselves—in the comfort and security of our own homes? How many major changes begin with a few moments of intimate thought or conversation in a bedroom, or sitting at the breakfast table or on the deck? In such ways a quality personal space stimulates us to stretch the limits as no other environment can.

Whether Callie thinks great thoughts in her home remains anyone's guess. However, as we saw when she got that new toy from Merilee's brother, she feels much more comfortable exploring new things in her own environment. In fact, accounts of companion animals displaying extraordinary behaviors also often take place in familiar surroundings. Service dogs trained to function as the eyes, ears, or hands of their owners stretch the limits of their training every day. One not only fetches everything from shoes to razor for her wheelchair-bound owner, but also unzips his backpack and removes her ball so he can toss it for her. On a more mundane level, many owners who worried about how the dog would respond to the new baby because of the animal's leeriness of strange infants are delighted to discover that their own child stimulates the dog to develop a whole spectrum of "nanny" behaviors.

Another example of how a secure space can stimulate learning occurs when Whit and Merilee enroll Callie in obedience class.

"The first few weeks I felt so mortified by her behavior, I almost quit," Whit confesses. "She just didn't seem to get it in class. But as soon as we brought her home and put her through the same routine, she caught on in no time. Then we'd go back to class the next week, and it was like she'd never heard the commands before."

Although most owners want their dogs to obey basic commands and feel comfortable in a variety of environments, shy animals or ones accustomed to a quieter household, like Callie, may find the class setting so daunting that they just can't concentrate.

"That's what Merilee said, too," Whit acknowledges, grinning sheepishly. "She reminded me of the times when I gave a presentation perfectly in front of the mirror or to her, then got all tongue-tied at the actual meeting."

Realizing that Callie needs to learn the setting as well as the commands, Whit and Merilee arrange to work with their pet in the training center before the other owners and dogs arrive. As Callie becomes more comfortable in those surroundings, the appearance of other owners and dogs bothers her less and less.

"Sometimes I wondered why we didn't just sign her up for private lessons since being with the group was so difficult for her," Whit admits as he tosses the border collie her fuzzy ball. "Would that have been easier for her?"

Initially, perhaps, but that approach wouldn't address the issue of the dog's discomfort around others. Because her owners want Callie to feel at ease and respond to basic commands in strange environments, they still would need to accustom her to these. On the positive side, the confidence many dogs gain from performing even simple tasks well at home often enables them to handle strange environments more easily, too.

Spaces may restrict growth and development in other ways as well. Whit and Merilee gave up vacations, dinners out, expensive vehicles, and other nonessentials to save for a home of their own because they found their downtown apartment so cramped and noisy.

"Whit's chair took up half the living room in the old place," Merilee recalls. "And the walls were so thin we had no privacy at all. It was hard enough to think with all the racket, let alone think great thoughts."

The same thing happens to dogs. The last chapter described how raising pups in restricted or chaotic environments may permanently affect their mental development. For sure, we all want a stable pup or dog capable of going with the environmental flow, but we need to look at that realistically. Even the most stable animal can't compensate for an environment that doesn't challenge it enough, or one that frustrates rather than stimulates its positive growth and development.

For example, one owner of a high-energy dog wanted me to prescribe Ritalin—a drug commonly used to treat hyperactivity in youngsters—because it "works so well in kids." In less than a year, the owner had tried so many different training methods that it made me jittery just to hear about them all. This dog didn't perceive her home as a serene environment, but the owner didn't see—or didn't want to see—how her beliefs and the resultant physical, mental, and emotional environment they created caused her dog's problem. Even more sadly, the dog didn't fit the pattern of a hyperactive animal at all; she would settle down if you simply ignored her, and she had never destroyed anything in the home. However, the idea of a quick-fix pill fit the owner's belief structure so perfectly that *she* couldn't settle down long enough to permit the in-depth workup necessary to determine true hyperactivity. When I refused to prescribe any medication without this testing, I never heard from her again.

Stimulating Space Check

Think about your home as a place capable of stimulating your new pup or dog to grow: Do you consider your home quiet or active? If your home is active, what is the source of the activity: Family members? Pets? Visitors?

Learning Space Check

Think about your home as a learning space for your new dog: Are there times when your home is less active than others when it might be easier for your pet to learn new things? Do certain parts of your home provide fewer distractions that could interfere with training? If not, could you make changes that would create a learning space for your new pet?

The Sensual Space

The ability of an environment to elicit memories can pack a potentially powerful behavioral wallop, even though few of us consciously consider this aspect of our homes. Obviously if a place evokes positive memories, we feel more relaxed and comfortable there than if it evokes negative ones. This quality is particularly relevant to dog owners because studies of memory indicate that when it comes to storing data, our brains work a lot like our dogs'.

For example, Merilee cut herself with a carving knife while preparing dinner two years ago when she and Whit lived in the city. Whit rushed her to the emergency room of the nearest hospital, an overcrowded, understaffed inner-city facility. There they waited more than four hours for an intern to stitch up Merilee's hand, bandage it, and give her a tetanus shot. Merilee completely forgot about the incident—until she took Callie in for her first veterinary exam.

"As soon as I smelled that antiseptic, it all came back in such vivid detail, I thought I was going to throw up," she recalled later.

Although we humans consider ourselves a visual species compared with our dogs, odors and sounds jog our memories more than visual cues. The aroma of a cup of cinnamon-apple herbal tea can send our minds drifting back to Grandma's house or our sixth birthday when Mom served that incredible apple pie aglow with candles. A car backfires, and people and dogs raised in serene settings may leap upward in surprise, their minds blank, while those raised in war zones dive for cover as memories of past battles cascade through their heads.

In spite of this, we pay scant attention to how important those familiar scents, sounds, and sights are, not only to our sense of place but also to our sense of self—until we're cut off from them. This fact came home to me dramatically several years ago when I did a stint of traveling that involved visiting 10 cities in 10 days while living out of a single carry-on bag. I arrived at the last stop, San Francisco, after midnight and left the hotel before six the next morning to attend a conference. When I got back to the hotel after dark that night, I walked into the room, stood in the short entryway with the bathroom door on one side and a mirrored closet door on the other, took in the grey tweed carpeting and pale green walls—and had absolutely no idea where I was. I could have been in virtually any hotel room in any city in the country. Worse, because I'd run out of most of my own travel-sized toiletries and had purchased others as substitutes, I didn't even *smell* like myself.

I'd never before felt so disoriented. When I walked into the room far enough that I could see my carry-on on the luggage carrier, I practically lunged at it in my haste to get out my baggy old T-shirt or anything familiar. Nor do I remember a time when my dogs smelled more deliciously doggy, and home more wonderfully "homey," than when I returned home from that trip.

Considering how much more our dogs' senses dominate their world than our senses do ours, we can only begin to imagine what kinds of memories the scent of Whit's leather chair, Merilee's shampoo, or Callie's own beloved, well-chewed fuzzy ball elicit in the pup. Just as Pavlov's bell awakened a strong-enough memory of food to make his dogs salivate in anticipation, so our dogs may attach meaning to sensory cues we scarcely notice or don't even experience ourselves.

For example, when I want to take the dogs out, I'm often too lazy to go into the office and turn on the answering machine, so I'll simply take the kitchen phone off the hook. Although I'd love everyone to believe that my dogs represent the epitome of canine decorum, the truth is that whenever I suggest a walk my hound mix, Watson, leaps vertically in the air, and Violet runs in circles issuing sharp barks. I never connected these events until the day a repairman took the kitchen phone off the hook, the hound leaped, and the corgi barked and ran in circles.

"Them dogs always act like that?" he asked, edging away from this somewhat demonic display.

"Only when I take the phone off the hook," I replied, realizing that I'd unwittingly duplicated Pavlov's famous experiment.

The incident illustrates how visual cues—just like sounds and odors—can trigger sometimes complex canine memories and sequences of behavior, the cause of which may not occur to us until after the fact. Most dog owners easily can recite similar connections their pets make once they think about it. Based on studies of pups raised in chaotic environments, the strongest connections appear to occur in the least cluttered sensory environments. This doesn't mean that the dog raised in a relatively quiet, fairly odor-free environment will make *better* connections when it associates a sound, sight, or scent with an activity, but rather that these connections will be *stronger*. Dogs who routinely accompany their veterinarian or vet tech owners to work couldn't care less about the smell of antiseptic, while the shy little poodle who visits the clinic once a year for her vaccinations begins trembling the instant she catches a whiff of it.

Can we use this knowledge to our advantage when we try to create quality shared spaces for ourselves and our dogs? Yes, provided we remember that they don't see our homes exactly the same way we do.

Sensual Space Check

Thinking of your ideal dog and any function bred into it, walk through your home listening to all of the different sounds: television, radio, CD player, computer games, canaries chirping, kids bickering, traffic, and barking dogs outdoors. Then focus on the scents: dinner cooking, hair spray and aftershave, wood smoke, the dirty diaper pail, the lemon furniture polish. Next evaluate your home visually, not only considering its details, but also with an eye toward motion. Finally, think about your home as a source of memories elicited by those sounds, scents, and images.

After you collect all this sensory data, rate your home as an environment in which a pup or dog could learn and create good memories. If your home strikes you as too limited and quiet, what could you do to spice it up? If you think it's too hectic, how could you tone it down?

The Functional Home

For many household pets the home environment also constitutes its workplace. Because our dogs see establishing and protecting the territory as their primary "occupation," especially in our absence, it helps to recognize the qualities that would create a comfortable work environment for our pets, too.

Naturally, humans put the most emphasis on any threats the workplace may pose to their well-being.

"You're kidding!" snorts Whit. "Once I knew where the fire exits were, I didn't worry about safety."

True, but Whit works in the data-processing division of a company that distributes office supplies, not a particularly high-risk occupation. However, suppose he worked as an undercover agent for the Drug Enforcement Agency and routinely found himself in potentially threatening environments. In this workplace, he surely would think about exits and other escape routes because his life could depend on such knowledge.

Do our dogs function more as office workers in placid environments or as undercover agents in hostile territories when we leave them alone to perform their protective functions? That depends on the animal, its relationship to us, and the environment. Suffice it to say that an animal lacking experience and confidence left alone with its instinct to "Take care of house" probably feels about as secure as you or I would if asked to perform a five-kilo drug-drop at midnight in a ghetto torn apart by gang wars.

"How can you possibly compare my house to a war zone?" Merilee demands somewhat irritably.

Merilee feels irritated by the analogy because she forgets that dogs live in a world of sights, scents, and sounds we can't even begin to comprehend. They have a hearing range hundreds of times more sensitive than ours, in terms of both volume and sensitivity, including sounds in the ultrasonic range. They can detect motion in even the dimmest light and can also see color, but not the same way we do. And what a range of scents they sniff and analyze! Depending on the breed, a full 10 percent of their brains may be devoted to processing scent data, compared with a human's meager 1 percent. Touch? Even newborn pups will respond defensively to any touch. At the other end of the spectrum, Pavlov's Effect of Person proved that the mere touch of a person can alter a dog's heart rate by as much as 100 beats per minute. Consequently, it seems safe to assume that any tactile stimulation will affect the animal somehow.

Thanks to their rich and complex perceptual ability, our dogs spend most of their time living in a world we can barely comprehend. When we interact with them, by their choice or ours, they focus on our world, but when we leave them alone, they naturally take the broader canine view. Moreover, our perceptual limitations make it difficult for us to help our dogs determine what, among all the stimuli that assault them, poses a legitimate threat to the territory and which input they can safely ignore.

When Callie hears a strange noise beyond her owners' hearing range, she begins to bark.

"It's nothing, Callie," they assure her.

However, chances are it probably *is* something to Callie, and she interprets their assurance to mean she needn't worry about what she heard rather than that she heard nothing at all. If she accepts this assessment, she stops barking. If she doesn't, she continues. Then her owners can choose from among a variety of training techniques that run the gamut from ignoring the dog to using physical force to teach her not to bark at "nothing."

Each dog must work out to its own satisfaction which of the sensory input that it receives from the environment poses a threat and which doesn't, and that takes time. Dogs who live in quiet rural homes whose peace is violated at most by a daily delivery to the mailbox at the end of a long driveway and a monthly visit from the meter reader don't receive nearly the exposure to novel stimulation as animals living in the city. On the other hand, I recall one city dog who moved to the country and became frantic when acorns dropped on the roof from the ancient oak tree growing next to the house. And, just as our ever-vigilant-on-the-job undercover agent may turn into a laid-back family man in his own home, so the dog who ignores all kinds of sensory input while it happily romps with us evenings and weekends may behave quite differently while on the job protecting its and our territory in our absence.

In addition to wanting to work in an environment in which we feel reasonably safe, we want one whose demands match our capabilities. Although Whit and Merilee may joke about finding jobs that pay them a fabulous salary for doing nothing as they trudge off to work every day, we know from recent mind-body studies that a lack of function can undermine human health and happiness every bit as much as our dogs'. The opposite holds true, too. When Whit's company reorganizes and he winds up trying to do the job of three people, he develops an ulcer within a matter of months. Thus, we define a quality workplace as one whose demands fall within our capacity: while we relish the opportunity to grow in any environment, we want it to stimulate us within what we consider our achievable limits.

What does this mean to our dogs? Let's write Callie's job description from both her owners' and her own points of view. Whit and Merilee's description of what Callie does looks like this: "Play, eat, and sleep with us when we're home. Play, eat, and sleep alone when we're gone."

Callie's description of her job looks quite different: "Play, eat, and sleep with Whit and Merilee when they're home. When they're gone, protect territory. Notice any unusual sounds, scents, or sights. If stimulus comes from indoors try to track it down. If from beyond a closed door, scratch at the door. If it comes from the boxes in the spare bedroom, paw through them. If sound, scent, or sight comes from outdoors, sneak onto the couch in the living room and look out the windows. If I still can't locate it, and the threat seems real, sound alarm barks to scare it off. If that doesn't work, urinate or defecate to mark territory."

And that barely begins to tell the story. Callie could repeat that sequence every time she smells, hears, or sees something she considers novel which, for a young pup, could be practically everything. If her environment offers her the opportunity to explore sufficiently to satisfy herself that no real threat exists or if it protects her from sensory input, she begins to relax in her new home. However, if she can't determine the source of the stimuli and she can't get away from them, then she feels more like Whit trying to do the work of three people.

Review what you discovered when you evaluated your home for scents, sounds, and visual stimulation. Because many dogs spend more time playing and working in their homes than their owners do, we need to perceive our homes in terms of these dual canine functions, with an eye toward balance. We want our dogs to feel secure in our homes, but not so secure that they won't interact with others who visit us. Nor do we want them to feel so secure that they can't cope with a new environment.

Veterinarians increasingly encounter a behavioral phenomenon called *separation anxiety* in which the pet becomes so dependent on its (usually highly anthropomorphic) owner and home that it goes to pieces when separated from them. When these animals succumb to illnesses that normally would require hospitalization to provide optimum care, the owners must treat them at home or on an outpatient basis because the psychological effects of hospitalization would undermine any treatment. This can prove a tremendous burden for the working owner. However, these human-animal-environment combinations also serve as potent object lessons for those tempted to create highly anthropomorphic relationships with, and overprotective environments for, their pets.

If you intend to add another dog to your household, walk through your home again, this time with an eye toward how any other animals currently divvy up your space. Not only will this help you determine any areas your new pet could claim as its own, but it also will reveal any territorial hot spots over which the animals might clash.

Canine Environmental Tension Relievers

Having considered the factors that go into making a house a home for us and our dogs, let's move on to some simple ways to merge human and canine needs. First, make a list of all your environment-related rules. A typical prospective dog owner's list might look like this:

- No house-soiling.
- No destruction of any of our possessions or the house itself.
- Must stay in kitchen or family room.
- Must stay off all furniture.

"Our list looked just like that!" Whit marvels as Callie lounges on the foot of the bed playing with one of Whit's old slippers.

Puppies have a way of doing that. When my old dog died, I decided to get a new couch to replace an old love seat that had jokingly become known as the "dog couch." Before I did, however, I asked my husband how he felt about any new pets sleeping on the furniture.

"Absolutely not," he declared. "I'm tired of picking dog hair off my clothes."

"No problem," I confidently assured him. "I'll simply train the new dog to stay off of it."

Then I went out and bought a dark green couch and matching chair guaranteed to attract every pet hair in the universe. Then I got my corgi.

The first night I left the pup sleeping contentedly in her bed in her fiberglass carrier and went to sleep myself. A short time later, I felt a soft, warm, squirmy feeling in my left armpit.

"Why is this dog in the bed?" I mumbled sleepily.

"She's so little," my spouse murmured. "Surely you can't expect her to sleep on the floor."

"She wasn't on the floor," I yawned. "She was in a crate with a warm fuzzy blanket she dearly loves."

"Shhhhh," he replied. "She needs her sleep."

After making a mental note to stock up on vacuum cleaner bags, I fell happily asleep with the dog.

Because pups do have a way of worming their way into the hearts and beds of even the most experienced and resolute owners, it makes sense to formulate a plan flexible enough to cover all the bases. Had I known that my previously dog-neutral spouse would fall head over heels in love with our new pup, I most certainly would have chosen furniture upholstered with a smooth, densely woven fabric, such as denim, and I wouldn't even have considered anything that didn't come with removable pillow covers.

Originally, I did cover the couch with a flannel sheet that I routinely washed, but I gave this up for aesthetic reasons: I bought the couch because I liked it, and I never got to see it. When one of my sons stopped in and jokingly thanked me for protecting his legacy so carefully, I initiated a new plan. I removed the sheet and dubbed one side of the pillows "dog" and the other side "company." When company comes, I flip the pillows over to reveal a fresh, relatively dog hair–free surface. As soon as they leave, I flip them back to the doggy side. When the rest of the couch starts looking doggy, too, I'll spruce it up with slipcovers made in a smooth, densely woven, easily washed fabric.

I also kept the old love seat, moving it into a common area adjacent to the kitchen and covering it with one of those do-it-yourself slipcovers that consists of a single piece of fabric with an elasticized band that forms a skirt. Because this fabric is too thin to tolerate much canine use, I cover the back and pillows with a color-coordinated piece of denim. A washable natural wool rug in front of the couch, a pot of geraniums beside it, and two birdcages above give this pet nook a country cottage look with which both the pets and I can live.

The desire for an environment that looks attractive and can be easily cleaned comes up repeatedly when dog owners describe the ideal human-canine home. In addition to removable pillow covers or slipcovers and washable rugs, wood floors win hands-down over wall-to-wall carpeting. Not only do wood floors simplify cleaning up dog hair and any canine accidents that may occur, but they also make flea control much easier. In addition, both humans and animals with allergies fare much better in these environments. This goal of "cleanability" limits many pets to the kitchen with its vinyl flooring. However, given that the dog's territorial needs include the freedom to explore, such an environment-sparing rule may create a great deal of tension for the animal.

"Surely you don't expect people to turn a new pup loose in the house and go off to work!" Merilee shudders at the thought.

Not at all, although the concept of confining the pup raises more than a little trepidation. Depending on the pup's original environment, in its owners' absence it may happily—and gratefully—adopt a fiberglass kennel or crate kept in a secure place such as their bedroom. Placing the kennel or crate within a wire exercise pen, or even a child's playpen for smaller pups, gives the animal a "yard" to go along with its house. Put an old sweater or sweatshirt inside the kennel, and spread a plastic dropcloth underneath it to create a secure and easy-to-clean home base.

Owners who confine a pup or dog in this way don't do it to punish the animal, but rather to provide it with its own private, personal space to use in their absence when the animal doesn't want (or lacks the confidence and experience) to protect the territory. Once the dog becomes house-trained, the owner can remove the exercise pen and leave the crate for the dog to use at its convenience. Used in this manner, it provides a haven to which the shy pup or old dog can retreat when the household bustle becomes too much for it to deal with comfortably. It's also much easier to teach young children not to bother Callie when she's in her "home" than to stay away from her when she looks "tired" or "grouchy."

When owners use kenneling in this way, most dogs come to view their crates as a home within the home. Some dogs continue to use them for their entire lives, while others seek out alternative places where they feel secure in the owner's absence or when things get too hectic in the household.

Most working owners start out using crates as sanity-savers. Regardless of how bad we may feel about denying a pup total freedom, we must weigh that regret against how we feel when we come home after a wretched day at work and discover puddles, piles, and chewed-up furnishings. If we can dismiss all this with a smile, fine. But if we scream at or smack the dog, or spend the next day at work feeling guilty about swatting the pup the night before *and* worrying about what it might be getting into now, the pup's freedom hardly frees owner or pet from mental and possibly physical pain.

On the other hand, improperly crating a pup can yield equally disastrous results if the owner uses crating as a substitute for training and quality interaction, or if the animal won't tolerate the approach. Although my corgi loved her crate as a pup and accepts it when we travel and visit others, my hound, who spent all but five weeks of his first three and a half months in a shelter, resisted crating from day one. Moreover, he resisted in a way I could never figure out. I'd leave him in his crate in the bedroom, and when I returned an hour later I'd find its top, bottom, and door lying on the floor with the screws arranged tastefully around it. Although I admit I was tempted to search him and the area for concealed screwdrivers, and even wondered if the corgi and/or the cat provided outside assistance, I assume he figured out some way to jump in the crate such that he worked the metal bolts loose from the plastic nuts. However, I never succeeded in catching him in the act.

In spite of all the effort to which Watson obviously went to get out of his crate, though, once out of it he never did any damage in my absence (except chew up whatever the diabolical cat knocked off the counters). Consequently, I chose to let it go. Although I would like him to feel comfortable in a crate for his own sake, his behavior makes it clear that I'm up against some deeply rooted early experience. While he fits into my environment very well, an owner who insisted on crating would find him an exasperating and intolerable pet.

"When we crated Callie, we just did it because we thought it was the right thing for us to do," Whit points out.

Whit's observation may reflect more personal preference than knowledge, but we already know how the owner's beliefs can influence the success of any human-canine interaction. Even though I've encountered situations in which crate-training theoretically would take a huge amount of territorial pressure off a particular animal, I know from sad experience not to recommend it unless I believe the owner fully understands and supports the concept and its underlying philosophy. If the owner views crating and penning as "putting the dog in jail," not only won't the technique work, but it will make any problems worse. In these situations, restricting the destructive or house-soiling pup to the kitchen or even the cellar may work much better simply because the owner believes in the approach.

"That sounds like more of that doggy voodoo," Whit laughs.

Yes and no. Consistency lies at the heart of any successful change. Owners who believe in the rightness of their approach will work much harder at making that belief a reality. As long as it lies within the dog's physical and psychological capacity to fulfill the owner's expectations, few problems arise, and some pretty amazing results can occur. However, if the owner expects a submissive pup to cope with all the territorial violations that may crop up in an apartment building in a bustling community without showing signs of stress—house soiling, whining, chewing, maybe chronic digestive or other medical problems—the owner's determination will do the dog more harm than good.

If you want to crate or isolate a pup or dog, ask yourself why. If it's because you can't bear the thought of anything happening to anything in your home, pets probably don't fit into your idea of a quality space. Nor will crating work if you want to use it to avoid intimately interacting with the animal and accomplishing the necessary training and confidence building that will enable it to live freely and without fear in your home. However, if you see it as a sound way to meet your own *and* your dog's needs in your particular environment, then by all means do it.

If you get a purebred pup, talk to the breeder about crating. Some breeds and lines of dogs adapt to it better than others. Some breeders of small dogs use large fiberglass carriers as whelping boxes and then dismantle them so the pups become used to the bottom half as beds. Animals raised in such environments can be a godsend to busy owners who want a crate-accepting animal because they worry about their furnishings in their absence, or because they travel and want to take the dog with them. (Many motels will accept pets, but only if they stay in a crate in the owner's absence.)

As I noted with Watson, some animals from shelters or pet stores react poorly to crating. Others embrace it so thoroughly that they can't live anywhere but in a crate. If the dog resists and you want to limit its range in your home, use the combination method, leaving the open crate in a confined area such as a large exercise pen or the kitchen. If the dog resists this, bite the bullet and give the animal free run of the house; go out for a five-minute walk, and see what happens. When you return you may well discover, as I did, that nothing happens at all.

When we evaluate our environments in terms of a particular dog's needs, we seek to balance its need to explore and feel free in its space with its concurrent and contradictory need to feel safe and secure. Given all the factors that go into the human and canine definitions of a quality space, reaching that balance seems impossible. However, if you just keep the basics in mind and talk to other dog owners, especially those who own the kind of dog you like and share the kind of relationship and environments you want to share with yours, your own unique definition of a quality human-canine environment will emerge.

A dear friend's home welcomes the visitor with an array of paintings, books, plants, antiques, and musical instruments that immediately identify it as a very personal and well-loved human space. On the mantle sits a small engraved sign informing visitors that this lovely space is maintained solely for the comfort of the owners' *animals* (so many dogs, cats, birds, mice, and rats that I've lost count) and anyone who doesn't like it can leave. When I look at that home, I can't imagine that comfortable couch without a greyhound or a shaggy terrier sprawled out on it along with a cat or two. This delightfully synergistic environment didn't occur overnight, of course, nor does it represent a finished product. Like all human relationships with pets, it represents a work constantly in progress, evolving and changing to fit the owners' and the animals' changing needs.

4

A Meeting of the Minds

How the Principles of Pack Behavior
Shape Our Relationships with Our Dogs

When Pete Mattson starts his own marketing consulting business in his home, he revels in the fact that he can now work with his dream dog at his side. He gets an English bulldog pup, Cynthia, and in a sometimes deliberate, sometimes subconscious revolt against the rigid policies of the autocratic corporation for which he'd previously worked, Pete takes a democratic approach to her training.

"None of those high-handed 'comes,' 'sits,' or 'stays' for my dog," Pete boasts. "She's my best friend."

By the time Cynthia celebrates her first birthday, Pete's wife, Jane, doesn't have the heart to tell him how much she dreads being alone with his canine best friend when he goes off to visit clients because the dog becomes a fur-covered tyrant during his absence. Nor does she confide how many of her friends have stopped visiting her because Cynthia makes them feel so uneasy.

Of course, all of this does come out when Cynthia bites one of the Mattsons' grandchildren.

———————

While the last chapter discussed how we and our dogs go about arranging our homes so that each can claim a unique personal territory within the shared space, this chapter focuses on how we arrange the mental territory.

I approached this material with some trepidation because of a troublesome paradox I see plaguing more and more human-canine relationships. At the same time that a lack of human leadership within the human-animal pack causes the majority of canine behavioral problems as well as many medical ones, this owner response occurs more as a backlash to a mistaken idea about what constitutes leadership rather than as the result of a conscious choice not to lead.

My own experience and discussions with professionals, students, breeders, and owners convinces me that many people perceive dominance (the so-called alpha status) and subordination *emotionally*, a perception that interferes with their ability to analyze their relationship with a dog objectively. Consider this classic example of canine interaction:

Two strange dogs meet in the park. They sniff noses, circle, and sniff rear ends. One dog puts his front paws on the shoulders of the other. If the other dog goes down, rolls over, and exposes its abdomen, no fight occurs. Under certain conditions the subordinate dog also will urinate.

Humans who observed this neutral canine display over the years coined the highly charged phrases "top dog," "underdog," and "yellow-bellied coward" to describe the participants and their activities. Not only does the alpha animal become linked with the emotionally charged "top dog" in many people's minds, but it also becomes synonymous with "A-1" and "Numero Uno."

Worse, many people erroneously associate these same terms with sporting events during which a competitor wins by beating an opponent.

In addition to preferring "leader" over "alpha" to disengage the concept from as many of these misleading and emotional associations as possible, I also prefer the term "subordinate" to "submissive" for the same reason. When Pete recalls his interactions with a boss he found particularly demanding and hard to get along with, he perceived his own response as submissive rather than subordinate.

"I gave into that little weasel again," he berated himself disgustedly after the event.

Jane would later perpetuate this villain/victim view of dominance and submission when describing the event to her sister.

"Poor Pete. I feel so sorry for him when that jerk picks on him."

While changing "alpha" to "leader" and "submissive" to "subordinate" may seem like little more than a word game, bear in mind that the issues discussed in this chapter lie at the heart of many of the most serious human-canine problems. The more we can disengage these from the misconceptions that permeate our society, the more objectively we can analyze our true leadership skills.

Emotional Pecking Orders

Many of us owe our ideas about pack structure, dominance, and subordination to Norwegian zoologist T. Schjelderup-Ebbe. In the early 1900s Schjelderup-Ebbe studied chickens, noting particularly the phenomenon that occurs when an unfamiliar group of hens is put together.

"The pecking order!" Pete Mattson exclaims, correctly guessing the name of the behavior the scientist first described.

But what does it mean for a group to establish a pecking order?

"The way I see it, at first everybody jockeys for position. But after a while the biggest, toughest bird comes out on top, and he pecks all the others to keep them in line. The number two bird pecks all the birds except number one, the number three bird pecks all those except the top two, and so on. The bottom bird gets pecked by everyone."

Given Pete's view of subordinate animals as "henpecked" and his negative feelings regarding his former boss, we can appreciate why he didn't want to treat Cynthia as a member of a pack. But, before we accuse Pete of anthropomorphism, let's look at the science behind this phenomenon.

Schjelderup-Ebbe's studies of how chickens established a social order appealed to other ethologists who then studied a wide variety of other species, including mammals. They discovered similar relationships, but because some species don't peck each other, they referred to the phenomenon as *rank order* or *dominance hierarchy*.

This view pervaded scientific thinking through the 1950s and '60s and was championed by the great ethologist Konrad Lorenz. In his classic book *On Aggression* Lorenz described what contemporary ethologists now view as his and his supporters' "masculine utopian vision." According to Lorenz, a few male animals (to whom he referred as the "senate") acquired all the authority necessary to make and carry out all the decisions for the good of the entire community. Western European and American male-dominated societies that championed male political, academic, military, and religious leaders (as well as a male god) as "top dogs" naturally embraced these findings because they validated their own beliefs. After all, wouldn't you like a theory that proved your own superiority?

However, these scientists neglected the fact that they set up the rules for dominance in such a way that only those males who they wanted to perceive as dominant could become dominant. In human society, if the political process gave women little or no say and required great wealth to participate, that society would likely wind up with wealthy men in positions of power who might possess few or no true leadership qualities.

Subsequently, when scientists of both sexes began studying animals of both sexes and all ages for longer periods of time, a different picture began to emerge. Consider the following list of characteristics describing a particular male monkey in a troop of animals:

- Does not lead the group.
- In a skirmish, moves to the center of the group and lets the males at the periphery fight.
- May not be the most sexually active.
- Interferes little with the group's arrangement.
- May charge others to break up fights.

Do these characteristics describe the behavior of a dominant or a subordinate animal?

"Definitely subordinate," Pete volunteers immediately. "He doesn't show any signs of dominance at all except maybe breaking up fights. Given his other qualities, I bet he only does that because someone forces him to."

Wrong. Pete's belief that this *dominant* animal actually displays subordinate behaviors provides another clue to how he and many other dog owners get into trouble with their pets. Obviously, if you don't know how a leader should act, you'll have a hard time acting like one consistently.

Let's see how this plays out in the human-canine arena. One day Cynthia sprawls out right in the area where Jane Mattson wants to work. When Jane lightly nudges the pup with her foot, the bulldog growls at her.

"Don't be so mean to her," Pete rebukes his wife. "She's trying to sleep."

Later when Jane returns home after running some errands, Cynthia practically bowls her over.

"Look how much she loves you!" Pete laughs.

In this situation, Pete's mistaken view of dominance leads him to accept two dominant canine displays in the name of love.

Not only that, in the process of doing so he concurrently, but unwittingly, defines himself and Jane as subordinate. However, Cynthia's problems don't arise because Pete perceives Jane's dominant response to a dominant canine act (growling) as mean, or because he dismisses other dominant canine actions (jumping up) as loving. The dog's problems arise because her owners don't *know* which canine acts communicate dominance.

Canine Dominance Check

Before reading on, think about each of the following canine behaviors and indicate whether you view each as dominant (D) or subordinate (S), and whether you would reward (R) or punish (P) it.

• nudging	• growling
• jumping up on people	• snapping
• leaning	• biting
• licking	

Add any other behaviors or notes that might help you further define your own views of pack structures.

Pete considers the four canine behaviors in the left-hand column subordinate displays which he rewards, and the three in the right-hand column dominant ones which he disciplines "depending on the circumstances." Jane describes Cynthia's nudging and leaning as "bossy," but not enough so that she'd discipline the dog for displaying these behaviors. On the other hand, she finds growling, snapping, and biting intolerable "because of the grandchildren."

The Making of a Leader

To help you sort out your beliefs and feelings about leadership, let's put Schjelderup-Ebbe's chickens to work again and see what the studies actually revealed about the nature of dominance and subordination.

First, even though most people automatically imagine the top bird in the original study as a rooster, Schjelderup-Ebbe studied only groups of hens. Second, the henhouse did not become a bloody battlefield, nor was the "lowest" bird pecked to death. Fighting occurs because of a *lack* of social structure, not because of its presence. Third, for any given pair of birds, a quick peck or look usually sufficed to establish the order. Fourth, although the birds tended to maintain their place once they established it, they didn't necessarily form a linear hierarchy. In fact, so many variations can and do occur within a group that many scientists now use the phrase *dominance relationships* rather than *dominance hierarchy* to describe them. One scientist even went so far as to describe the pecking order as a "pecking puzzle." Just as a hen forms a unique relationship with every other hen in the henhouse, our dogs may evolve intricate strategies to maintain stable relationships with everyone with whom they come in contact.

What images come to mind when you contemplate these familiar dominance-related phrases?

- struggle for survival
- battle of the titans
- survival of the fittest
- winner take all

Most of us envision some sort of one-on-one, energy-intensive interaction with brute force ruling the day.

In reality, such a view of dominance makes little sense because it wastes too much time and energy. When we discussed territoriality in the last chapter, we noted how animals lacking a sense of place won't eat, drink, or reproduce. Consequently, the more time an animal spends fighting to establish and protect its territory, the less it can devote to eating and drinking, and the weaker it becomes. The weaker it becomes, the less likely it can win a fight.

Moreover, those who fight run the risk of injury which will further increase their vulnerability. Considering the ultimate goal, mating and passing on one's genes to successive generations, constant fighting presents several major drawbacks:

- If there's no time to eat or drink, there's certainly no time to mate.
- Weakness and injury could knock an animal out of the game of life as well as the mating game.
- While the battle rages, any potential mate could get bored and go off with someone else.

Therefore, we can see why it would benefit an animal to possess qualities that would enable it to compete successfully for food and mates in the most energy-efficient manner. Put another way, it makes sense to move the leadership game out of the physical realm and into the mental arena as quickly as possible. Ethologists list five approaches that may work singularly or in combination to help animals achieve this goal:

- resource holding potential (RHP)
- the confidence effect
- the bystander effect
- aid from others
- individual recognition by others

Because owners and dogs also wittingly or unwittingly use these same approaches to enhance or undermine their relationships with others, we need to know more about them if we want to establish a stable pack with our dogs.

Might and Right

Ethologists refer to a dominance strategy that depends on the ability to win fights as an animal's *resource holding potential*, or RHP. Within a group of animals, RHP tends to function as a self-limiting phenomenon over time. Initially the biggest and strongest males claim the most territory, food and water, and mates. As expected, their mates give birth to more, bigger, and stronger offspring. Eventually a group emerges whose physically similar members spend more and more of their time fighting each other for dominance.

It comes as no surprise that when physical force serves as the primary criterion for leadership, turnover tends to run rather high. In the human-canine pack such physical-force–based relationships sour in two ways. First, if force-oriented owners can't muster the wherewithal necessary to sustain their position, they may give up the dog.

"I just don't have the time and energy to handle a big dog like this," says Jane Mattson's sister as she whaps her leaping Airedale on the head with a rolled-up newspaper for the 10th time in five minutes.

However, owners who do find the time and energy to maintain the physical approach also experience a high pet turnover. Another reason the Mattsons resist anything that even hints at exertion of any kind of dominance over their dog comes from watching their neighbor, Jack Nesbitt, a retired military man. Jack favors German shepherd dogs and heavy-handed training techniques, and he'll talk for hours about his confrontations with various animals to "teach them who's boss."

"Just about the time I get them straightened out, though, they come down with diarrhea or some other chronic problem," he admits, snapping his fingers at the sleeping shepherd who rushes to his side with ears flattened and tail tucked. "It's a damn shame after all the time and effort I put into training them."

When Jack reminisces about his all-time-favorite dog, Sultan, he views their relationship quite differently from the way a behaviorist would.

"What fights that dog and I had!" Jack laughs at the memory. "Most of the time he behaved pretty well, but every once in a while he'd get it into his head that he was in charge. Then

I'd have to wrestle him and pin him down. He bit me pretty bad a few times, but I never let him get the best of me."

Whereas Jack remembers Sultan fondly because the dog repeatedly challenged his position as leader, in reality Jack lacked any true leadership skills.

"You're kidding!" exclaims Pete Mattson, who always wanted to believe this was true, even though Jack's military background argued against it.

Remember that the various displays between animals function to keep the peace, not to perpetuate war. The fact that Sultan kept acting up clearly communicated that he *didn't* recognize Jack's dominance, no matter how much physical force Jack used to subdue him. If the dog truly had respected his owner's authority, a simple word or look from Jack would have sufficed to terminate the confrontation. In reality, Jack and Sultan functioned more as male littermates vying for the top position than as a human leader and well-behaved dog.

Think about that when you test a new pup or a litter for dominance by holding the animal down on its side or back. The pup should settle, not struggle. And you should be pleased when it does so in a relatively short time because that's a sign of a stable pup. If, on the other hand, you find yourself feeling pleased that the pup's "spirit" or "spunk" causes it to continue its struggles which you must counter with more physical force, your definition of a stable human-canine pack and leadership may result in a less-than-rewarding human-canine relationship.

While some owners may indulge in continual hand-to-paw combat with their dogs to settle leadership disputes, a surprising number of others willingly cede that position with little struggle. When Cynthia growled at Jane for nudging her, Jane backed off immediately when Pete told her to. Compared with Sultan, Cynthia hardly needed to expend any energy at all to communicate her dominance. Soon the bulldog doesn't even need to waste energy growling.

"I can tell just by the look in her eye when she doesn't want me to do something," Jane tells her son as she sits down on the uncomfortable straight-backed chair rather than disturb the pup lounging in Jane's favorite recliner.

Human Dominance Check

Think about how you would feel if your dog growled at, snapped at, or bit you. List the circumstances, if any, under which you would consider such displays acceptable. Do these same conditions apply to all members of your household? What would you *do* if your dog growled, snapped at, or bit you? What would you do if the dog did it to someone else?

The Confidence Effect

Within the scientific community, the fact that winners tend to keep winning and losers tend to keep losing comes about as a result of the *confidence effect*. Scientist T. Burk's studies of field crickets revealed that the top-ranking cricket won 93 percent of its subsequent confrontations following a win, but only 39 percent of those after a loss. The bottom-ranking cricket also benefited from the confidence effect, but not nearly as much: it won 33 percent of its fights after a win, but only 19 percent after a loss. Other studies indicated percentages of 90 percent for winners and 20 percent for losers; that is, a winner stands a 90 percent chance of winning again, while a loser faces only a 20 percent chance of bettering its opponent.

"So, what do crickets have to do with dogs?" asks Jane Mattson as she tiptoes around the sleeping Cynthia.

A great deal, it turns out, because similar studies of other species indicate that the confidence effect applies just as much to mammals. Consider Jane's relationship with Cynthia. When Pete first got the pup, Jane immediately labeled the bulldog "headstrong" and "stubborn." When she lightly nudged the pup with her foot and the pup growled, how did she feel?

"I was surprised and a little frightened," Jane readily admits. "But she was still small, and I wanted to do something to make it clear to her that we wouldn't tolerate that kind of behavior."

At this point the Mattson leadership scenario falls apart because Jane didn't know what to do, and Pete rejected any use of force. So, rather than cheerfully snapping a leash on the pup and taking her on a jolly, fast tour of the house to assert their leadership position, the Mattsons let the behavior go. Score: Cynthia 1, the Mattsons 0.

Like many other owners, the Mattsons want to believe only the best of their pup. Because of this, they chalk Cynthia's behavior up to the fact that she just was having a "bad day," or that they did something that legitimately upset her. Unfortunately, both of these explanations do little more than assign blame; they do nothing to solve the problem. As a result, Cynthia's dominant behavior persists, but with one critical difference.

When Cynthia growls at Jane the second time two weeks later, the dog feels much more confident about her position in the Mattson household. She charges into and out of the house in front of them, jumps up on them and everyone else who comes into their home, sleeps on their bed, and obeys commands only when the mood strikes her. Meanwhile, Pete's fledgling business takes off, and he spends more and more time away from home. When Cynthia begins menacing rather than jumping up on visitors in his absence, the Mattsons label that behavior "protective."

All of these human-canine interactions not only reinforce Cynthia's leadership position in the Mattson pack but also indicate that her owners *accept* this arrangement. Given this setting, it comes as no surprise that Cynthia doesn't hesitate to growl when Jane tries to move the dog's food dish, or that Jane backs away immediately. Whereas Jane at least considered giving the pup a good shake the first time Cynthia growled at her, the second time Jane considers such a show of force suicidal. In terms of the growling, Cynthia can claim two wins to the Mattsons' none. In terms of claiming the leadership position, the dog's score is considerably higher.

In Chapter 1, I spoke of that almost mystical quality known as presence, and alluded to what I call the "leap of faith." Confidence and presence are inextricably entwined. If we lack confidence in ourselves and our relationship with our dogs, we communicate that to them and others in countless subtle and not-so-subtle ways. This combined effect determines our presence. Given the confidence effect, we can appreciate what happens when an owner cedes the leadership position to the dog. Jane and Cynthia essentially entered their first power struggle with the deck stacked in Jane's favor by virtue of her size and species. However, if Jane doesn't play her hand shrewdly, she begins the next game with the deck firmly stacked against her.

Under those circumstances, Jane's lack of trust in Cynthia, her dread of a possible confrontation, and her mixed feelings toward her husband who wanted a dog in the first place, loves the animal so much, and won't *do* anything to make her behave all combine to undermine Jane's presence. She tries to jolly the bulldog, but her high, strained voice sounds like a submissive whine to Cynthia. Jane's movements become jerky and hesitant, further communicating her lower position in their human-canine pack. She refuses to establish eye contact with Cynthia, telling herself she's ignoring the dog, but in reality trying not to do anything that might incite the pup. Given such a lack of presence, Jane most likely will lose rather than win all future confrontations with her pet.

Now suppose Jane decides she doesn't want to live like that and goes to the library or bookstore, selects some training books or videos that appeal to her, and studies them carefully. As she begins teaching Cynthia basic obedience commands, her confidence begins to grow. Does that mean that Jane's home free? Maybe, but maybe not. Remember that our dogs need a sense of function every bit as much as we do. Although behaviorists and trainers traditionally proposed putting bossy dogs into some sort of training program in order to communicate human leadership to them, this isn't necessarily a cure-all for whatever ails a given human-canine relationship. Some of the most firmly entrenched canine tyrants I've encountered routinely take home blue ribbons in obedience and agility. These animals of strong function perform well because they love to perform, not because they recognize their owners as leaders. The acid test comes not from how well Cynthia does what she *likes* to do, but rather how well she does what she doesn't like—such as come when Jane calls her rather than keep playing with her dog pals, or hold a down/stay when she'd rather investigate that knock at the front door.

Ideally when owners of bossy dogs initiate some kind of a training program, their confidence grows, and the animal gracefully cedes the leadership position. However, this is where the leap of faith comes into play. Owners who *believe* their dogs will accept human leadership fare much, much better than those who don't. Unfortunately some of those whose dogs respond to them in what the owners consider a threatening manner approach this backwards: they expect the dog to recognize their leadership *first*, then they'll act like leaders. However, as long as they don't trust the dog, they'll communicate this through their lack of presence thereby greatly decreasing the odds of achieving the very goal they want most to achieve.

Owners who do muster the courage to make the leap of faith fall into two groups. Some restructure their packs using a combination of training and environmental changes that enable them to feel confident the dog will never threaten them again, or that they'll be able to handle it if the dog does. Others consciously or subconsciously create a challenge situation one final time. One day Jane comes flying into the living room to answer the phone and accidentally kicks the bulldog sleeping in the doorway. The two of them freeze, their eyes lock while the phone rings unheeded, and in that instant, Jane makes the leap and assumes the leadership position once and for all.

"Sorry, kiddo," she apologizes, giving the dog a quick pat on the head as she reaches for the phone, "but I told you not to sleep there."

Cynthia yawns and moves to her chair on the other side of the room.

Such self-evaluations always play a critical role in the selection of the perfect canine companion, but are especially important for anyone considering animals from shelters or rescue groups because these dogs may have problems that require well-developed human leadership skills.

Confidence Check

Review those behaviors on your Canine Dominance Check list that you labeled dominant and that would require discipline if your dog displayed them. Now note *how* you would discipline the dog (yelling, hitting, isolating, distracting) and how you would feel at that time (pleased, sad, guilty, betrayed, neutral).

Not-So-Innocent Bystanders

Ethologists use the term *bystander effect* to refer to the tendency of a third party observing a confrontation between two animals to attack the loser. In purely survival terms, it makes sense to align yourself with a winner, the individual who best can benefit you and your offspring.

"That's like kicking someone when they're down!" Pete protests.

Perhaps, but even though our hearts may go out to the underdog, sometimes we inadvertently become involved in such "primitive" scenarios ourselves. For example, the notorious biting incident at the Mattsons' described at the beginning of this chapter occurred during a family reunion when two of the Mattsons' young grandsons engaged in a mock battle. When the older child picked up a pillow and began batting the younger, Cynthia bit the younger child. Although those present viewed this as an unprovoked, vicious attack on an innocently playing youngster, we can see how an animal lacking a clear sense of its position within the human pack might automatically make such a response.

More commonly, we see the bystander effect occurring in multiple-dog households, and it merits consideration if you're contemplating the addition of a second dog. In this situation, the owner yells at or otherwise disciplines one dog, and the other dog attacks that animal too. To put it mildly, this puts the owner in an awkward position. Pulling off the attacking dog not only puts the person in a good position to get bitten, but also gives the disciplined dog enough breathing room to fight back. Now the owner must contend with two biting dogs instead of one. Because the probability of a person's simultaneously subduing two fighting dogs approaches nil, whatever the owner hoped to communicate about his or her leadership to the first dog vanishes in the ensuing fracas.

Once again, prevention offers the most time- and energy-efficient approach. Work with and train the dogs separately first, then with each other. If bystander confrontations arise between the dogs, stay out of them.

"It says here you can break up a dog fight by pulling the hind legs out from under the *loser*," Pete remarks as he leafs through one of Jane's dog-training books. "That must be a misprint."

No, it's not a misprint. Because fighting wastes time and energy, animals resort to it only when they can't establish a pack structure by other, more efficient means. When dog-to-dog confrontations occur, we can simply stand quietly and let the animals work it out, or we can pull out the hind legs of the loser, thereby helping the winner win sooner. Because the animals fight for position, once they determine that, the winner may give one last nip, and that ends it.

"So, why not break up a fight with two of your own dogs that way?" asks Jane.

You shouldn't under those circumstances because the pack dynamics differ in two critical ways. On the one hand, when Jane takes Cynthia for a walk and a stray dog attacks the pup, the stray obviously doesn't recognize Jane's authority, and her chance of convincing him to do so borders on zero. In this situation, it makes more sense for Jane to do whatever she must to end the fight quickly to protect her dog from injury. That means either doing nothing at all or pulling Cynthia's hind legs out from under her.

However, let's suppose the Mattsons purchase a second bulldog, Amanda, a year after they get Cynthia. The Mattson pack now consists of humans in the leadership position, with Cynthia as number two and Amanda as number three. If Jane yells at Amanda, and Cynthia dives in to give the younger dog a few quick licks of her own, the entire display simply reinforces the existing pack structure, and no problems arise. But suppose Jane yells at Cynthia and Amanda goes after the older dog, not to show dominance over Cynthia but rather to show her support for Jane. Pulling the more dominant Cynthia's legs out at that time would confuse both dogs rather than resolve the issue.

A variation in this second scenario could occur as Amanda and Cynthia grow older. If at some time Amanda decides she should dominate the canine pack of two, a power struggle will ensue. Because this is a dog issue—that is, neither dog challenges Jane's or Pete's leadership—the dogs need to settle it themselves. Owners who try to interfere simply increase the tension, prolong the event, and sometimes make any skirmishes between the animals more intense.

Owners of multiple animals who don't recognize human leadership may experience one final, extremely harrowing, variation of the bystander effect. Here, one of the animals gets hurt and begins whimpering or howling in pain. If the person who attends the animal doesn't act in a manner that conveys confidence and presence, the other dog(s) may attack the victim. Why remains unclear. Perhaps something about the injured animal's or the owner's behavior makes the other dog(s) think the owner caused the injury. We do know from the bond studies that, just as we and our animals can calm each other, so we can upset each other, too. Consequently, we owe it to our pets to maintain our presence when they get hurt, for three reasons:

- It will help them feel better.
- Their feeling better will help us feel better.
- It will keep any bystanders from interfering as we try to help the injured animal.

Also note that dominant human displays directed toward members of others species (cats, birds, horses) can precipitate the canine bystander effect too. One owner told of her dog attacking her $2,500 parrot when she shouted at the bird to get off the kitchen counter. Unfortunately the bird did, and landed right in the path of the dog.

Regardless of what precipitates a canine bystander response, always remember that your confident and calm presence can help speed resolution of even the most troubling situations.

Human confrontations also may precipitate the bystander effect, and family arguments turn many a family dog into a basket case. Pete yells at Jane for forgetting to mail an important report, and Cynthia snarls at Jane too. More stable animals who recognize both of the combatants as leaders may become frightened and confused, wanting to align themselves with someone to relieve the tension, but uncertain with whom. Some may slink out of the room or huddle next to one owner or the other to protect or be protected by that person, depending on their relationship. Animals in multiple-dog households may attack *each other* in an attempt to relieve their anxiety.

If you normally resort to loud arguments to settle disputes in your household, get the human problems straightened out before you get a dog. Otherwise you'll just add the dog's stress-induced medical and behavioral problems to the fray. For certain, no dog ever solved a human relationship problem: it may distract people from their problems for a while, but it won't make them go away.

Bystander Check

Think of all the human-animal and human-human confrontations that occur in your household. Then imagine those same confrontations occurring with your new dog at your side. Does your knowledge of the bystander effect alter how you would behave? If so, how?

A Little Help from Some Friends

In groups of social wild animals, individuals may ally themselves with others to ensure their position in the pack. In general, such alliances usually occur among relatives, but they may also include outsiders. In areas of scarce territory and resources, for instance, some birds will help their parents feed and raise their young rather than mate and reproduce themselves. While this looks like the epitome of subordinate behavior—hanging around to feed someone else's young—in fact it functions as an effective strategy to procure a territory and win a chance to reproduce in an extremely limited environment. By doing this, young females may inherit a nest site when an older female dies, and young males may claim portions of the territory too far from the nest site for the dominant male to protect while he's busy mating and feeding offspring.

Do our dogs form such alliances? Indeed they do. Surely every dog lover has heard tales of dogs who know that one person will let them get away with a behavior another person in that same household won't tolerate. Although Cynthia knows that Jane doesn't want her to sleep on the bed, she also knows that Pete couldn't care less about his wife's rule; as soon as Jane leaves to run a few errands, Cynthia sneaks into the bedroom. If she fails to hear Jane's approach until she comes into the room, the dog streaks out the door and hunts down Pete wherever he may be, leaps into his lap, and acts totally innocent. Similarly, we need only to observe where the dog sits during the human mealtimes to determine who, if anyone, feeds the animal from the table.

Such alliances cause minimal problems and may even form an endearing part of the relationship if the dog remains healthy and well behaved. However, if behavioral and/or medical problems plague the animal, all owners—and especially new ones— need to take a closer look at any existing alliances.

For example, if Pete binds Cynthia to him by giving her snacks that result in weight gain and/or digestive problems, this alliance hardly benefits the dog. On the behavioral front, while Pete may find it appealing when Cynthia runs to him when she violates Jane's wishes, he undermines Jane's leadership position every time he condones this canine behavior. Similarly, if he insists that Amanda and Cynthia not square off to settle their own pack structure because he thinks of Cynthia as the top dog and doesn't want anything to change that, his devotion could make Cynthia's life more complicated instead of more comfortable.

If you plan to bring a dog into a household with other people, make sure everyone agrees on what constitutes human leadership in order to avoid troublesome alliances that could undermine the animal's behavior, and your relationship with these people as well as your new pet.

Dream Dog Alliance Check

Think about your dream dog in terms of alliances. Do you see your new pet as "my dog," "the kids' dog," or specifically aligned to any other particular member of your household for some reason?

Who's in Charge Here?

The final behavioral concept, individual recognition by group members, tends to generate more than its share of human emotion. Viewed from the standpoint of time and energy conservation, few would argue with the soundness of a system that utilizes some quick and obvious cue to denote dominance. When military man Jack Nesbitt attends a meeting at the Pentagon, one look at his uniform tells everyone whether to treat him as a superior or subordinate. Nor do the younger men expect the retired officer to demonstrate how he acquired that rank before they defer to him. Because Jack jumped through all the dominant/subordinate hoops before, he doesn't need to prove himself anymore.

However, showy signs of superiority can become a drawback, too. Within the animal kingdom, we see dominant animals sporting bright plumage or heavy antlers just like soldiers or athletes displaying their medals. While these adornments may attract females and intimidate other males, they require a certain amount of energy to create and maintain—which explains why these animals shed their finery at the end of the breeding season. Imagine Jack in his dress uniform with all its medals trying to move undetected through hostile territory. Whereas his uniform triggers immediate respect from those within his own circle, it makes him an easy target when he steps out of that group.

Recall the old cliché, "Clothes make the man." When a male moose brandishes that magnificent rack of antlers, we see it as evidence of a clearly superior animal who demonstrated great physical and mental ability to achieve this rank. However, within the domestic canine population, genetic manipulation allows humans to shortcut this process, creating dogs people define as dominant simply because they *look* dominant.

Such a misguided approach precipitated the problems currently besieging breeds such as rottweilers, German shepherd dogs, Dobermans, and pit bulls. Whereas the original working animals impressed people as superior because of a combination of physical, mental, and personality traits, some unknowledgeable breeders focused solely on creating an animal with a physically intimidating appearance. One result is that when these animals do something wrong, people remember the misdeed and its perpetrator much more clearly—and negatively—than similar behaviors displayed by members of other breeds.

We see the same phenomenon in dog owners, too. Just as every officer isn't necessarily a gentleman, so every human can't claim dominance over a dog simply by virtue of walking upright and possessing an opposable thumb. In fact, some of us must work darned hard at maintaining a quality leadership position in a human-animal pack. In general, most dogs view men as more dominant than women and women as more dominant than children unless those people communicate otherwise to the animals through their actions. In general, we can also say that intact (unneutered) animals lean more strongly toward playing by dog rather than human rules in a human-canine pack.

Now, before you go accusing me of sexism and political incorrectness, please note that I came to accept this pack structure after more than 20 years of working with dogs and owners, discussing the issue with behaviorists, trainers, and breeders, and reading the (unfortunately scarce) scientific literature on the subject. I'm convinced that, whether we like it or not, dogs do recognize our sex. Not only that, but they may also respond differently to children going through puberty, pregnant women, or those in various phases of their menstrual cycle. Reports of biting attacks of women by males of species as varied as dogs and pet iguanas show a correlation between the phase of the animal's breeding season and the woman's menstrual cycle. If the male dog lives near a female dog in heat or the iguanas are in their breeding season, if the woman has a close relationship with the pet and is premenstrual or menstrual, the males become aggressive.

"You're kidding!" laughs Jane Mattson. "Sounds like more of that doggy voodoo."

Not by a long shot. All animals, including humans, release powerful chemical compounds called *pheromones*, substances so potent that a single molecule of a particular one from a female moth will cause male moths a mile away to drop everything and fly *upwind* to her. For many years we humans denied that such trickery could fool our superior brains, but recent research indicates the opposite. Like those testy male dogs and iguanas, men asked to sniff slides of smears taken during various phases of a woman's monthly cycle responded much more negatively to those taken during premenstrual and menstrual periods of least fertility.

Although the idea of an animal relating to its owner as a mate seems bizarre, it makes perfect sense. Recall from Chapter 2 how we humans championed domestication because it reduced the sense of species self and permitted those animals to accept us as one of them. Once they do that, they'll naturally apply the rules of their particular species game to us if we don't teach them otherwise. When other animals of its own species come into heat, these animals tune in to that message and expect their owners to become more receptive to their attention, too. If the human female's scent communicates, "Bug off, creep," while a female dog down the street broadcasts, "Come hither," we can see how a male spaniel could become aggressive toward the owner.

Moreover, although neutering will diminish this response because it removes the ovaries or testicles (the major source of sex hormones), it doesn't completely eliminate it for three reasons. First, neutering doesn't eliminate *all* sex hormones, and some animals maintain higher postneutering levels than others. (It's not unusual to see a neutered dog rapturously clutching its embarrassed owner's extremities or locked in an ecstatic embrace with an accent pillow on the couch while the owner chatters nervously about the weather.) Second, it appears that pheromones released by intact animals during the breeding season may stimulate neutered animals, too. Third, just as domestication decreases the animal's sense of species self, neutering diminishes its sense of its sexual self. When the behaviors or pheromones of intact animals in the area elicit these vague shadows of normal sexual behavior, the neutered animal must try to cope with its feelings as best it can. Owners commonly describe these animals as "anxious" or "edgy," two feelings that suffice to make a more dominant animal—or one thrust into that position in the human-canine pack—of either sex less tolerant of human behaviors that it considers unacceptable.

In addition to communicating sexual messages, animals may communicate their pack position via scent. In species as varied as cockroaches and mice, dominant animals produce pheromones that broadcast their status as well as their species and sex. Although some ethologists contend that this scent makes these animals dominant, other scientific studies—including ones done on men—indicate that testosterone levels rise after a success and drop after defeat. This suggests that the scent likely follows the behavior. Other studies demonstrate that the most dominant animals of some species, including canids, may secrete pheromones in their urine that suppress sexual development and/ or reproductive behaviors in other members of the group of both sexes.

One fact of particular importance to prospective dog owners is that almost everyone who works with animals believes that animals can smell or sense fear, even though no concrete data exists to substantiate this. We do know that some well-trained bomb-sniffing dogs can detect certain forms of human skin cancer before physicians can, picking up substances in concentrations as low as several parts per quadrillion (1 followed by 15 zeros). Think about Cynthia applying even a small fraction of that canine sensory sensitivity to the far more dramatic bodily changes that Jane experiences when Cynthia first growls at her and she backs off: Jane's pulse quickens, her stomach flips, she begins to sweat. Does it seem likely that her pet would miss all of these changes? Given the bond studies that tell us we and animals can affect each other's heart rate, pulse, and cholesterol levels without realizing it, doesn't it seem likely that they would respond to something as potent as our fear? Given the ability of some dogs to detect impending seizures in their epileptic owners up to hours in advance of the event, doesn't it seem likely that our dogs would sense our strong feelings at other times, too?

Unfortunately, although little data exists on how negative emotional states affect our body chemistry and that of those around us, even less exists about the effects of positive ones. Still, the idea that the holy grail of presence could include the sweet (pheromone) scent of success in addition to more fluid body motion and a lower, firm, but gentle tone of voice does intrigue most dog lovers.

Mixed Messages

Although our dogs most likely can detect even the subtlest messages from us, they may interpret them quite differently from what we would expect. When the Mattsons first get Cynthia, the puppy's adorable appearance and Jane's lack of experience with dogs lead Jane to coo baby talk to Cynthia under normal circumstances and to use a hesitant, almost apologetic tone when she gives the pup a command.

"Please, Cynthia, don't chew on the rug," Jane pleads with the pup. "It makes Mommy so sad, and you don't want to make Mommy sad, do you?"

Unfortunately, everything about Jane's tone and demeanor communicates subordination rather than leadership to her pet. Even if the naturally dominant Cynthia did happen to stop chewing the rug at that moment, she would more likely do this because she got bored with the activity than because she recognized her owner's authority.

Because social animals *need* to know their place in our packs as well as our homes in order to relax, dogs will attempt to fill any leadership void out of necessity. Couple Cynthia's lack of training to establish human authority with Jane's soft, sweet voice and hesitant demeanor, and we can see why the dog assumes the dominant position in their pack of two. Similarly, we can understand why the pup feels obligated to police up the activities of the visiting grandchildren.

What kind of pack do Pete and Cynthia form? We already know that Pete's size, deep voice, and other male characteristics prime Cynthia to perceive him as the leader. Consequently, when he refuses to accept this responsibility, she gets thrust into an unnatural leadership position. Within the past decade or so, the emergence of the so-called kinder, gentler male has wreaked havoc with more than a few human-canine relationships because some dogs perceive these men as wishy-washy and indecisive rather than either kind or gentle.

Once again the dog's territorial and perceptual senses come into play. A young, inexperienced pup such as Cynthia needs someone to set limits and relieve her of the full burden of protecting the entire territory. When Pete's words and body language communicate subordination, the pup becomes confused, disoriented, and edgy. While Pete thinks his own behavior communicates, "You're my best friend, and I don't want to make you do anything you don't want to do," Cynthia sees it as a dereliction of duty, and that forces her to fill the leadership void herself.

Unfortunately, dogs who are unwittingly or deliberately thrust into the leadership position by their owners often wind up biting someone. Because these animals take a more territorial view of their owners—that is, they view the owner more as a possession than as a leader and companion—they may bite people who visit the home, or who approach the owner in the dog's presence away from the home. If the stranger does anything the dog perceives as threatening, it attacks, even though the person's action might appear benign to the people involved. Whereas a dog who recognizes its owner's leadership takes its cues from that person regarding what poses a threat and what doesn't, dogs in human-canine relationships such as Cynthia's with the Mattsons know from experience that they can't count on their owners to provide this valuable input. These animals therefore must play by dog rather than human rules, and that might mean lunging at the minister who happens to wear the same aftershave as the letter carrier who maced the dog last week.

While the dog thrust into a leadership position may bite non-family members because it perceives them as territorial violations, it also may bite its owners for social reasons. For example, Cynthia snarls at the meter reader because the man violates her space. However, she snarls at Jane when Jane nudges her, because dog rules say subordinates don't interrupt the leader's rest. Moreover, not only will the naturally dominant dog who assumes the leadership position in a human-canine pack growl at or bite owners who break rank by such actions as disrupting the dog's rest, moving its food dish, or speaking to it harshly, but naturally subordinate ones thrust into the leadership position can become so frustrated with their owner's refusal to accept that responsibility that they bite *the owner* rather than the person who comes to the door. Although it may smack of anthropomorphism, imagine how abandoned 15-pound Cynthia must feel when forced to bark and snarl at whoever or whatever pounds on the door because kinder, gentler, six-foot, 180-pound Pete refuses to assert his leadership position by teaching her to sit when someone arrives, thereby relieving her of this protective function.

Children add their own twists to the human-canine pack structure. Up until the age at which they become toilet trained, most children communicate their subordinate status by virtue of the fact that they soil their diapers in the dog's presence, though neither the child nor the owner might make that connection. More commonly dog owners feel pleased when the dog becomes devoted to (protective of) the child. As long as the parents assume the leadership position over both dog and children, few problems arise. However, if parents refuse to set limits for both, look out.

Dogs who perceive children as their possessions may become anxious when infants begin to walk. Consider Cynthia's relationship with the Mattsons' various grandchildren. She immediately knows from Pete's and Jane's response that the children are valuable property. The infant in the group poses no problem to the pup because he spends most of his time lying on his back sleeping or soiling his diapers (i.e., displaying pure submission). Three-year-old Emily, on the other hand, gets into everything, and Cynthia won't take her eyes off the child for a minute.

"Isn't that cute!" gush the adults. "Cynthia won't let Emily go near the stairs."

As long as Emily responds to Cynthia's body blocks and nudges or the adults move the child away from the stairs when the dog displays the behavior, this analysis of the problem works okay. But let's look at another very common child-dog interaction as it relates to human leadership. This time Cynthia nudges Emily away from her food dish, which everyone also agrees is cute. When the toddler persists, Cynthia snaps at her.

How people respond to this situation depends on their views of leadership. Pete may see Cynthia's behavior as so frightening that he angrily grabs the pup and smacks her, such a surprising show of dominance that it may shock the pup into snapping at him, too. Or suppose Pete takes her food away entirely.

"I'll teach you to snap at someone around your food!" Pete snaps at the dog.

In addition to the identity crisis precipitated by a non-leader's sudden show of dominance, this method further muddies the waters on two fronts. First, by taking up the food in such a manner, Pete communicates loudly and clearly to Cynthia that humans *can* take her food, exactly what she feared in the first place. Removing the food under such circumstances therefore makes the dog even more leery of people around her bowl. Second, although Pete may get away with this tactic, Jane would never consider doing it, and the toddler certainly can't. In the end, Pete only teaches the dog not to snap at *him* when she's eating, which she never did anyway.

In another scenario, Jane makes excuses for the dog's behavior under these same circumstances: "Cynthia's not used to being around children. I'll move her food and water bowls to the back bedroom where no one will bother her."

Here, the owner attempts to restructure the environment to avoid, rather than confront, the leadership problem. It's one thing to enter someone's house and see the dining room chairs piled on the white couch to keep the dog from sleeping on it in the owner's absence. It's quite another, when the Mattsons warn visitors, "Oh, don't sit there. That's Cynthia's chair. And stay out of the back bedroom. She doesn't like people in there with her food. And don't make any sudden moves, or rustle paper. She *hates* that."

Owners who refuse to accept the leadership role get themselves caught in a downward spiral of negative dog behavior. The Mattsons start out with one rule that says, "Don't bother Cynthia while she's eating," then add another and another until conversation about their pet contains more and more comments that begin, "Cynthia's a great dog as long as you don't . . ." Although they might be able to keep track of all those rules, inevitably a visitor to their home can't.

Let's go back to the kitchen and consider an approach to the food problem that solves it in a more positive manner. Instead of putting all of Cynthia's kibble in the bowl at one time, the Mattsons keep half of it in a cup on the counter. As the pup eats, they toss a few pieces into her bowl as they walk by. They encourage other adult guests and then the grand-children to do the same. In such a way the dog comes to associate people around her food dish in a positive rather than negative way.

"How does that communicate leadership?" asks Pete, who would die if anything happened to the wriggling toddler he holds on his lap.

Even though no show of force occurred, the solution communicates human leadership because it solves the problem for the entire spectrum of humans who might interact with the dog. Compare this with snatching the food away, a limited approach that might affirm the leadership position solely of the person who removed the food. Teaching everyone to stay away from the dog's food or, worse, giving the dog its own room in which to eat communicates nothing whatsoever about human leadership.

Another time of increased child-canine tension can occur when dogs and children go through puberty. Given what we know about pheromones, we can appreciate why puberty can be as trying for our dogs as for our kids. Many times owners notice that the perfectly trained dog suddenly appears to have forgotten everything they ever taught it, a feeling famil-iar to parents of young teens. Just as children make their moves toward independence at this age, so do our dogs, and the pack structure often must change to accommodate these developments.

For example, Cynthia viewed the Mattsons' two grandsons as subordinate littermates when she first met them as a young pup. The children rolled around on the floor with her and squealed in delight when she jumped up and licked them. The boys also roughhoused with each other and laughed when Cynthia tried to get between them. When the children visited the second time, the older boy was going through puberty and so was Cynthia. In pheromone terms, he was making the transition from youngster to young adult. In canine behavioral terms, that meant Cynthia's former subordinate littermate now ranked as a possible contender for her leadership position in the Mattson pack.

Now the dog faces a dilemma: should she cede the leadership position to the older boy or prevent him from taking over their pack of three?

In a previously described incident, Cynthia attacked the younger boy because she recognized the older boy's authority, and the younger child fell victim to the bystander effect. However, suppose as she matures, too, Cynthia decides she doesn't want to defer to the older child anymore. Suppose this time when the boys begin roughhousing, Cynthia views the older child as a threat to her territory—the younger child—as well as to her pack leader status. Under these circumstances, instead of getting between the two children or attacking the younger, she attacks the older child.

From these examples we can see that humans and dogs form dynamic pack structures and even more intricate pecking puzzles than those famous chickens. The dog may relate differently to each member of the household, and these relationships may change over time. Because how the dog relates to those in its human-animal pack affects how it relates to others, these internal changes also affect how the dog views visitors to the home and strangers on the street.

The more you know about your personal leadership style and that of those in your household, the more easily you can select a training, exercise, feeding, and medical approach that will enhance this view.

Personal Pack Structure Check

Think about the pack structure in your household. Where do you want your new pet to fit into it? Whom do you want your new dog to obey?

The Human-Canine Power Balance

Keeping all that in mind, consider the following list of behaviors:

- jumping up on people
- sleeping on the bed
- going in and out of doors in front of people
- pawing, bumping, pressing against, or licking people

"What's wrong with them?" Pete wants to know. "They still seem like perfectly normal dog behaviors to me."

Exactly. In fact, the list includes some of what we consider the most endearing canine displays. While my exuberant corgi charges after her bone, I welcome the warmth of the hound leaning against me as we watch this spectacle in the cold New Hampshire winter air. How many owners instantly forget the rotten day at work or the gridlock on the commute home the instant they set eyes on that leaping dog, beside itself with joy at their arrival?

Unfortunately, that doesn't change the fact that every one of these behaviors expresses as much canine dominance as growling or biting. This fact creates a dilemma for me because not only do I deal with a lot of aggressive dogs, but I also see the number of these cases increasing nationwide. I always champion a preventive approach because it saves owners time, money, and energy in the long run. At the same time, though, I recognize what a potent, positive emotional charge many people assign to these behaviors and what a crucial role they play in many solid relationships.

So, what to do? For one thing, when an animal crosses the line and threatens someone's safety, owners must stop all of the aforementioned behaviors because they all communicate canine rather than human dominance. If Jane smacks or otherwise disciplines Cynthia for growling at the meter reader and then lets the dog jump up on her or sleep on the bed, she confuses the dog rather than teaches the dog who's in charge.

Further complicating the process, some dogs resist ceding the leadership position in such a way that they make the owner feel *guilty* about insisting that they do so. In several situations, dogs banished from their owners' beds became so upset that they vomited or developed diarrhea—a very strong incentive for all but the most determined owners to give in to the animal!

Many times I'll recommend that owners use a Gentle Leader collar because its structure gently, but very effectively, communicates human dominance by applying pressure around the dog's muzzle and the back of its neck. Because even the slightest pressure in these behaviorally sensitive areas on the animal's body communicates dominance, dogs who don't want to cede their position can engage in some downright dirty psychological warfare to induce their owners to remove the collars, rubbing their faces against the owner, on the furniture, and on the floor in an effort to free themselves of it. They whimper, whine, and moan. Even the most resolute owners (usually those facing the prospect that the *next* person the dog bites will sue) entertain fleeting thoughts that the collar contains some noxious substance or that their dog suffers from some rare allergy to the collar's fabric. If the owner remains firm, the dog's efforts may intensify to the point that it rubs until sores appear, further convincing the owner that there's something terribly wrong with the collar.

However, those owners who combine the collar with a fast-paced training program, jolly the dog through all the changes, and praise it lavishly when it succeeds find that the collar gives them an amazing amount of control. That control increases their confidence, which affects their presence and begins to reverse the downward spiral.

"So, should we put our foot down the instant we get a new pup, or what?" asks Jane.

First, I don't see the process of establishing ourselves in the leadership position as at all heavy-handed. You can stop a pup or adult dog from leaping up on you simply by ignoring it and having anyone who comes into your home do the same. In a matter of one or two weeks, visitors will trigger calmness rather than chaos in your pet.

Not only will this reduce the chance that Rambo will send Great Aunt Harriet flying, but it also takes a great amount of tension off the dog. Studies indicate that dogs possess marvelous built-in clocks that can trigger the ones who engage in high-spirited greetings to gear up for the event as much as an hour beforehand. If the expected owner is held up in traffic or decides to go out to dinner or do some shopping after work, the dog must languish in a state of "homecoming interruptus" until the owner arrives. For some animals that might mean increased gut activity, particularly if the owner usually feeds the dog shortly after arriving home, priming the animal for a bout of vomiting or diarrhea. For others, it might mean chewing on the rug or digging at the door to relieve the tension.

As far as sleeping on the bed, it depends on the pup. If you lost your heart to a dominant little fur ball that ran up your leg, keep him off the bed because consistently asserting your leadership from day one will pay big dividends later on. Although many busy owners have reveled in the discovery that they could instantly housebreak a pup by allowing it to sleep with them (because most dogs would rather die than soil their beds), owners of dominant animals come to rue this decision when they wind up sleeping with a dog who nips their toes when their movement disrupts its sleep. If you still envision your dog curled up at the foot of your bed and you select a dominant animal, make sure you assume the mantle of gentle but firm leadership from day one.

It also makes sense to train your pet not to charge in and out of doors in front of you, for practical as well as behavioral reasons. When Cynthia flies out the door for her evening walk, Pete's laughter at her behavior gives way to a yelp of surprise and pain when he slips on the rain-slick walk and goes flying into the rosebushes. Nor does Jane find it humorous when the muddy pup charges into the house after her walk. How much simpler just to teach the animal to sit at the door and wait for the owner's signal to exit or enter!

Pups and dogs who lean, lick, and paw also communicate dominance. If Cynthia wants to go out, she rests her head heavily on Pete's thigh and stares at him as they sit together on the couch.

"Isn't she the smartest little pup!" he exclaims as he puts down his paper and takes her out for the eighth time that evening.

Granted we all want our dogs to alert us when they need to relieve themselves, but Cynthia only noses around the yard during her numerous jaunts. If we look at this human-canine interaction in terms of the classic progression of stimulus–proper response–reward, what do we see? We see the dog giving the owner the stimulus: *"Stop reading your paper and pay attention to me."* The owner makes the proper response: Pete puts down his paper and takes the dog for a walk. Then Cynthia rewards Pete by leaving him alone until she wants him to pay attention to her again.

Given what you now know about human-canine pack structure, what's wrong with that picture?

"It's backwards," Pete sighs. "But even though I understand what you're saying, the idea of having a dog who doesn't sleep next to me or jump up when I come home or lick me. . . . Well, I'm not sure that's the kind of dog I want."

Ten years ago I would have felt obliged to inform Pete that he *must* eliminate these behaviors if he didn't want his relationship with his dog to come to a horrible end. I now realize that such rigid tactics turn more owners off than on. True, in order to make a lasting change in our dog's behavior or our relationship, we must respond consistently—and unemotionally—until we and the dog internalize that change (i.e., until we both come to accept it as a normal part of our lives). Once we do that, however, a certain amount of *inconsistency* not only will do little harm, but can actually strengthen the desired behavior. Consequently, once the Mattsons establish human leadership in their human-canine pack, they don't need to exert it all the time. Periodically they can allow Cynthia to get away with something because both they and she feel confident of their positions.

In the past I hesitated to mention this, fearing owners wouldn't adhere to any new training, exercise, feeding, or medical program long enough to make it normal for them and their pets. But, I discovered that just the opposite holds true. People will more consistently implement any necessary changes for four or six weeks or even six months if they know they can cut the dog some slack after that. Not only that, but something almost magical often happens.

"When we first stopped letting Cynthia jump up and lick anyone, I felt like the scum of the universe," Pete recalled later. "That first week, I even marked the days off the calendar. But she caught on really fast and was so thrilled when Jane or I praised her for fetching her ball or learning a new command, I forgot all about my bad feelings."

The Mattsons began the program believing themselves caught up in a villain/victim power struggle with their dog, but they ended it as leaders in a wonderfully stable and loving relationship.

Personalized Leadership

Get out your lists again and analyze them in terms of leadership. For example, Jane and Pete Mattson both realized they prefer a more anthropomorphic relationship with a dog based equally on their personal feelings and the information they gained after reading Chapter 1. Their canine want list looked like this:

- breed: bulldog
- sex: female
- age: pup
- color: doesn't matter
- temperament: spunky, high-spirited

The Mattsons decided they wanted a bulldog because they loved the breed's look, and a female pup because everyone told them females and puppies were easier to train. They wanted a spunky, high-spirited pup because "things are so quiet around here with the kids gone." At the end of Chapter 2, they felt confident they could meet the needs of an animal of this particular breed given their orientation, limits, and lifestyle. By the end of Chapter 3, they also felt confident that they could provide a comfortable home for a bulldog and that such an animal wouldn't violate their sense of place.

Unfortunately, however, the Mattsons picked Cynthia before they worked through their feelings about pack structure and leadership.

"In retrospect, we should have listened to the breeder," Pete admits. "She suggested a quiet pup she felt would suit our personalities better, but we were determined to get a dog who was more bouncy."

"Thank God we both work at home and could afford to get professional help when we got into trouble," Jane adds. "Our kids' lives are so hectic I know none of them could have helped, no matter how much they loved the dog."

Personal Leadership Style Analysis

Do you want a dog who comes the instant you call? Or does it just need to start ambling in your direction? Would you feel comfortable physically restraining your ideal dog if it became necessary? If, for example, you describe yourself as a peace-loving 110-pound woman, what would you do if your ideal male Great Dane snapped at your child? The child who lives next door? The meter reader?

Next, put yourself in the Mattsons' shoes and imagine how you would respond to each of the situations in this chapter. Then run every worst-case scenario you can think of in terms of your lifestyle, your environment, you and other members of your household, and any visitors to your home, and note your responses. Do you feel you have to win all the time, or only in certain situations? If the latter, what kinds of situations? Does everyone in your household agree with you? How do you define a "win"? Will you feel like a leader if the dog just stops doing what it was doing, or do you need to see some other act—such as crouching, submissive urination, tucked tail—that indicates it recognizes your authority?

Granted not everyone is born a leader of men. However, given a clear understanding of our orientation toward dogs, the dog's sense of self and function, and human-canine pack dynamics, even the shyest person can assume the leadership position and offer his or her pet all the benefits of a stable mental as well as physical environment.

Now that we've examined the four most critical components of every human-canine interaction, let's use that knowledge to select the training, exercise, feeding, and medical programs that will provide a solid foundation upon which you and your new dog can build a long, happy, and healthy relationship.

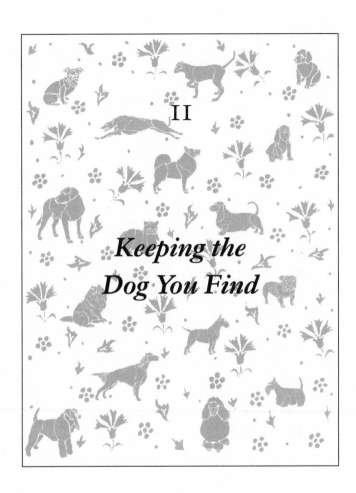

II

Keeping the Dog You Find

5

Training a Keeper

Selecting the Best Training Program to Fit You and Your Dog

"Today I'm going to teach you to sit," Dr. Alex Waterman says with a yawn as he fast-forwards through the last 10 minutes of the most recent addition to his growing collection of dog training videos.

His Irish wolfhound pup, Rory, leaps exuberantly at the prospect, then drags his owner toward the park for the promised event.

Once there, Alex selects a spot near a busy playground to desensitize Rory to children while he trains him. In five minutes the owner gives the pup the sit command 13 times in a tone that escalates from gentle pleas to enraged threats, all the while pushing down on Rory's rear end, yanking up on his collar, yanking down on his collar, and calling him everything from "good dog" to "bad dog" to "bonehead." If Rory displays even the slightest inclination to sit, Alex gives his pet a treat. Throughout the session, Rory's eyes follow the boisterous activity of the children, parents, balls, swings, and bikes in the playground behind his owner.

"What a loser!" Alex rants in disgust. "I've tried five different training methods and you just don't get it!"

Considering that Direct Book Service's 1996 *Dog and Cat Book Catalog* lists more than *five hundred* dog training titles and that even the smallest animal shelters in the tiniest towns offer some sort of training and/or behavioral counseling, you might suppose that everything that could be said on the subject has been said. Nevertheless, despite the wealth of information available behavioral problems remain the primary reason that human-canine relationships fall apart. And even though Alex and other frustrated owners might complain about dogs getting dumber, more than a few dogs out there surely must grumble about the decline in human intelligence, too.

However, experience tells me that a lack of a compatible program, not a lack of intelligence, lies at the bottom of most training failures. Alex wastes much of Rory's prime puppy-training period experimenting with different methods rather than actually training his pet. To make matters worse, in the process of trying all these approaches, not only doesn't he teach Rory anything positive, but his lack of consistency actually reinforces the pup's bad habits. Alex began with a stack of training books, then switched to videos, which he watches while he eats a late dinner. During one of these he falls asleep, only to wake up convinced that the expert told him Rory would outgrow his unruly and destructive behavior. Unfortunately, by the time Alex finds the time to replay that video and discover that the expert said no such thing, Rory's bad habits have become even more entrenched. Surely neither we nor our dogs need the cerebral capacity of rocket scientists to realize that all of this does little to create a stable relationship with a well-trained pet.

Similarly those who bring older dogs into their homes also may miss that brief but valuable window of training opportunity that opens during the animal's first weeks in a new household. When Molly McKinnen adds an 18-month old female Chesapeake Bay retriever, Juno, to her household, she spends the first two months making excuses for the dog's behavior, chalking any problems up to the dog's troubled past. By the time Molly decides that, troubled past or no, she doesn't want to live with an ill-mannered dog, Juno has claimed a good-sized chunk of Molly's territory as her own and refuses to relinquish it without a fight.

In both of these situations, the owners lack a clear understanding of their orientations toward dogs, the limits they placed on their relationship, their dog's needs, their environment, and their own leadership style.

Tailor-Made Training

Review your previous comments about the ideal training program, then answer the following questions: What do you expect from a training program? What human needs must it fulfill: Time? Cost? Location? What canine needs must it address?

For example, Alex's hastily scrawled notes look like this:

- basic obedience
- house- and kid-safe
- half-hour a day max
- at-home program

Given such a simple want list, Alex should experience little difficulty finding a training program that meets his criteria. Compare his list with Molly's:

Expectations

- stop barking when tied outside

Human needs

- no harsh discipline
- small class
- nice teacher
- not too expensive

- not more than an hour's drive
- meets Tuesday or Thursday nights
- class ends before holidays

Canine needs

- Juno must enjoy program
- nice dogs in class

Although some of the entries on Molly's list may strike us as oddly idiosyncratic, this greater detail provides her with valuable insight that will help her find the best training program for her pet.

Once you decide what criteria you want a training program to fulfill, you need to find a program that meets those needs.

"Be serious!" laughs Alex. "I don't have time to sort through 500 programs!"

Few owners do, which is why we need to impose some order on the seemingly chaotic collection of training options. To do so, let's begin by dividing them into four basic categories.

Do-it-yourself at-home methods

- Books
- Videotapes
- Audiotapes

Courses

- Animal shelters
- Kennel clubs
- Professional trainers
- Veterinary facilities

Private lessons or consultations

- Trainers
- Behaviorists
- Veterinary behaviorists

Away-from-home training

- With owner
- Without owner

By analyzing each group in terms of your orientation, any financial, time, emotional, or physical limits, your environment, your dog's needs, and your leadership style, you can considerably narrow the search for the most effective training program for you and your pet.

Owner Orientation and Training

How owners relate to their dogs has a direct bearing on the success of any training program. Alex tends to assume a chattel orientation toward Rory, which arises from both human and canine origins. For one thing, Alex generally feels uncomfortable intimately interacting with any human or animal. For another, knowing that Rory will weigh more than 100 pounds when he matures also spurs Alex to adopt a fairly objective, unemotional approach to his pet's training.

"I simply can't afford to have an untrained dog that size running around," Alex admits candidly. "My hours are so irregular, I need an animal I can trust in the house alone plus around other people." Almost as an afterthought, he adds, "And I want Rory to be a winner. I doubt I'll ever show him, but I want him to stand out in a crowd."

That almost-throwaway remark reveals an aspect of Alex's personality that will greatly affect the success of the method he chooses to train his dog. In addition to being aloof, Alex is extremely competitive. He views his work as a battle between himself and the evil forces of disease and injury. Although he would never admit it, his orientation resembles how he feels when his favorite football team clashes with their arch rival on the playing field. This view could lead him to seek out more heavy-handed, confrontational training methods, but that's not his style, either.

"I don't want to do the 'master of the universe' thing," he insists. "I just like the extra dimension competition adds."

However, this added dimension takes Alex's view of training programs out of the realm of pure objectivity because, even though training methods that primarily focus on competition and winning appeal to him, he doesn't have the lifestyle and inclination to pursue them properly. The upshot is that, even though Alex takes a chattel view of his dog, he paradoxically selects a training approach based on its anthropomorphic appeal.

Although psychologist Molly McKinnen doesn't consider her orientation toward dogs anthropomorphic, she got Juno for strictly anthropomorphic reasons. When she visited a kennel seeking a pup, Molly found the breeder to be an overbearing know-it-all who irritated her immensely. Rather than seeking out another breeder with whom she felt more comfortable, Molly asked to see all of the animals, far more alert to any weaknesses than strengths in the animals and/or environment. When she noticed Juno in a run by herself and listened to the breeder dispassionately rattling off a list of the dog's many problems, Molly immediately decided the breeder and the environment, not the dog, caused all of these. Instantly abandoning the idea of getting a pup and ignoring the breeder's insistence that she'd regret the decision, Molly claimed Juno as her dream dog.

"Maybe that dreadful woman didn't beat you, but I bet she didn't give you much love, either," Molly told Juno later. "Don't you worry, though. I'll make it up to you."

In addition to babying Juno and letting her claim all the furniture as well as the bed, Molly opts to use food treats to train the dog because "that awful woman doesn't believe in treats, but I'm not that mean."

Even if both the breeder's approach and the former environment had contributed to Juno's problems, Molly's idea of making up to her dog for these past human failings springs strictly from her own feelings rather than any knowledged-based analysis of the situation. Understandably, but unwisely, she selects a training method that appeals to her own emotions rather than addresses Juno's needs.

In both of these situations, we see owners who at heart want only house- and people-safe dogs who obey the most basic commands. However, because they didn't analyze their own orientations toward dogs first, they selected approaches that met only their own needs rather than their own and their pet's.

"But I did that," Alex counters as he dons his sweat suit and sneakers for another training foray in the park with Rory. "I picked a program to meet my needs as well as Rory's."

No, he didn't. In spite of the fact that Alex does take an objective, even remote view of his dog, he selects a training approach for emotional reasons and then responds emotionally when it doesn't work. Because of this, Rory winds up with the worst of both worlds: an owner who relates to him as chattel under normal circumstances, but also one who doesn't hesitate to assume an anthropomorphic orientation and project his own frustration and anger strongly on his pet when Rory does something wrong.

At the opposite end of the spectrum, Molly's desire to baby Juno to atone for all the dog's real or imagined past traumas leads her to adopt a training approach with a completely different emphasis. Although both kinds of training methods can work well, they don't work for these owners because they don't address their particular animals' special needs or take environmental and leadership factors into account.

Owner Training Analysis

Review your training program want list in terms of any anthropomorphic or chattel views you might hold toward dogs. Once again note with a "K"

or an "E" whether these preferences result from knowledge of a particular type of training program or your own emotion.

When Molly completes this exercise, she realizes that her
anthropomorphic views arise primarily from her emotions. Alex's
personal analysis, on the other hand, reveals that he leans more
toward a chattel view that arises about equally from knowledge
and emotion.

Purpose-Oriented Training

Because so many training options exist, the more clearly, specifically, and realistically you define what you want a program to
accomplish, the more easily you can sort through the many
options to find it.

"All I really care about is that Rory's good around other
people and animals, that he walks quietly on a leash, and comes
and stays when I tell him to," Alex reports. "I really don't care
whether he stands, sits, or lies down as long as he stays put when
I tell him to."

Given these goals, Alex probably would find that programs
specifically designed to train owners and dogs for competitive
obedience don't meet his needs. However, before he makes any
final decision, he should recall his remarks about wanting others to see Rory as an exceptional dog. Will it suffice if others see
his pet this way simply because of the dog's striking appearance
and stable temperament? Or will perfectionist Alex expect his
dog's behavior to outshine that of all the other dogs in the neighborhood, too? If he desires the latter, Alex needs to define the
purpose of any training more clearly before he begins it.

Those who want a dog to perform a specific function such
as competitive obedience, showing, agility, hunting, tracking,
sledding, or herding will save themselves money, time, and
effort—to say nothing of saving their dogs from confusion—by
selecting a training method that complements this purpose. If

Alex decides he wants to show Rory, he should focus on programs that emphasize conformation training and showing. Such specialized programs require that the dog obey basic obedience commands, and Rory easily can master these within a context Alex finds appealing.

While Alex seeks an overall training program with a specific goal in mind, Molly, like many other owners who select older dogs, takes a problem-solving approach to Juno's training.

"Juno already knows how to come, sit, and stay," Molly announces proudly. "She's perfect except for barking when I put her on her run in the backyard."

Although taking a problem-oriented approach seems both logical and efficient, it creates several predicaments. First, this approach rests solely on the owner's and/or trainer's ability to identify the problem properly. Without such a clear definition, an inexperienced or unknowledgeable owner can spend a lot of time, money, and energy treating a symptom rather than the cause of a problem. Consider these exchanges between Molly and two different trainers, Paul and Chris:

Scene I

Molly: I want to train my dog not to bark when I put her on her run in the backyard.
Paul: No problem. I'll just outfit her with a shock collar that will stop that in no time.

Scene II

Molly: I want to train my dog not to bark when I put her on her run in the backyard.
Chris: Why is she outdoors?
Molly: She hates her crate indoors.
Chris: Why is she in the crate?
Molly: She messes in the house when I'm gone. Plus I put her in there when I have company.

Chris:	How come?
Molly:	Well, one of the reasons I wanted a dog was for protection because I live alone. But Juno snaps and growls at everyone until she gets to know them, so I put her in the crate so she doesn't hurt anyone.

Because Chris knew enough to ask these questions, he uncovered the true cause of the problem—a lack of human leadership—as well as the much more serious threat posed by the dog's growling and snapping.

If you, like Molly, include protection among the canine behaviors you wish a training program to provide, a few words of caution are in order. It should come as no surprise given the numerous books, videos, and programs promising to help people teach their dogs to attack for "personal protection" (as opposed to such training for law enforcement work), plus owners who believe they can accomplish such training on their own, that the number of reports of unwarranted canine attacks is increasing by leaps and bites. Unfortunately, programs geared specifically to *stop* such negative behavior can't guarantee success in every case because treating these animals creates a terrible dilemma for their owners.

Recall what we said about leadership and that all-important quality known as presence. People who get or train dogs for protection, by definition, are frightened. Because of this, it's extremely difficult, if not impossible, for them to communicate presence and leadership to their animals. Instead, they communicate fear and subordination, which the dog picks up on, and which leads the animal to respond aggressively to what *it* rather than the owner considers a threat—the meter reader, the children in Halloween costumes, the plumber banging in the basement.

Theoretically, the owner can reclaim the leadership position by pursuing a program that begins with the most basic obedience training. Once the owner develops the necessary leadership skills and presence, treating the biting problem becomes a cinch. Without these, however, any shock or prong collars, hanging nooses, beatings, or other negative reinforcement applied to the dog when it attempts to bite will only create the illusion of a well-trained dog, one who simply doesn't bite whoever applied the punishment, but who still could very well bite a child or another dog.

I use the word *theoretically* when referring to such training because nothing we can teach the dog will change a fearful owner into a confident one. Without that owner presence, the dog trained or allowed to attack becomes the canine equivalent of a three-year-old child wandering around the house and yard carrying a loaded gun with the safety off. *With* that owner presence, knowledge, and skill to properly handle a dog for protection, the need for such an animal ceases to exist.

If you want a dog for protection, I strongly suggest you spend some time in the emergency room of your local hospital and see how much damage a biting dog can do. Police and medical reports indicate that dogs bite far more family members and other innocent people than potential murderers or rapists. Second, stock up on liability insurance before you get your new pet because you'll probably pay an arm and a leg for it afterward, if you can get it at all. And third, get yourself a good lawyer if you don't have one already.

One final fact to complete the picture: news reports of "dog heroes" over the years indicate that the most reliable protector when the chips are *really* down is the stable household pet who takes its cues from its owner.

A Week in the Life of Your Ideal Dog

Think about how you'd like to spend an average weekday and weekend with your pet. Jot down all the skills your new pet will need to know to make that an enjoyable experience for you both.

For example, if you envision yourself hiking with your new dog off-lead, you definitely need an animal who will come when called. Visions of taking your new pet with you to outdoor rock concerts should trigger the addition of training that will desensitize the animal to crowds and loud noise in addition to teaching it the basic come, sit, and stay commands.

Cost-Conscious Training

The costs of training programs span as broad a spectrum as owner income. Training book prices range from $4.95 for mass-market, do-it-yourself paperbacks to $50 or more for professional texts written for trainers and others seeking more detailed information. Most general texts run in the $12–25 range for quality paper or hardback editions. Audiotapes and videotapes cost from $19.95 to more than $65, depending on length and content.

Fees for classes also vary a great deal depending on length, content, and the credentials of the teacher. Some animal shelters, kennel clubs, and even towns sponsor low-cost classes (in the $15–25 range) conducted by well-qualified individuals. These sponsors operate on the belief that the more well-trained dogs in the area, the fewer strays, abandoned animals, biting incidents, and other dog-related complaints they'll encounter. Because subsidizing these courses can save these organizations a great deal of money and mental anguish in the long run, they consider it a sound investment.

Veterinarians who understand how the dog's behavior can affect both its health and its relationship with the owner also may offer reasonably priced ($35–45) puppy classes for their clients and/or the general public. Some classes focus primarily on accustoming the dog to handling and on the development of social skills such as interacting with other dogs and people, while others also teach basic obedience.

Classes offered by professional trainers can run from $40 to more than $100 for a six- to eight-week session. One-day seminars by nationally recognized trainers and behaviorists cost an average $85–150, weekend sessions $125–200, and weeklong sessions up to $1,000. Some of these follow a lecture/demonstration format where participants listen and observe, while others invite owners to bring their dogs and learn how to work with their own pets. One fun alternative, Camp Gone to the Dogs in Putney, Vermont, offers owners lectures on such varied topics as canine health and legal issues; classes in obedience, agility, therapeutic massage, grooming, and other canine activities; plus access to some of the top canine experts in the country for private consultation. Fees for on-site housing, food, and all classes run $685–750 per person and dog (double human-canine occupancy—i.e., the dogs stay in the same room with their owners).

Fees for private lessons and consultations range from $30 to more than $150 an hour. Trainers who work with dogs at their own facilities without the owner charge $500–1,000 per week, and some require a minimum two-week stay. Prospective owners considering this approach should read the in-depth discussion of how to select a behavioral consultant in William Campbell's *Owner's Guide to Better Behavior in Dogs* (Alpine, 1995). You can also access this same discussion on the Internet at:

http://www.rogueweb.com/petbehavior

When you tally up the cost for any training method, don't forget to allow for any add-ons. These may include additional books, workbooks, videos, collars, leashes, distraction devices, or other items the instructor uses in the training process. Although you already may have included some of these items in your new dog's budget and some are relatively inexpensive, the cost of others can mount up.

Regardless of the equipment involved, don't begin your training program without it. When Alex grabs a highly recommended training book and jogs to the park with Rory, he discovers the program uses a noisemaker to attract and hold the animal's attention. Lacking that, Alex tries snapping his fingers and whistling, but these sounds blend in with those from the busy playground and confuse his dog, as well as frustrate Alex.

Or consider what happened to Molly. She saved her pennies for months to enroll her new dog in classes conducted by a famous trainer. During the first class the trainer strongly recommended Molly switch Juno to a limited-edition all-natural diet and fortify it with obscure supplements, all available only from the famous expert. Although Molly really couldn't afford these products, she had already paid for the course and feared her failure to comply would damage her relationship with the trainer.

Given Molly's tight budget, why didn't she train Juno herself? As is the case with a lot of owners, the program's high cost greatly increased her commitment to its success.

"After scrimping for those classes, there's no way I'm going to miss one, or not do the homework assignments," she vowed. "Besides, knowing that the trainer and other owners will be watching Juno's performance each week makes me much more conscientious about working with her at home."

Some trainers and behaviorists require that the dog receive a physical examination prior to the consultation because concurrent medical problems plague a surprising number of ill-behaved dogs. Some, myself among them, will focus primarily on the bond side of the behavior, and refer the owner to a trainer for routine obedience or agility work in addition to recommending changes to correct a specific problem. Others prescribe psychotherapeutic drugs (more on this in Chapter 6), some of which can cost a small fortune.

If you'd like to attend a camp or extended training sessions with your dog or send your animal to a professional for training, don't forget to add in the cost of transportation, food, and lodging if these aren't included in the overall price.

Regardless of what option you choose, determine all of the stated as well as any hidden costs. Going over-budget won't only depress you, it also can cause you to resent the program and your dog for wiping out your savings.

Training Finances

Review your budget for your new dog in terms of the training options discussed in this chapter. Can you afford the one(s) that appeal to you? If not, list any alternatives you think might enable you to achieve comparable results more economically.

So Much Training, So Little Time

As noted in Chapter 1, even owners with limited spare time can effectively train a dog. The trick is in selecting an approach that you can comfortably accomplish in the time available. This means not only surveying your options before you get a dog, but also making your selection early enough that you can adapt the process if necessary to meet your needs.

If you opt for a do-it-yourself book, that means getting the book and reading it from cover to cover first. Although some people think do-it-yourself videos take less time, that's not always the case. Studies indicate that the average person finds it difficult to concentrate on even the most slickly produced video for more than 12 minutes at a time. This means that even if Alex could stay awake for the entire 60-minute training tape after a night on call, chances are he'd need to watch it several more times before he could digest its entire contents. Because of this, many owners find it easier to adhere to a program that breaks down the material into specific lessons or other more manageable blocks. Regardless of what do-it-yourself method you select, preview *all* of the material first, then study each section in detail before trying the approach on your dog.

Before signing up for any class or private lessons, you should also know how long the sessions will last and the amount of daily training time built into the program. Although to someone like Molly it sounds like a bargain to spend two hours or an entire day with the greatest trainer in the universe, both people and dogs can take only so much, and some can take less than others. Classes should contain a mixture of events, including lecture, show-and-tell, and working with your own or someone else's animal.

"Juno would never sit still while someone talked," Molly remarks dubiously.

Maybe not at first, but most dogs quickly learn to sit still by watching other dogs and/or because their owners ignore them. As a result, even though these quiet interludes give the dog a break while the owner learns the rationale behind the next step of the training, the dog continues learning, too.

By the same token, no matter how hectic Alex's schedule gets, he gains nothing if he holds marathon training sessions on his days off and weekends but does nothing the other days. Because consistency is critical, five minutes a day will accomplish a lot more than an entire day once a week. If Molly lacks the time to achieve all that the instructor expects between classes, the experience could prove more frustrating than beneficial for both her and Juno in the long run.

Another aspect of time that deserves mention involves the training concept called *timing*. Because all dogs and people maintain their own unique sense of time, the success of any training program depends on the compatibility of the two. Although we may never give it much thought, most of us expect our dogs to respond to a command within a certain amount of time. For instance, Alex expects Rory to ignore all the activity in the playground and immediately come running the instant he commands, "Come." After all, the nurses with whom he works in the operating room instantly obey. On the other hand, Molly doesn't care if it takes Juno a few moments to come as long as the command does cause the dog to move in her general direction.

Problems naturally arise when owners and dogs maintain different senses of time. Rory's laid-back approach to life drives intense and aggressive Alex up the wall; Juno's fast-paced style drives her laid-back owner crazy, especially when the dog drags her down the street. To get the maximum benefit out of any training program, you need to determine your and your dog's timing and make any necessary changes. In my experience it works best for the owner to slow down or speed up to match the dog rather than to expect the dog to change its timing while learning other new skills.

Molly begins running with Juno, doing fast-paced turns and figure eights until Juno learns to focus on her, then she gradually slows down to the pace she wants. This might represent a minority opinion in some training circles where the dog must perform a certain act within a specific time frame. However, I find that owners of fast-paced dogs get better results from a fast-paced program that they then gradually slow down to match their own pace than they do from screaming at the dog to slow down *and* respond to their other commands simultaneously.

Obviously if you want to compete with your dog in obedience, you should use a training program that develops the timing required in these events. However, if you want only a well-behaved pet, don't hesitate to juggle the timing to fit your own and your dog's needs.

If you're considering using training videos, be aware that many attempt to pack a tremendous amount of information into a relatively brief presentation. Depending on the quality of the editing, this may result in what appears like a frenetic pace for dog and owner alike. Although Alex much prefers this approach, Molly finds it nerve-wracking and disorienting. More to the point, even if Alex finds the timing of the presentation acceptable, that doesn't automatically mean Rory will agree. That's why it's a good idea to evaluate every training program for time flexibility in three areas:

- Can I fit this program into my available free time?
- Can I adapt this program, if necessary, to accommodate my sense of timing?
- Can I adapt this program, if necessary, to accommodate my dog's sense of timing?

Training Program Time Analysis

Before you get your dog, read your training book, watch your training video, or sit through an obedience class or two, and ask yourself these time-related questions: Does this pace seem too hectic and rushed? Does the session appear to drag? Does the instructor insist on all people and dogs adhering to a fixed standard of time? Do I feel comfortable with any fixed standard? What would I and/or this instructor do if my dog possesses a different sense of time?

Heart-to-Heart Training

At the top of the list of emotional limits that can affect the training process is the degree to which an owner endorses the philosophy underlying the program. I became aware of this variable years ago in medical practice when a group of owners began bringing in dogs with diarrhea on the same morning every week. It turned out that, rather than succumbing to some rare, time-sensitive virus or parasite, all of these animals attended the same obedience class taught by a particularly heavy-handed individual. The owners found the experience so trying and felt so sorry for their pets that they stopped at McDonald's on the way home from class and shared a burger and fries with their dogs. The tension of the course plus the nutritionally questionable treat proved more than the canine gut could handle, and the animals developed diarrhea.

"What should I do if I don't like the way the trainer handles my dog?" asks Molly.

Ideally, you check out the trainer and class before you enroll so you don't get yourself and your dog caught in this predicament. If the trainer refuses to allow you to do that, look for another trainer.

"What if that person teaches the only class or the only one I can afford?" Molly counters. "Isn't that better than nothing at all?"

Although I want to say, "It depends," experience forces me to say, "No." Owners who disagree with the philosophy of a training method or who don't like the person teaching the course communicate this to their animals in a thousand subtle and not-so-subtle ways. In addition, these negative feelings may cause the owner consciously or subconsciously to sabotage the program.

For example, although Molly considers choke collars inhumane, she signs up for a program that uses them anyway. She puts the collar on Juno for class but doesn't use it at home when she works with the dog. This creates multiple problems for owner and dog alike. Wearing the collar only during class confuses Juno, so she doesn't learn what she should there. Because the trainer's methods depend on the use of the collar, when Molly tries to implement these techniques at home without it, she confuses the dog even more.

If Molly believes that this structured class will work best for her and her dog, she should discuss her feelings about the collar with the trainer. While most trainers opt for the method that works best for the majority of the class, they'll usually propose alternate approaches for certain students if the need arises. Obviously, however, if the owner doesn't inform the trainer of the problem, that person might not otherwise recognize it in a hectic class of 20 dogs.

If the trainer Molly chose can't or won't provide or accept alternatives, then she should seek an alternative herself. With all the options out there, any new owner should be able to find a suitable one. More and more veterinarians and veterinary technicians, for example, take an interest in behavior, and they often can provide valuable information about their favorite methods as well as link owners up with trainers who hold similar views. Personnel at animal shelters, rescue groups, kennel clubs, and pet stores also often serve as information clearinghouses.

Above all, only neutral or positive feelings should arise from the training process. Whether at home or in a class, the instant you feel yourself getting uptight or angry, back off. Take a break, or take your dog for a brisk walk or run through a series of fast-paced figure eights until you both calm down.

Although active dogs respond well to a more active training program, that doesn't mean owners should yell at them. Yelling and shouting serve only to desensitize a dog to its owner's voice and its own name. In addition to ignoring unruly dogs during consultations, I speak to their owners in a calm, quiet voice. When I do, dogs who are normally yelled at not only settle down, they actually move closer to me as if to hear what I'm saying. I recall one very excited animal who totally ignored his big brawny owner's booming orders but responded immediately when I *whispered* those same commands.

At the opposite extreme, an angry word to a more timid animal may devastate it. When Alex roars, "Sit!" in a fit of anger, Rory not only sits but also crouches, trembles, and urinates submissively. Now Alex faces two equally unproductive courses of action. One, he can apologize to Rory for frightening him and attempt to jolly the pup back into a more positive learning frame of mind. This can take a fair amount of time, the lack of which caused Alex to grow impatient and yell at his dog in the first place. Second, Rory's fearful response may make Alex feel so guilty that he yells at the dog even more.

"You little coward!" he berates the pup, even though he's far more angry at himself than at his dog.

Without a doubt fear undermines the training process more than any other human emotion, and although people who openly fear handling their own animals pose definite training challenges, owners who *won't admit* their fears complicate the process much, much more. If Molly admits her fears, the trainer can recommend special confidence-building exercises. However, if Molly denies those fears, she may reject one training program after another because "it's too heavy-handed (too intense, too insensitive, etc.) to meet Juno's special needs."

Regardless of what reason Molly gives, she really rejects these programs because all of them ultimately require her to assume leadership over her dog, and she's afraid to do that. Until she recognizes this, no program will work for her, and she and Juno will remain trapped in a vicious cycle. Because Molly fears her dog, she's afraid to train her. The lack of training causes Juno to behave in a manner that frightens her owner, which further undermines Molly's resolve to train her dog.

Training Emotional Limits Check

Carefully consider any philosophical or emotional limits you bring into the training process. If you feel strongly about any training devices, acknowledge it now so you don't wind up cursing the trainer who uses them under your breath every Wednesday evening for six weeks. Be brutally honest about any emotional shortcomings you may have as well as any strengths. If you can't take criticism, if you get angry or frustrated when things don't go your way, or if you would burst into tears if your dog growled at you, jot it down, but also note your willingness to ask others for help, or your saintly patience.

All owners occasionally say or do something to their dogs that they regret, just as all dogs do things from time to time that their owners find regrettable. However, by selecting a program and/or trainer with a philosophy that complements your own, recognizing the potent role your emotions play in the training process, and having the presence to back off when your feelings interfere with rather than enhance the process, you can make any type of training a positive emotional experience for you both.

Light- and Heavyweight Training

Training programs that accommodate the entire range of human physical limits also await the new dog owner. Sports enthusiast and active competitor Alex can find books, audiotapes, and videotapes that focus on the special needs of the athletic dog and teach owners how to incorporate sports psychology into the training process.

Just as some owners prefer to experience life at a brisker pace, so do some obedience class instructors. Rather than taking the dog to class, then later stopping off at the fitness center for a workout, owners who attend these canine classes can exercise with their dogs. Some instructors even incorporate elements of freestyle dancing (complete with music!) into the training, working the various commands into a peppy human-canine routine.

These more physical programs offer energetic owners several advantages:

- The self-conscious owner can more easily get caught up in the learning process.
- The shy or unruly animal doesn't have time to worry or act up.
- The programs combine human-canine exercise with training.
- Both owners and dogs find that the extra pizazz makes the training more fun.

"Forget that!" protests Molly. "I do enough running around at work! I want something slow and easy."

Even though many dog owners believe that they'd learn better in a more serene, less physical environment, the very act of putting a group of dogs together often negates this possibility. Some trainers do offer classes for children that take into account the younger pet owners' physical limitations, and these programs can do wonders for establishing human leadership, to say nothing of building the child's confidence. Carol Benjamin's *Dog Training for Kids* (Howell, 1988) remains the perfect text for at-home young trainers. Parents of young children who want to further ensure a positive training experience for their offspring also will find Brian Kilcommons's *Child-Proofing Your Dog* (Warner Books, 1994) a valuable addition to their dog owner's library.

I also recall hearing about a "low-impact" obedience course for senior citizens that got great results. In addition to senior citizens, the course attracted people of all ages with physical problems ranging from arthritis to carpal tunnel syndrome to immunodeficiency diseases. I hope we see more of these and other "special-needs" courses in the years ahead, for three reasons. One, we know from bond studies how particularly valuable pets can be to children, senior citizens, and people with physical, mental, or emotional impairments. Two, these people need special, less physical training techniques. Three, as the population grows older, more and more people will fall into this category.

For people with specific physical limitations who desire information about how to incorporate a dog into their lifestyle as either a companion or service dog, the Delta Society (289 Perimeter Road East, Renton, WA 98055–1329) serves as an excellent starting point. In addition to functioning as a clearinghouse for the increasing data on the human-animal bond, one of the Delta Society's four goals commits them to reducing the barriers to the enjoyment of animals in everyday life. The Society also offers information for pet owners who would like to train their pets to visit nursing homes and provide other positive pet experiences for people unable to own pets themselves.

If any group or private lesson strikes you as too physical or not physical enough, talk to the trainer. Because timing is critical in formal obedience, and because instructors often need to cover a lot of material in a relatively short period, they may sometimes forget that not everyone can keep up with them. Similarly, if the trainer asks you to do something you can't physically accomplish or can accomplish only with discomfort, say so. A good trainer will provide alternatives that better suit your needs.

Physical Limits Analysis

Review any physical limits that might affect your choice of a training program. Do you see yourself as more athletic like Alex or laid-back like Molly? Do you have any problems that might interfere with a certain kind of training program?

Know thyself. Although the image of the owner lacking the strength to physically restrain an unruly pet typically comes to mind when considering physical limitations, I recall one allergic owner whose best intentions to train his new dog vanished when he selected a program that met outdoors during the peak of goldenrod season.

Dog-Friendly Training

Like people of different ages, dogs of different ages require different training approaches. As noted, prospective owners who wish to train their new pups at home can choose from a wide assortment of books and tapes that address the special needs of this age group. If you hope to compete with your dog in obedience, agility, or other sports, or train it to hunt, herd, track, or pull a sled or cart, don't forget to check out the resources on this subject, too. Many include sections on how to train your pup to prepare it for these specific activities.

Because much of the general training literature as well as videos and courses pretty much take a "one-size-fits-all" approach, it behooves you to know as much as you can about your dream dog's needs beforehand. For example, different breeds may respond to owner orientation and distraction in different ways. An orienting stimulus causes the dog to establish eye contact with the owner, whereas a distracting one simply makes the animal stop what it's doing. Although some trainers see these as one and the same, I differentiate them because of the way most people intuitively relate to their dogs. In order to get Juno to establish eye contact with her, Molly calls the dog by name. However, if Molly wants Juno to stop doing whatever she's doing immediately, she shouts, "No!" and claps her hands.

Even though little breed-specific information regarding this aspect of training exists, we can make some general statements about how a dog's breed can affect its training. Irish wolfhound Rory, for instance, comes from a long line of animals bred specifically to hunt by sight and thus respond to even the subtlest visual cues. This group also includes Afghans, borzois, Scottish deerhounds, greyhounds, salukis, and whippets. When Alex holds his training sessions next to the busy playground, the sight hound pup becomes so overwhelmed with visual stimuli that he can't concentrate on his owner. When Alex moves the sessions into his secluded backyard, however, Rory quickly learns to respond to even the most subtle hand signal.

On the other hand, scent hounds, such as basenjis, bassets, beagles, bloodhounds, dachshunds, and Rhodesian ridgebacks, respond much more intensely to scent than to visual cues. My dear, sweet hound mix, Watson, pointed this out to me very clearly when we commenced educating each other. Unlike working breeds such as herding dogs which must juggle several concepts simultaneously, scent hounds prefer to deal with only one concept at a time, preferably an odor.

Never having owned a hound before, I set about training Watson as I did Violet, the sight-oriented corgi. Shortly after I got him, I took him to the grassy area in front of the house and did the sit routine.

"Whoa, is that dog brilliant or what!" I congratulated myself as he sat, then remained there without moving a muscle.

However, when I observed him more carefully, I realized he sat there because his mind was a million miles away processing some tantalizing scent that kept him glued to the spot. To test this hypothesis, I called him, I whistled, I jumped up and down and, finally (and only because I live in the middle of nowhere) took off my shirt and waved it at him. Nothing. If I needed any additional proof that this dog dwelt in a world of scent, the wind suddenly shifted, and his head drifted with it until he stared glassy-eyed at the hills to his left, still processing some wondrous message oblivious to me and his surroundings.

Further insight into how breeding may affect training comes from the world of food training. My aversion to giving dogs treats for good behavior goes back to my days in medical practice when I discovered that many owners don't wean their pets off the treats as these programs recommend. The treat and then other snacks and table food become symbols of love, precipitating relationship as well as medical disasters such as obesity and digestive problems when the dog gets older. However, I also realize that giving dogs treats can create near miraculous responses in many dogs, not to mention gratifying owners who believe their dogs expect more than just praise. Nonetheless, for health reasons I try to convince those who opt for this approach to use pieces of carrot rather than cheese, meatballs, or high-fat commercial dog treats.

Although many dogs respond positively to food training, others do not, a fact that may be breed-related. Sight hounds and sporting breeds such as retrievers quickly learn in which pocket their owners store the treats, and they automatically respond to hand motion in that direction. This gives rise to two behaviors peculiar to these dogs. As Rory sits in response to his owner's command, he simultaneously looks at the pocket in which Alex keeps the treats rather than at Alex. Second, if Alex inadvertently moves his hand near that pocket at some other time, this motion, too, will draw Rory's attention away from his owner.

Because getting the dog to focus on the owner for leadership as well as training purposes is a goal of virtually every training program, Rory learns only half the lesson. When Alex tries to replace voice commands with hand signals, he discovers he can't because Rory hasn't learned to look at him.

Owners of retrievers, spaniels, and other dogs who enjoy fetching a ball or toy note that their pets will respond much more reliably to that object than to food. One absolutely vicious cocker spaniel would allow me to do anything to her if she held her ball in her mouth and stared at her owner. While I initially found it rather unnerving to perform a complete physical examination (except for looking in the mouth!) on an unrestrained known biter, this extraordinary behavior so impressed me that after a while I looked forward to her visits.

Scent hounds pose a completely different treat-related problem. Unlike the sight hounds or sight-sensitive sporting breeds who must see the owner reaching for the treat before they make the connection between it and their response to a command, scent hounds can smell the food, often from an incredible distance. During another fact-finding training mission, I decided to see if I could use kibble to distract Watson from the tantalizing scents outdoors long enough for him to focus on me. That noble experiment also failed miserably. As soon as the 50-pound dog caught a whiff of the food, he raced toward me at full speed and literally tried to jump into my pocket. Although this would seem like a foolproof method to teach him to come, once I put that food in my pocket he became so excited he wouldn't let me get far enough away from him to test this hypothesis. Nor would he sit or stay anywhere except right next to me, either, and he did that only because it put him close to the food.

Not only did the presence of food prevent Watson from establishing eye contact with me, it wouldn't distract him if he'd locked onto some other, more tantalizing scent first, either. I could dramatically put my hand in the treat pocket, show him handfuls of kibble, and even throw it up in the air directly in front of him, but he couldn't care less.

Other dogs appear much more sensitive to sound. While some dogs adore squeaky toys, others despise them and will either try to rip them apart or hide under the bed to escape them. Some Shetland sheepdogs find certain modern phone bells and similar sounds irritating and bark like crazy whenever they hear them. Such dogs may not respond well to training methods that use sound to orient the dog. On the other hand, owners can effectively use these dreaded sounds as deterrents.

For example, my corgi hates squeaky toys with a passion, a fact I discovered when I bought her one shaped like a carrot. Because she loves carrots, I irrationally assumed she would love the toy. She didn't. Initially, I felt guilty about her response, but I quickly got over that when I realized that I could use the toy to keep her off of certain select pieces of furniture and even out of an entire room simply by placing it there. Whenever I squeaked the toy, she would freeze in her tracks, a real boon the day she decided to dig up all the daffodil bulbs I'd just planted. Eventually merely saying the word *carrot* precipitated the reaction; whereas her name causes her to establish eye contact, the word *carrot* caused her to avert her gaze. One day, however, the dreaded carrot disappeared. I looked high and low, but never found it.

Breed-Related Training Analysis

Review your material on your ideal dog and any training program with an eye toward any breed-related behaviors that could enhance or undermine the process. Does your dream dog's breed make it more sensitive to sight, sound, or scent? Ask breeders or people who own dogs of the breed you desire if their dogs orient more readily to a particular kind of stimulus or avoid certain others.

Functional Training

In addition to recognizing that dogs bred for different functions may possess physical differences that can affect their training, we can't ignore the dog's sense of function in the training process.

"But what if I only want a dog for companionship?" Molly asks. "I think maybe I'd like to do competition obedience sometime, but I don't have the time for it right now."

In spite of all the time, energy, and money that owners may invest in formally training an animal for a specific function, owners who get dogs "only" for companionship face a much more challenging task. Bearing in mind the important role that a dog's sense of identity plays in its health and behavior and how this relates to its sense of function, owners of companion dogs must find some way to give that animal a sense of function within their environments. Lacking this human input, the average household pet will attempt to fulfill its functional needs via one of three activities:

- protecting its territory
- obedience
- exercise

Most of us don't even acknowledge that the first exists.

"Rory loves everyone," Alex tells guests to his home. "He'd probably let a burglar steal the whole place!"

Maybe, but if Alex saw the way the pup responds to every sight and sound in his absence, he might not feel so sure of this. Nonetheless, most of us rarely consider our pets' territorial natures, much less how fulfilling or not fulfilling this function affects them. As a pup and young dog, Rory thinks of dashing in and out of his dog door, patrolling the perimeters of Alex's large fenced yard, and policing up the activities of the chipmunk population as a big game. As he gets older, though, he much prefers to spend most of his time alone sleeping.

On the other hand, protecting the territory overwhelms kennel dog Juno. Rather than providing her with a sense of fulfillment, it makes her feel threatened and inadequate.

Although responding to even the most rudimentary obedience commands can give our canine companions a sense of function, most of us view obedience training more as a rite of passage, like housebreaking; we do it when we get a new pup, then we forget about it unless problems arise. We rarely consider our dog's ongoing territorial function which often plays itself out in a restricted environment. Juno's breeder put the Chesapeake Bay retriever through a rigorous training program to prepare her for showing, then turned her into a kennel dog when she didn't develop the desired show qualities.

"That's why she has problems now," Molly reminds us. "If that woman had worked with her more, Juno wouldn't be so headstrong."

Like Molly, most of us immediately grasp why Juno's early training didn't do much for her in adulthood. However, because Molly dotes on Juno, she doesn't realize that the dog lives an equally, if not more functionally, restricted life in her new home. Once Molly ascertained that Juno would respond to come, sit, and stay commands, she considered the dog fully trained.

"I don't need to give her those commands," Molly boasts. "She's always right beside me and pretty much does what I do."

In fact, most owners give their pets few commands because most dogs pick up any human routines fairly quickly. Two weeks after Alex first commands Rory to sit before he takes him out or before they come back into the house, the pup automatically does this. Not only that, Rory also knows where Alex keeps the leash, and he gets much more excited when Alex dons his old romp-in-the-park sweat suit than his brief-walk-before-I-go-to-work sports coat. Rory likewise knows what time Alex feeds him, where Alex keeps the food, what his food dish looks like, and what "Rory," "walk," "ride," "food," and "no" mean. Not bad for a dumb animal!

Because the majority of dogs are quite intelligent and love to learn and please their owners, using obedience as a source of canine function-fulfillment makes sense for busy owners without either the time or the inclination to become involved in more formal functional pursuits. Rather than just teaching Rory to come, sit, and stay and then forgetting about it once the pup learns the commands or Alex needs the animal to perform these functions, Alex gives Rory commands throughout the day and genuinely praises the pup for responding properly. Although some may frown and challenge the political correctness of Alex's training Rory to fetch his paper and slippers rather than a ball or toy, it's difficult to ignore the dog's joyful expression when he accomplishes this task.

Functional Training Analysis

Review your material about your dream dog as it relates to function. Does your ideal dog possess a strong or weak sense of function? Can you incorporate your new pet's natural tendencies into its training program? How?

"There's no way I'm going to take up hunting!" Molly huffs, a sentiment shared by many sporting dog, hound, and terrier owners.

Nor do I think they should. However, the fact that we may disagree with the philosophy that resulted in the breed's creation doesn't automatically erase any canine functional needs that go with that breeding. Juno's breeder doesn't hunt either, and through trial and error she discovered that her dogs responded best to a training program that employs an AKC-regulation dumbbell, both as a training device and as a retrieving toy. Her dogs so enjoy retrieving, that they'll come, sit, and stay as soon as they see the object, knowing the owner will reward them with a quick game of fetch.

However, because Molly doesn't know how the breeder built this function into the training process, she gives Juno commands only as needed. Now Juno loses on two fronts. First, Molly's failure to supply the positive functional stimulus provided by the toy makes it necessary for the dog to try to fulfill this need some other way, and Juno now devotes all the mental and physical energy she used to expend responding to commands and retrieving her dumbbell to barking at every strange noise she hears. Second, even when Molly does give Juno a command, her ignorance of the complete sequence leaves the dog feeling unfulfilled. Ironically, Molly would never consider training a dog with food and then not giving it a treat after it properly responded.

"That's mean!" she exclaims with the utmost conviction.

On the other hand, the idea that her dog would take far more pleasure out of a brief game of fetch or even just *holding* her beloved dumbbell than a food treat as a reward never crosses the owner's mind.

We return again to a familiar theme: Talk to breeders and owners of dogs you admire. Find out what training methods they use, why, and what works best for them. Different breeds and even different lines may possess their own little idiosyncrasies that may enhance or undermine the training process. By learning about these first, you can select the method that best meets that animal's functional as well as physical needs.

Training Range Analysis

Before beginning this section, make a list of all the different places you would like your dog to go with you. Note any special social skills your dog might need—ability to walk on- or off-lead, ability to accept crowds, noise, etc.—to enable you to do this.

The Well-Appointed Training Scene

Having determined how our orientations and limits and our dog's needs can affect how we train our dogs, we need to revisit the subject of purpose-oriented training as it relates to the environment. As previously noted, I've met some dogs with horrendous behavioral problems who possess championships in obedience. I've met an equal number who will respond flawlessly to the owner's commands in the living room barring the presence of any strangers. These performances serve as valid indicators of the dog's trained status, but only if the owner doesn't take the animal anywhere else. If you want to take your dog to the park, in the car, to the shopping mall, or to visit your folks, then you should include these different environments in your training program.

A trainer of guide dogs for the blind told me about sending a litter of German shepherd dog pups to country homes to get them off to a good start in stable, wholesome environments. Unfortunately these idyllic surroundings did nothing to prepare the pups for the sensory chaos of the city where many visually impaired folks who need these dogs live. Even though the dogs could perform perfectly in their pastoral settings, they never felt comfortable enough in the city to become reliable service animals.

Fueled by the idea of all the places he wants to take his dog, Alex nails down the basics with Rory in their home and yard. Then Alex moves the action to a quiet corner of the park. When Rory masters that new environment, Alex moves him closer to the playground. Rather than seeing Rory's ongoing training as involving the completion of a series of lessons or mastering some specific commands, Alex focuses on the bigger picture formed by all the places he wants to take his dog and how he wants his dog to behave there.

If you get an older animal, you may need to initiate any training program in an environment the animal considers safe first, then gradually broaden its exposure to other areas. Dogs raised in chaotic and restricted environments may freak out in a class setting, a fact that should prompt their owners to adapt any training programs accordingly. For instance, you may decide to teach your pet the basic commands at home and merely visit and observe the local obedience class with the dog to accustom it to the new environment. Once the combination of home training and exposure enable the animal to feel more comfortable in that setting, you can enroll your pet in a class.

Consider this typical owner's obedience want list in terms of the different environmental conditions involved:

- accept grooming and handling
- walk on a leash without pulling
- walk through a crowd
- stay in position on command
- permit petting or examination by strangers
- accept strange dogs
- not panic when exposed to distracting conditions
- not bark, whine, howl, or destroy things when left alone

The variety of the items may at first make this appear to be more of a "wish" list. A dog who accepts grooming, petting, and examination by strangers elicits images of groomers and veterinary clinics rather than obedience classes. City streets and parks come to mind when we think about walking our dogs through crowds, stray dogs, and distracting conditions. Wanting a dog who remains calm when left alone reminds us of the desire to leave our pet in the car while we run into the post office, or of leaving it at a friend's home while we take in a movie.

While such needs appear so varied that no program could possibly address them all, in fact the American Kennel Club's Canine Good Citizen Program does exactly that. Moreover, many hospitals and nursing homes with pet visitation programs require that all canine visitors pass this program, so if that appeals to you, you can train your dog *and* prepare to visit shut-ins with your pet at the same time. Basically you train your dog with a group or on your own, then take a 10-part pass/fail certification test. Owners not interested in certification can use the program more as a guide and adapt or expand it to meet their specific environmental needs. For further information about the program, contact your local kennel club or the AKC or pick up a copy of Jack and Wendy Volhard's *Canine Good Citizen* (Howell, 1994).

Pack Structure and Training

Now we come to the final training question: Who will train the dog?

"Naturally I will since I live alone," Alex immediately replies.

It's true Alex lives alone, but does he want his dog to respond only to him and to those people Rory perceives as like Alex?

"Good Lord, no!" exclaims the athletic six-footer. "My parents are both elderly, and a lot of my friends have kids. I want Rory to respond to anyone who gives him a command."

In that case, Alex should teach his dog the basic commands and then ask these other people to do the same to establish across-the-board human leadership. Granted a dog who responds only to one person poses less of a threat than one who responds to no one, but single-owner control doesn't make the dog well trained no matter how well it responds to that individual.

Some puppy classes provide a wide range of people to interact with their canine students in a safe environment. In addition to children and elderly people, some of these classes include people with special needs. Any owner who has burned with embarrassment when his or her dog cowered and growled while the owner tried to converse with someone in a wheelchair can appreciate the value of this early experience. Also, if you think you'd like to join that growing group of dogs and owners who visit residents of nursing homes and other shut-ins, such varied experiences will give your pup a good head start.

Although dogs who learn to respond to owners with more anthropomorphic views and subordinate tendencies like Molly will usually respond to a broader range of people than animals trained by someone like Alex, it pays owners to train any dog to respond to the least capable person that animal could encounter in its environment. For most of us that means a child. In fact, because of the way dogs view the human pack structure, many busy parents discover that, contrary to what they initially believed, having their children train the dog can save a lot of time and effort in the long run. Even though the parents may need to offer a lot of support and encouragement to their offspring throughout the training process, a dog well trained by a child commonly views everyone older than the youngster as a leader. Compare this with Dad and Mom training the dog first and then inviting the kids to do likewise, a much more time-consuming process. Also, considering how many latchkey kids now fill our homes and how many parents see the dog as a source of comfort and security for their children, the dog should recognize the child's authority. Otherwise, the child will feel more intimidated than comfortable and secure when alone with the dog.

"Wouldn't it be easier just to hire someone to train the dog for them?" Molly wonders out loud.

One of the most frequent complaints voiced by reputable trainers who train dogs for others laments the erroneous belief that this approach will solve all of the dog's problems once and for all. It's simply not true, and any knowledgeable trainer will tell you that up-front. Not only will you need to reinforce any training in your own environment, you'll also have to shift the dog's focus from the trainer to yourself and to anyone else to whom you want the dog to respond. However, if you lack the time or confidence to initiate the training process, qualified trainers who take the dog for a few weeks and teach it the basics of human leadership as well as obedience can get things off to a fine start. These individuals also provide a valuable service for owners who select adult animals with problems that the owners can't resolve themselves.

Whether you send a pup for basic training or an adult dog for a bit of fine-tuning, thoroughly research both the program and the people running it.

Remember Molly's early experience: after saving for months to send Juno away for a two-week training session, Molly practically dies when the trainer demonstrates the heavy-handed techniques he expects her to use on her pet. Because such a program runs counter to Molly's beliefs and leadership style, it's difficult, if not impossible, to implement it in her own home.

Leadership Style Analysis

Review your notes about your personal leadership style as it relates to training. If necessary, revise your list, then add any other customized training criteria you developed in this chapter. The more you can limit the field and review possible programs before you get your dog, the more prepared you'll be to begin training your new pet immediately.

Molly defines herself as a low-key leader who feels more comfortable using positive than negative reinforcement. However, she also acknowledges that she wants her dog to respond positively to children. Even though Alex describes his leadership style as much more dominant and aggressive, he, too, wants to use positive rather than negative reinforcement to create a well-behaved pet who will obey everyone.

"But even if I knew I wanted a Chesapeake Bay retriever, how would I know what kind of temperament that animal will have?" argues Molly. "After all, I went to the kennel expecting to get a nice, stable pup."

You can never guarantee you won't give in to your emotions when selecting a new dog. On the other hand, the more clearly you see yourself and your future pet in your particular environment and the more objectively you consider how you'll train that dog to do what you want it to do to fulfill both your own and its needs, the less likely emotions will cloud your judgment.

Imagine Molly first seeing Juno and openly discussing the dog's special needs and training options. Imagine her going home and pondering this as it relates to her personal needs, limits, environment, and leadership style.

"But then maybe I wouldn't have taken her," Molly declares. "And Juno would have spent the rest of her life miserable in a kennel."

Not necessarily. Perhaps someone with the knowledge, skill, time, and environment to fulfill Juno's needs would have adopted her if Molly hadn't. Such a happy outcome could occur just as easily as Molly's image of the dog rotting in a cage. If Molly decides she really does want Juno and then considers what she must do to make life mutually rewarding for herself and such a dog, she might spend several weeks making Juno-compatible changes in her environment and selecting and previewing the training program that will best meet both their needs. Not only will this save this busy owner a tremendous amount of time, it will help ensure that the dog's training marks the beginning of a long and rewarding relationship rather than a necessary burden of pet ownership.

Now that you know how to select the best program to give your dog the necessary social grace, we need to examine the burgeoning array of training aids that promise to transform even the most thick-headed doggy demon into a well-behaved canine saint.

6

Baits and Switches

Determining If, and What, Training Aids Will Work for You and Your Dog

Marty Cabliano and his son, Tim, want only the best for their English setter pup, Luke, and that includes an aesthetically pleasing buried electronic fence.

"This'll keep him safe," Marty tells Tim as he adjusts the collar containing the receiver around Luke's neck.

A week later, a freak thunderstorm triggers the pup's collar, and the terrified animal frantically races around the yard in an effort to escape the electrical shocks while his equally horrified owners tear after him. In a panic, Luke crosses the fence and runs into the road, directly into the path of an oncoming car.

Luke's leg will heal in six to eight weeks, but it will take a lot longer to repair the damage to his self-confidence, to say nothing of his relationship with his owners.

The idea of a training aid that promises a quick fix can easily seduce dog owners during their weakest moments. This chapter will help you understand how the owner, dog, environment, and pack structure may affect the use of training aids and vice versa. When Marty Cabliano adds "new pup owner" to the juggling act that already includes "professional" (he's a computer software designer) and "single parent" (he's the proud father of an active teenager), his already complex life becomes even more so. The day Marty dashes into the house, slips in a pile of puppy-do, and stumbles over the chewed remnants of Tim's clarinet case on his way to answer a phone call from a neighbor ranting about Luke's incessant barking, he understandably grasps at any straw that promises to cure his dog's problems instantly.

In reality, though, none of the products currently on the market can produce an instant cure, even though some manufacturers may claim they do. Nonetheless, busy new owners grappling with the fallout of negative behavior often project their own, unrealistic expectations onto these products, then feel cheated when the devices don't work, or even make the animal's problem(s) worse. Marty reads an ad for a combination electronic training collar/containment system and envisions it curing all of Luke's problems. In a flash, the collar will help him instantly train the pup not to bark, and the containment system will enable him to leave Luke outdoors safely, thus instantly solving the pup's house-soiling and destructive chewing problems. When Marty tells his aunt, Helen Sorenson, a very active senior citizen, about this miraculous system, she wonders whether it would solve all her problems with Dandy, the four-year-old fox terrier she adopted from the local shelter.

The bewildering and expanding array of training aids available spans the spectrum from the most sophisticated to most simplistic, but the options can be divided into five broad categories:

- electronic devices worn by the dog
- handheld electronic devices
- electronic devices placed in the environment
- drugs
- low-tech options

Before we can determine whether a particular training aid will work for a particular pet and owner in a particular environment, though, we first need to understand how these devices work.

The Wired Dog

Virtually all of the electronic devices designed for canine wear attach to special collars, and almost all claim to help owners perform one of three functions:

- accomplish general training
- stop or limit barking
- confine the dog or keep it away from certain areas

The basic training system consists of a collar with a built-in receiver and a separate, battery-powered portable transmitter. Depending on the design, the transmitter sends out an electrical pulse of variable strength and/or duration, a sound, or a combination of sound and electrical stimulation, all of which theoretically inhibit negative behavior. Some collars emit an audible tone that precedes the electrical stimulation, while others use sound only to reward positive behavior. Originally designed to train hunting dogs, these systems can transmit electrical or sound stimulation to animals anywhere from 250 yards to more than a mile away.

"When you say 'electrical stimulation,' do you mean a shock?" asks Helen Sorenson, hugging Dandy protectively.

Yes, I do. I use the word *stimulation* because the ads and literature for these products use that terminology. However, most other people, including the trainers who use them, refer to them as "shock collars."

Although anti-barking collars use the same negative-reinforcement principle as electronic training collars, they're self-contained systems triggered by the barking dog's throat vibrations. Some systems respond to all barks, whereas others contain timing devices that don't punish the dog's alarm or protection barking; some even include voice recognition chips that respond only to the barking of one specific dog. Also, instead of electrical stimulation, some models emit a high-frequency sound when the dog barks, while others beep at the first bark and transmit an electrical pulse only if the barking continues. Another system releases a pungent burst of citronella, an odor most dogs dislike, whenever the animal barks.

Other electronic collar systems promise to keep the dog out of specific areas. Marty purchased one for Luke that creates a 10-foot-diameter "force field" around the transmitter which Marty placed in the bottom shelf of the bookcase containing his and Tim's tennis trophies. As Luke approaches this area, the transmitter activates a beeper on the pup's collar. If Luke continues moving toward the transmitter, the collar emits an electrical charge. Another system Marty considered consists of a collar and electrified mats which the owner uses to block the forbidden area. When the dog steps on the mat, it receives an electrical shock from the collar.

Electronic containment systems designed to confine a dog outdoors utilize a buried electrical wire that triggers an adjustable electrical pulse (with or without prior audible warning) in the dog's collar whenever it approaches the wire. Depending on the model, these systems can contain very small to very large animals in a space up to 25 acres. A variation uses sound transmitters rather than buried wire. When the animal approaches one of these, the collar emits a warning tone. Owners may set the system to emit an optional pulse stimulus if the dog continues moving toward the boundary.

The Wired Owner and Environment

Like electronic collars, electronic handheld devices promise general training and/or anti-barking benefits. They use the same principle as mechanical devices such as the trusty ultrasonic dog whistle, or chains or disks which, when tossed at the dog's feet (not at the dog), produce a sound that distracts the animal from its activities and orients it toward the owner. Handheld electronic devices all emit sound and come in two basic styles. One transmits bursts of ultrasonic sound which the owner uses to gain the animal's attention and/or emphasize commands. The other produces an irritating ultrasonic sound burst to discourage misbehavior plus a more soothing audible tone to reward desired responses.

Handheld devices specifically designed to stop dogs from barking work the same way. When Helen presses the button on hers, it emits an irritating high-pitched sound. Because anti-barking devices, like the other handheld training aids, theoretically enhance rather than replace owner interaction, they possess a much shorter range (1–25 feet) than remote-controlled training collars.

A variation on the handheld theme takes the form of a device Helen attaches to Dandy's leash. As soon as the dog starts pulling, the gadget emits an audible tone, Dandy turns toward Helen to investigate, and she establishes eye contact and gives him the command to heel (i.e., walk beside her).

Likewise, training aids designed to discourage various canine behaviors in the owner's absence use either electrical stimulation, irritating sound, or a combination of the two. The simplest consists of a snapping device similar to a mousetrap with a wide, flat base that Helen places next to her kitchen waste receptacle. When Dandy steps on the base, the device snaps and frightens him away.

When Luke touches special mats placed on furniture or other off-limits locations in Marty's home, the pup receives an electrical shock. Vibrations trigger other devices to emit audible alarms to frighten him and alert his owner to the misbehavior. More sophisticated systems emit high-pitched sounds—with or without flashing or strobe lights—when they sense heat, sound, or motion anywhere from 10 to 50 feet from the transmitter. Others create a sound barrier by transmitting sound just above human hearing range which animals find irritating.

The Drugged Dog

For years, veterinarians have prescribed various tranquilizers, such as acetylpromazine (Acepromazine), for dogs excessively distressed by veterinary visits, thunderstorms, or long-distance travel. When used properly, these substances dull the dog sufficiently that it no longer reacts to the previously upsetting circumstances, but not so much that it can't function. Although tested and used extensively, these drugs do produce different results in different animals, and it can take a while to determine the effective dose for a particular animal. When Luke and Dandy receive the identical dose per pound of body weight, Luke can barely keep his eyes open, while Dandy acts more agitated than usual; a third dog shows no effects of the drug at all.

In addition to periodically drugging dogs exposed to certain upsetting conditions, owners now can opt to use certain human psychotherapeutic drugs, such as busparine (Buspar), amitriptyline (Elavil), and fluoxetine (Prozac), to treat canine behavioral problems ranging from aggression to separation anxiety. Although researchers are currently exploring the therapeutic value of at least 10 different behavior-altering drugs, the media focus primarily has been on fluoxetine (Prozac), the most frequently prescribed human antidepressant in the country, but among the drugs least prescribed by veterinarians.

Unlike veterinary tranquilizers whose development and usage has resulted in a considerable amount of data regarding their effects and side effects over the years, the newer psychotherapeutic drugs offer some unique challenges. First, as we know from our discussion of owners, dogs, and their environments, defining a particular canine behavior as a problem, let alone one that requires medication, depends a great deal on subjective judgment.

"Geez, Aunt Helen, why don't you get that poor dog something to calm him down?" Marty complains after he dog-sits for Dandy one weekend and the terrier refuses to eat or drink and licks one foot raw.

"Don't be silly, Dear," Helen Sorenson soothes her nephew. "According to the man at the shelter, Dandy's mother did exactly the same thing. It's how he shows he loves me."

Second, all of these drugs fall under the heading of "experimental" when it comes to their use in animals, even though the manufacturers may have conducted some preliminary studies on laboratory dogs. This doesn't automatically mean these substances are unsafe. However, it does explain why veterinarians who prescribe these drugs expect owners to:

1. Provide a detailed description of the animal's problem.
2. Agree to any medical workup necessary to eliminate other problems that might cause the behavior or interfere with the drug's activity or metabolism.
3. Monitor the animal closely for any sign of negative side effects as well as benefits.
4. Conscientiously implement any training or other programs that would permit the elimination of the medication over time.

Finally, veterinarians may use certain drugs to treat behavioral problems in dogs that physicians use to treat entirely different conditions in humans. Although propranolol (Indural) may help control aggression in dogs, most people take the drug to control angina or high blood pressure. Consequently, if Helen takes the drug herself and a veterinarian prescribes it for Dandy, she must constantly guard against the tendency to compare her own dosage and response to the drug to her dog's dosage and response.

Nonelectronic Persuaders

Among the low-tech, nonelectronic training aids we find crates, exercise pens, gates, collars, halters, harnesses, and muzzles. The use of crates and exercise pens was discussed in Chapter 3. Some owners prefer to use gates rather than crates or exercise pens to block their new pet's access to certain areas of the house until it's housebroken. Although Dandy was house-trained when Helen got him, she crated the terrier in her absence until she felt she could trust him in her home. Then she gave him free run of the house except for her sewing room, which she blocked off with a gate.

Training collars come in halter, choke, and prong versions. Halters such as the Gentle Leader system discussed in Chapter 4 cause Luke to turn toward Marty when his owner applies pressure to the leash. A nylon, chain, or leather choke collar will tighten around the pup's neck, whereas a prong collar will tighten and the metal projections on its inner surface will dig into Luke's neck under those same circumstances.

The anti-pulling harness Helen buys to keep Dandy from dragging her down the street encircles the dog's chest and front legs and applies pressure in the "armpit" area when he tries to forge ahead. Some versions attach to the dog's collar, while others are self-contained. The harness she puts on the terrier to stop him from jumping up limits his motion by looping around his chest, abdomen, and hind legs.

If Helen decides that muzzling Dandy will teach him not to snap, she can choose from three basic models. One consists of two attached Velcro-secured bands she slips around Dandy's muzzle and neck. The second, a nylon or leather sleeve held in place by straps that fasten behind the dog's head, covers the entire muzzle. As its name implies, a wire basket muzzle consists of a wire basket that fits over the dog's muzzle and leather straps to hold it in place. Unlike other muzzles, the basket muzzle permits the dog to open its mouth slightly, thereby avoiding the serious problems that may arise when a muzzled animal drools excessively or vomits.

Training Aid Appeal Self-Evaluation

Consider each of the training options described in this section. List those you would consider using on your dog and the circumstances that would lead you to do so. Also list those you wouldn't consider under any circumstances.

Marty will use anything necessary to keep Luke from becoming a nuisance or destroying his possessions. Helen doesn't like the idea of shocking or muzzling Dandy, but if he attempted to bite her, she'd try anything to stop the behavior.

Owner Orientation and Training Aids

Given their busy lifestyles, most contemporary owners want to train their dogs initially or correct behavioral problems that crop up as quickly and inexpensively as possible. However, many times their relationships with their dogs, far more than any deficiency in the training program or aid, sabotages their attempts to do this. Anthropomorphically oriented Helen Sorenson is consumed by guilt every time she crates Dandy.

"Poor little baby," she coos sadly, kneeling in front of the crate. "Mommy's so sorry she has to lock you up like that."

Naturally Dandy tries to reach his distraught owner, and that makes her feel worse. After several weeks of this highly negative emotional reinforcement, Dandy develops diarrhea whenever Helen confines him.

At the opposite end of the spectrum, even busier and more distracted Marty's chattel view causes him to crate Luke with food and water far longer than the pup's psychology and physiology can endure. Instead of a housebroken pet who perceives his fiberglass carrier as a haven, Marty creates a neurotic dog who fouls his own sleeping and eating area and, naturally, hates his crate.

The more complex the training aid, the more critical the role the owner's orientation plays. When Marty and Helen visit the store that sells the combination training collar/containment system that Marty read about, the salesperson wisely asks both of them to hold the collar or, better yet, put it around their own necks with the contacts pressing into their skin while he triggers the device.

Marty does so without hesitation and reacts only slightly when he feels the shock. Helen, on the other hand, doesn't even want to touch the apparatus, and she screams when it shocks her.

"I could *never* do that to Dandy!" she cries. "That's terrible!"

"Then you definitely shouldn't buy one of these systems," the salesperson insists.

In my dreams. In reality, many people buy these systems through the mail based on the limited and glowing information available in their ads, or on a pitch rattled off by a salesperson who may know little more about the product—and even less about canine behavior—than they do. When anthropomorphically oriented owners deliberately or accidentally experience the shock after they get the system home, their negative feelings completely thwart their use of it. Helen puts the collar on Dandy and cringes when she gives him a command, dreading the shock. The dominant terrier interprets his owner's hesitancy as subordination, a perception that greatly lowers the probability he'll respond to the command. Helen's lower lip trembles and her hands shake as she zaps her beloved but unruly dog. You don't need a PhD in canine behavior to realize that such human-canine interactions do nothing to improve the dog's behavior but a lot to confuse the animal and undermine the relationship.

Unlike Helen, who remained uncomfortable with the idea of shocking her dog even after she had read and reread the upbeat training manual that came with the system, Marty feels so comfortable with the technology that he ignores the directions entirely. Instead, he puts the training collar on Luke, sets the transmitter at the highest level ("to get the fastest results"), and commands the pup to sit. Just as Luke figures out what Marty wants him to do and begins to lower his rear end, Marty loses patience and zaps him. The terrified pup freezes in terror and urinates submissively. Marty zaps him again, this time for urinating on the rug.

In this situation, technology-loving Marty completely ignores Luke's needs and the variations built into the equipment to meet those needs.

Similarly, owner views can affect the success of other training devices. Because the ultrasonic sound emitted by the handheld distraction device doesn't bother her, Helen assumes it doesn't bother Dandy, even though the literature that comes with the device clearly states that it works because dogs find the sound irritating. Consequently, while she could barely bring herself to zap her dog with an electrical impulse, she doesn't hesitate to blast him with sound. Although Helen initially gets what she considers spectacular results, the dominant terrier soon grows accustomed to the sound and ignores both it and his owner.

Because Marty's not home enough to use a handheld distractor effectively, he opts to put an electrified mat on the couch when he's gone. In his mind's eye, he envisions Luke responding to this in a typically Pavlovian way: Luke will touch the mat, get zapped, and stay away from the couch. However, this linear, rather mechanistic chattel view of the situation fails to take Marty's lifestyle and environment into account. Sometimes he forgets to turn the system on, or the mat winds up on the floor or even in Luke's bed next to the couch where Marty or Tim drop it when they want to use the couch. Further contributing to Luke's confusion, Tim often invites the pup to join him on the couch in Marty's absence, in spite of Marty's strict rule banning the dog from the furniture.

Or consider what happens when Helen comes to visit the Cablianos. She walks past the bookcase where Marty and Tim keep their tennis trophies and practically leaps out of her skin when she triggers a motion-sensitive alarm.

"For heaven's sakes!" she gasps as she struggles to slow her pounding heart. "Why don't you move the trophies where Luke can't reach them?"

"No way!" Marty retorts. "I refuse to rearrange my home for a dog."

In this situation, Marty's vision of a well-behaved dog as a four-legged robot leads him to use devices capable of undermining his relationship with other *people*, as well as with his pet.

How do anthropomorphic and chattel orientations affect the success of behavioral drug therapy? Dogs on psychotherapeutic drugs pose several challenges to their anthropomorphic owners on similar medication. If Helen experienced positive results with Prozac herself, for example, she might automatically expect Dandy to respond likewise.

"I can't understand why the veterinarian insists I monitor you and your behavior so closely," she tells her dog gaily. "I'm on the same drug, and I feel perfectly fine."

In fact, Helen feels so good and believes Dandy behaves so much better that the idea of training him to eliminate the problem behavior and weaning him off the drug strikes her as silly. Because of this, she fails to implement the suggested behavior modification program as directed because she can't commit herself fully to it.

Marty's more chattel-oriented views of his pup cause him not to monitor his pet, either, but simply because he expects the setter to take care of himself. When he accidentally spills Luke's medication and the pup gulps down an extra tablet before Marty can stop him, he tells his son, "I'm sure he'll throw it up if it bothers him."

Unfortunately, Luke doesn't, and Marty and Tim spend several very long hours waiting to hear from the veterinarian who is treating their pet's convulsions.

Owner Orientation Analysis

Review your analysis of the different training options you consider acceptable and the circumstances that would cause you to use them. Then note whether these arise from knowledge (K) or emotion (E), anthropomorphic (A) or chattel (C) views.

Marty's and his aunt's lists look like this:

	Marty	Helen
electronic collars	yes (KC)	no (EA)
handheld devices	no (EA)	yes (KA)
environmental devices	yes (KC)	no (KA)
drugs	yes (EC)	yes (EA)
low-tech options	yes (EC)	maybe (KA)

Marty credits his work in the computer industry for his knowledge and faith in electronic collars and environmental devices.

"But even though I understand the technology behind those handheld sound-makers, I just don't like them," he adds. "On the other hand, I know nothing about those drugs and have no time or desire to find out, but I wouldn't hesitate to give them to Luke if I thought it would cure any problem quickly. And frankly, all the other nonelectronic devices strike me as so innocuous, I wouldn't hesitate to use any of them."

Helen sees that same list of training options quite differently, always projecting her anthropomorphic views on the situation with or without any supporting knowledge. Does this mean her views carry less weight than Marty's? Not at all. It only means she approaches dog ownership in her own unique way. Let's put the two of them into some real-world situations and see how they fare.

Techno-Finances

Many owners maintain high expectations for some of the new training aids because they cost a great deal. If Marty decides to teach Luke to stay in the yard using traditional boundary training methods, he needs a collar, leash, and training book or video, for a total cost of $25–50. If he opts for an electronic containment system, however, he can expect to spend from $150 to more than $500. If he wishes to distract Luke from negative behavior or gain his attention, he can blow an old-fashioned audible dog whistle ($3) or an ultrasonic one ($15), or toss a specially designed chain ($3), disks ($8), or his car keys ($0, provided he doesn't lose them in the backyard). If he prefers something more high-tech, he can purchase a handheld device that emits a single, irritating tone for around $20, or one that emits negative and positive sounds for $30–40. If he wants to use a training collar that produces an audible tone as well as an electrical pulse, he can expect to spend $200–600.

To keep Luke away from the trophies in the living room, Marty can move the trophies or shut the door ($0), block the door with a gate ($25–50), put an electrified mat in the doorway ($85), place a plug-in transmitter on the shelf containing the forbidden objects and place a collar that emits both sound and electrical stimulation on Luke ($100), or install an indoor containment system to block off the entire room ($200).

You can see that some of the latest high-tech technology doesn't come cheap. However, an old saw definitely holds true: You get what you pay for. When Marty saw the price of the state-of-the-art containment system, he looked at his checkbook balance and bought a much cheaper one that lacked lightning protection. When lightning triggered the collar and Luke panicked, leaped the barrier, and got hit by a car, the $500 veterinary bill wiped out those savings and more. Anyone who plans to use a containment system in a suburban or urban environment also should make sure electronic garage door openers and other devices won't trigger the dog's collar, either.

Some training and containment systems come with poorly made collars that soon break, a definite drawback because replacements can cost more than $100. Other systems don't offer replacement collars at all; when the collar breaks the owner must start all over again.

Also, don't forget that any systems that depend on house current function only as long as the power doesn't go out. On the other hand, battery-powered systems require careful monitoring, too. Those that use disposable rather than rechargeable batteries cost less, but buying replacement batteries can eat up that difference, particularly if the system doesn't use standard batteries. Note that some rechargeable systems require a special battery charger, which will also add to the cost.

Although some drugs used to treat behavioral problems cost little, the monthly bill for medicating a medium-sized dog with some of the new psychotherapeutic drugs can exceed $100. In addition, owners incur the cost of the veterinary examination and behavioral consultation ($75–150 per hour plus any follow-up visits), and any tests necessary to eliminate medical problems and/or monitor the drug's effect on the animal's physiology ($100 and up).

"Do I really need to do all that just to get some pills for a perfectly healthy dog with a behavioral problem?" asks Marty dubiously.

Probably not—as long as everything goes right, and assuming both the veterinarians who prescribe the drugs and owners who use them bear in mind that these substances weren't designed for use in dogs. This means that doing anything less than a thorough workup requires excellent rapport and communication between the owner and the veterinarian, as well as the owner's willingness to carefully monitor the animal for signs of problems.

Prices for crates and pens to confine animals span a wide range, too. Crates average $25 to more than $100, depending on the size and model. You can pick up an old wooden playpen at a yard sale for your new pup for around $10, or spend $50 to more than $200 for a portable exercise pen with or without a pad under it and a top over it. A more permanent 8' × 4' × 6' chain-link fence enclosure will cost about $400–550, depending on whether you install it on bare ground, gravel, or a cement base.

Chain, nylon, or leather choke collars range in price from less than $5 to more than $20; chain or leather prong collars roughly $10–35. Expect to spend about $15–35 for a halter-style training system, depending on the dog's size and whether you purchase just the halter or a complete package that includes an indoor training lead and a training booklet. Both anti-pulling and anti-jumping harnesses fall in the $15–25 price range. People who fear that their pets might bite them or others can purchase a muzzle for less than $10 to more than $20.

Training Aid Financial Analysis

Before going on to the next section, review any financial limits you established for your new pet, then compare these with the cost of any training aid that appeals to you. Can you afford these? If not, list any other, more economical alternative that might meet your needs as well.

High-Tech Time Limits

Even if not a single ad or piece of promotional literature proposed any of the products mentioned in this chapter as time-savers, harried dog owners seeking a quick fix probably would still view them that way. In reality, though, virtually every one of these approaches requires a certain amount of skill, knowledge of the dog's personality and behavior, and, most certainly, the willingness to use the product *properly* for however long it takes to achieve lasting results.

Helen purchases her handheld ultrasonic trainer and thinks, "What's to know?" as she sound-blasts Dandy for chewing on her slipper while she talks on the phone.

Actually, there's a great deal to know, especially the fact that the most effective and humane training involves anticipating the negative response, then distracting the dog and orienting it toward you *before* it happens. So, while time definitely matters when owners employ these devices, don't think of them as time-savers. Rather, their successful use depends on the owner's *timing*, and that may require a great deal of time (plus knowledge and skill) to develop.

When Helen sound-blasts Dandy after five minutes of slipper chewing, she might discourage him from chewing slippers in her presence, but she does nothing to teach him to stay away from her slippers in the first place. Compare that approach with deliberately leaving her slippers out, observing Dandy surreptitiously from behind her newspaper or the kitchen door, then distracting him the instant he sniffs the forbidden object. The latter definitely will produce good results, but it also takes much more time than simply pressing a button.

We see a similar paradox with the training collar systems designed to give the dog an audible warning prior to the electrical shock. The warning means nothing if the owner doesn't have the knowledge and skill to trigger the device soon enough for the dog to respond to the sound and avoid the shock. Owners who lack this crucial timing end up routinely shocking their dogs, and creating neurotic rather than stable, well-trained pets.

Luke wanders around the yard wearing his electronic training collar while Marty and Tim shoot baskets in the driveway. Suddenly Marty notices Luke trotting toward them from the now ravaged flower bed with the remnants of a tulip hanging out of his mouth. Marty swears, grabs the transmitter, hits the sound warning button once, and then immediately zaps the pup with a maximum-level shock. The pup freezes and drops the flower.

"What's wrong with that?" asks Marty. "He shouldn't be digging up the flowers."

Exactly. However, Marty's response did nothing to teach his dog not to dig up the flowers. He taught the pup not to carry a flower to his owner. And the same principle holds as true for a whap of rolled-up newspaper as a zap from a high-tech electronic collar. The unfortunate paradox posed by many of these devices is that the people who have the knowledge, skill, and timing to use them properly don't use them, whereas those who lack these prerequisites do, naively thinking the device automatically will confer these vital training essentials on them.

Electronic containment systems also require a great deal of time to install and use properly. All come with training flags that the owner—or someone else—places within the confines of the electrified perimeter and then teaches the dog not to cross. If the owner does this properly, the dog never approaches the boundary and thus never gets shocked. Basically, then, the electrified system merely acts as a backup to plain, old-fashioned boundary training wherein the owner establishes a boundary— the sidewalk, flower beds, or even a row of empty boxes at the edge of the front lawn—and teaches the dog not to go beyond it, first while leashed and then when off-lead. The success of the containment system therefore relies on the owner's ability and willingness to devote the necessary time to teach the animal its boundaries *first*.

Even more than electronic devices, drugs can create the impression of instant success. In fact, their sometimes near-miraculous effect on aggressive or frightened dogs makes it extremely easy for busy owners to forget that the problem exists and disregard all those other changes the veterinary behaviorist recommended.

"Dandy acts like a completely different dog since I started giving him those pills," Helen marvels. "He's so calm and relaxed, not at all snappy like he used to be."

For some owners, only the thought of possible risks to their pet's health from long-term drug use prompts them to find the time to tackle the underlying cause of the behavior. For others living on a fixed income like Helen, the high cost of the drug may provide the necessary stimulus to make the needed changes.

Finally, some owners keep their dogs on drugs because they lack the time and commitment to do anything more than eliminate the *signs* of the behavior. Because little data exists on the long-term effects of these substances, however, we don't know whether these animals will develop more time-consuming medical problems down the road.

Regardless of what path owners who opt for psychotherapeutic drugs choose, properly defining the animal's behavioral problem, eliminating any possible medical problems, selecting the right drug, determining the most effective dosage, and monitoring the dog for side effects does take time.

The same principle holds true for the selection of less complex training aids. If Helen can instantly stop Dandy from jumping up with an anti-jumping harness, that seems so much faster and easier than recognizing the dog's behavior as a sign of a human-canine leadership problem and initiating all the changes necessary to rectify it. However, while the harness gives immediate results, it does nothing to stop the terrier's other dominant behaviors or resolve the pack problems in the household.

Training Aid Time Check

How much time did you allot to train your dog? Does that estimate include any time necessary for you to educate and train yourself to properly use any acceptable approach *first*? If not, can you free up that time from your schedule?

High-Tech Emotion

Despite the fact that even the most sophisticated computer lacks feelings, it seems that the more high-tech the training approach, the stronger the human emotions it elicits. People who adore electronic devices give them complete credit for their wonderful relationship with their pets, while those who hate them unduly blame them for myriad canine problems. In a similar vein, some praise psychotherapeutic drugs as godsends; others dismiss them as an ill-conceived and dangerous option. In reality, however, the sound blasters, shock collars, and pills have no power whatsoever to harm or enhance a dog's behavior or its relationship with its owner, any more than their less sophisticated counterparts. That power lies solely in the minds and hands of the people who use them.

For example, Marty imbues Luke's electronic training collar with a considerable emotional charge. Because it cost so much, Marty erroneously believes it will immediately and effortlessly train his dog to do whatever he wants. When this doesn't happen, he becomes angry and impatient. While some of these systems include "overcorrection protection" in the collar, presumably to compensate for fluctuations in the current that might harm the dog, both owners and dogs would benefit from additional programmable circuitry that monitored human blood pressure, too: when the owner's blood pressure exceeds a certain level, the system would automatically shut down.

Until that happy day, people who choose these devices must remind themselves and every member of the household that the devices are *not* toys. In certain situations, their transmissions rank them as weapons. No dog deserves to circle neurotically or chew itself raw because the kids played "Power Rangers" with the collar transmitter or ultrasonic training device, or Dad zapped the dog when it sat in front of the television during the final play of the Super Bowl. Owners with limited control of their own emotions armed with electronic devices pose a major threat to their dogs. At best, we can pray the animal will learn to ignore the stimulus—and the owner—entirely. At worst, the owner will create a dog with serious behavioral and medical problems.

It should go without saying that anyone who maintains strong negative feelings about these approaches shouldn't use them. However, when we're rushed for time, or the neighbors complain, or we see an ad with a picture of a happy family with a happy, perfectly trained dog thanks to such a system, we waiver.

"I really do hate those ultrasonic devices," Marty admits. "But after the mess we got into with that shock collar . . ."

Whether a different approach will succeed depends on Marty's willingness to learn the theory behind the device and how to use it properly. In other words, he must be willing to replace his emotions with *knowledge*. When he does this, his negative emotions may give way to at least neutral, if not positive ones, a transformation that will greatly enhance his chance of successfully using any device. On the other hand, if his study reveals what he considers sound reasons for not liking this approach, he can refuse to use it for logical rather than purely emotional reasons.

The same holds true for positive emotions. The fact that Helen champions ultrasonic devices "because they don't shock the dog" does nothing to provide her with the knowledge, timing, and skill required to get good results from this approach. Nor does her blind faith in the ability of a drug or muzzle to instantly cure Dandy's aggression serve her, her dog, or their relationship well.

Training Aid Emotional Analysis

Time for another break, this one to review your list of acceptable training aids in terms of their emotional appeal. What enables you to envision these on your new dog's horizon? If it's just a feeling, what kind of feeling: Impatience? A desire to work with your dog? A desire to placate or please other members of your household? Once again, the more detailed and specific your self-evaluation, the less likely you'll select a training aid that won't work for you or your pet.

Stretching the Physical Limits

Most people equate "high-tech" with "lightweight," and indeed none of the high-tech approaches discussed in this chapter requires much physical strength. In theory, this makes them ideal for people with physical limitations. For example, arthritis makes it difficult for Helen to apply leash corrections, clap her hands, or snap her fingers loudly enough to distract Dandy, but one quick burst of sound from the handheld training device gains his attention immediately.

Another physical aspect of electronic training aids revolves around owner perceptions of what these products can and cannot do. I don't recall any promotional material that showed anything other than a happy, off-lead animal responding to the device. While no one would doubt the visual appeal of such rosy scenes, they represent the ultimate goal rather than the starting point for most owners. This raises the question: What do you intend to do if the dog ignores the stimulus?

"Well, I guess I'd give him the stimulus again and hope it works," Helen offers tentatively.

Helen's hesitant reply misses the mark. Owners who train their dogs off-lead, and especially owners who lack the where-withal to control the animal physically if necessary, depend on their *presence* to communicate their authority to their dogs. Any-one like Helen without the knowledge and experience required to generate presence, should keep a lead on the dog until it rec-ognizes the trainer's authority. If you question your ability to con-trol your dog physically outdoors using a leash, begin any training inside.

On the other hand, we see owners like energetic teenager Tim Cabliano who find it difficult not to interact physically with their pets. Tim puts the electronic training collar on Luke and takes the pup outdoors for a workout.

"Come!" he shouts exuberantly to the pup sniffing the wheels of Tim's bike 25 feet away. Tim hits the sound button on the remote control. Luke pauses but doesn't come. Tim stamps his foot and moves toward the pup angrily.

"I'm warning you, you better get over here if you know what's good for you!"

Luke looks at Tim, senses his owner's anger, becomes fright-ened, and implements the fear-flight response. Tim charges after the pup, zapping him twice—once for not coming, and the sec-ond time for running away. The electrical stimulation totally dis-orients Luke, causing him to forget all about Tim, the command, and everything else but escaping from the electrical shocks. He runs blindly until Tim stops shocking him long enough to make a flying leap and tackle him. At that point, Tim begins smack-ing the dog for "misbehaving."

In this scenario, the highly physical owner completely misses the point that the goal of all training aids from the simplest noisemaker to the most sophisticated electronic device remains to *replace* displays of physical force with something else. Conse-quently, any additional physical display doubles the dog's punishment, often for doing something it completely forgets during the painful and confusing interval following its misbehavior.

This doesn't mean that owners must stand like statues when they use a training aid. On the contrary, all kinds of collars, halters, harnesses, and distractors work best when owners not only move with the dog, but also know the animal so well that they can anticipate any problem, distract the animal and orient it toward them, give the dog something positive to do, and praise it—all in one smooth motion. With a little bit of knowledge and effort, Tim could set a high-energy training pace that would satisfy his needs for activity as well as train his pup, a program that would enable him to act with rather than react to his pet.

"I could never do that," Helen declares with conviction.

Given her physical limitations and her older dog's unruliness, Helen certainly couldn't maintain the pace necessary to keep Dandy focused, but she can actively involve herself in her pet's training in other ways. Owners who use distraction devices often intuitively gesture toward themselves with it when they want the dog to look at them. Others discover that they automatically point to the ground when they want the dog to sit. Animal behaviorists have long recognized what they refer to as the "Clever Hans effect," named after a horse who learned to read his owner's body language so well that it appeared he could add and subtract. Owners who train their pets without the aid of any devices often rely on their awareness of their body language and tempo because it figures so prominently, and enjoyably, into the training process. The opposite also holds: those who depend on devices to train their dogs often don't recognize the extent of the body language messages they communicate to their pets.

We noted before how Dandy immediately picked up on Helen's cringe before she hit the shock button on the training collar. Similarly, if she gives him an orienting burst of ultrasonic sound but happens to look out the window because she can't hear it, her dog will associate the sound with *not* establishing rather than establishing eye contact with her.

Keep in mind that even the most sophisticated, device-driven training technique maintains its own physical rhythm. The more owners recognize their own physical limits, the more easily they can select a device that complements them. Once Helen realizes how her own body language affects Dandy's responses, she trains him only when she knows she can give the process her undivided attention. Some owners who view training as hard work prefer to do it first thing in the morning when they feel fresh. Others who see it as a way to unwind save it until the end of the day.

Personal Physical Limits Evaluation

Think about any physical limits you noted in Chapter 5 that might affect your selection of a training aid. Would the training aids that appeal to you make it easier or more difficult for you to train your dog given those limits? Could you adapt the aid to meet your physical needs? How would you handle your pet if it failed to respond to the device?

The Device-Driven Dog

How these different training aids affect the dog depends solely on the knowledge and skill of the person using them. Computer experts often say that a computer can't make a bad business good, but it definitely can make a bad one worse a lot faster. The same applies to any aid that an owner perceives as a quick fix rather than an adjunct to a well-thought-out training program.

In addition to all the previously mentioned potential for these devices to confuse or even hurt the dog if used improperly or inconsistently, a few additional dog-related points bear mentioning.

Recall that some breeds and specific dogs respond much more strongly to sound than others: a sound burst that orients the dog to an owner 25 feet away may cause it to cower in pain when the owner stands 5 feet away. Some dogs flee from sounds that orient others. Whereas owners can modulate the volume of a dog whistle, handheld devices lack volume controls, and the dog gets all or nothing unless the owner shields the device with a heavy coat or blanket.

Before investing in such a device, try one of the less expensive manual ones, or even a squeaky toy or clicker to see how your dog responds. This is particularly advisable for older, adopted animals who may be less adaptable, or who may have experienced negative sound encounters.

When Dandy was nine weeks old, his previous owners thought he'd like the Fourth of July fireworks display as much as they did. In fact, it—and all sudden sounds since then—terrified him.

In addition, although sound- rather than shock-emitting anti-barking collars might seem more humane, that's true only if the sound doesn't cause the animal pain.

If you intend to bring a second dog into your household and plan to use a sound device on your new dog, bear in mind that the other dog will hear it, too. When Helen uses the sound trainer to orient Dandy, her other dog immediately responds as well. However, when Helen ignores the other dog, it resumes chewing her shoe. By the time Helen gets Dandy trained, her other pet totally ignores her.

In this situation, Helen either should train Dandy away from the other dog—not a very practical solution considering a dog's hearing range or when using distraction to correct negative behavior—or train both animals using the device.

Most electronic training collars offer multiple levels of electrical stimulation, and their instructions recommend starting with the lowest. As previously mentioned, some also emit a warning tone that enables the dog to avoid the shock altogether. However, dogs differ and owners should never reject as a "baby" any animal who reacts strongly to the lowest level by howling, cowering, urinating, and/or defecating. Although we can't know for sure whether such animals experience pain or fear, they certainly experience *something* strongly enough to inhibit rather than enhance any learning process.

Studies of wild animals wearing electronic tracking collars indicate that the devices can cause uncollared members of the same species to react to collared animals differently and vice versa. Sometimes the collar will elevate that animal's status within the pack. Occasionally, however, animals will perceive the electronically collared individual as a threat and attack it. To prevent this, owners of multiple animals should closely monitor the collared dog's interactions with other dogs in the household.

Owners also should carefully monitor the electronically collared pet's interactions with animals of all other species (including humans), even those with which the dog has interacted positively in the past. In addition to other animals responding negatively to the collared animal, some collared dogs become very edgy and intolerant of previously tolerated behaviors in others.

Still on the technology front: although good-quality, properly installed containment systems that confine properly trained dogs might appear to solve all of a busy owner's problems, four issues warrant careful consideration before selecting this approach. First, dogs are conditioned-response animals. If Marty doesn't spend the necessary time using the flags that come with the system to teach Luke to associate the shock with crossing the barrier, the pup will associate the shock with whatever he happens to notice when he triggers it. That means the letter carrier, the toddler playing next door, or the cookie-selling Girl Scout walking up the driveway.

By the same token, dogs who do associate the shock with the barrier and either leap it for some compelling reason or cross it during a power outage may be extremely reluctant to come back into the yard. When Luke crosses the barrier one Saturday, he refuses to come when Marty calls him from within the yard, even though he normally responds instantly to the command. When Luke crosses the barrier one Wednesday after Marty and Tim leave for work and school, the confused pup sits in front of his home whimpering until it begins to rain. Then he huddles under a neighbor's porch until Marty comes home eight hours later.

Third, even though most dogs wearing the collars won't cross the barrier, owners sometimes forget that the barriers do absolutely nothing to keep children or adults from coming *into* the yard. Consequently, never use such systems to contain a dog with aggressive tendencies because the lack of a physical barrier implies that visitors can trust the animal. Nor should owners of animals they consider trustworthy automatically assume this will hold true once the animal gets shocked by the system. If Luke associates the shock with the toddler next door, he may react aggressively when the little girl just can't resist the urge to visit the cute little puppy one morning.

Some lawyers go so far as to maintain that no dog should be left within an electrified containment system without the supervision of someone with complete voice or hand-signal control over the animal.

Of course, it goes without saying that such a system won't prevent a demented or unscrupulous person from entering the yard and harming or stealing the dog, either. A canine variation on this theme may occur when the owner leaves a small or submissive animal within the confines of an electronic containment system, and a more aggressive animal charges into the yard and attacks it.

Every night Helen's neighbor's shepherd roams the neighborhood, marking Helen's yard along with everyone else's. When

Helen leaves Dandy unattended in the yard, the shepherd perceives the terrier as an intruder and attacks. Although a fence would keep the shepherd out, or the lack of any barrier would permit the younger, faster terrier to outrun his attacker, the containment system forces Dandy to confront his adversary and take a beating.

A final containment-system consideration relates to multiple-dog households. In several known cases of interdog aggression that occurred or intensified after the installation of a containment system, two factors came into play. First, prior to the installation of the system, the owners never left the dogs outside unattended, with the result that the dogs always played by human rules at these times. Once left on their own, however, they reverted to dog rules and got into territorial disputes that spilled over into the house.

Second, these owners noted that, even though they felt more secure knowing the system contained their pets, the dogs appeared edgier. It comes as no surprise that these busy owners also admitted that they didn't spend the time necessary to teach the dogs not to approach the barrier, but rather counted on the electrical shocks to train the animals for them. Although it is always important, it's particularly important in a multiple-dog household that all animals be totally boundary-trained and recognize human leadership *before* their owners turn on the power.

Whether certain breeds of dogs respond differently to different psychotherapeutic drugs remains anyone's guess until researchers compile sufficient data on sufficient numbers of animals for sufficiently long periods of time. Just as with tranquilizers, we do know that certain drugs don't work on certain dogs, and some experience more side effects than others, which certainly indicates that individual differences occur. Until the data exists, again it behooves owners who choose this option to monitor their animal's health and behavior with particular care.

If you're considering a particular breed of dog, breeders and breed clubs can provide the most specific information regarding all of these alternatives. Because of the controversial nature of some of these approaches, don't get discouraged if you hear views that span the love-hate spectrum. Just apply the same criteria to these views that you do to your own: Do they represent anthropomorphic or chattel orientations? Do they arise from knowledge or emotion? By doing so, you can sort the wheat from the chaff and get a more balanced view of which, if any, of these approaches will work best for your chosen dog.

Also beware of another breed-related paradox: breeders who have the most knowledge and experience with the use of a particular alternative are also telling you that the *need* for such a device exists in their breed or particular line. All kinds of warning bells should go off in Helen's head when the breeder insists that she *must* use a prong or shock collar on her new dog. A busy person with limited time, money, and/or ability to master the skills these devices require would be much better off considering a breed or line known for its positive response to *people* rather than devices or drugs.

Dream Dog Training Aid Check

Summon a mental image of your new pup or dog and carefully consider any personality or temperament qualities on your want list. Recall what you know about this particular breed or type of dog. Then think about your definition of a well-trained dog. Compare all of this with your list of acceptable training aids. If you get the kind of pup you want, what purpose will your chosen training aids serve? Helen noted that she wanted a sweet, gentle puppy, but listed a prong collar among her acceptable training aids. Note any similar inconsistencies in your own beliefs or those of any others in your household.

The Training Aid–Assisted Environment

The environmental concerns associated with training devices fall into two categories: maintenance and neighbors. Obviously a battery-powered system works only as long as its battery works. Marty and Tim congratulate each other for how well Luke's training progresses only to watch the pup's response dwindle to practically nothing. By the time they realize that each thought the other had replaced the batteries in the system, they had to start all over again.

Or consider what happens to Helen. She spent weeks working with Dandy and developing her own skill and timing with the distraction device to teach him the down command.

"I just know that tonight he's going to get it, once and for all," she boasts to Marty.

Helen puts the dominant terrier through a few relaxing exercises working up to the big moment when her pet will finally internalize the command.

"Down," she orders firmly, ready to distract Dandy the instant his attention wanders.

Thanks to all she's learned in the preceding weeks, Helen senses rather than actually sees Dandy begin to break the connection. With lightning speed she hits the button.

And nothing happens. Dandy looks momentarily confused, then ambles toward the kitchen while Helen stares stunned at the silent object in her hand. The moral? Don't forget to check your batteries.

Ideally, you should buy a system with a low-battery indicator light and replace or recharge the batteries as soon as it comes on. Lacking that, check the literature that comes with the product. Some manufacturers estimate battery life spans. Barring that, replace or recharge the batteries on a regular schedule.

Although pet owners might occasionally encounter a neighbor who objects to their use of an electronic training collar, containment system, prong collar, halter, harness, or muzzle, more commonly nearby neighbors object to sound-emitting systems. Devices designed to scare animals away from certain areas often do a pretty good job of scaring neighbors and their pets, too. Marty's neighbor finds no fault whatsoever with the anti-barking collar that keeps Luke quiet in his owner's absence, but he finds the alarms from the vibration-sensitive detectors that Marty leaves near his trophy shelf, the couch, and the doorway to his office nerve-wracking.

If you intend to use one of these devices, listen to the sound it makes before you buy it. Then tell your neighbors what you intend to do, and let them hear what it sounds like, too. If properly used, these systems should enable you to train your pup or correct any negative behavior in a matter of weeks, and most neighbors willingly will put up with that if it means adding a well-behaved animal to the neighborhood. However, you must do your part, too. If Marty only sprinkles noisemakers around his house, he does nothing to ensure his pet's good behavior in other areas.

Environmental factors can also influence the success or failure of drug therapy. Obviously someone needs to be home to give the dog the drug as directed. In addition to that, the more stable the environment, the more easily the owner can detect any positive or negative responses to the drug. "That kind of defeats the purpose, doesn't it?" asks Marty. "It seems to me you'd want to use drugs to tone down a jumpy dog in a hectic household."

Granted, the more hectic the household, the more the owners want and need a well-behaved dog. Nonetheless, the more controlled the environment, the more accurately owners can establish both the drug's safety and its effect on their particular pet. Helen starts Dandy on a drug to control his aggression and calls the veterinarian who prescribed it with a progress report a week later.

"Dandy did vomit several times, but I had company for the weekend and they brought their cat, and that always upsets him. Plus he got more snacks than he usually gets, and . . ."

Because of all the variables Helen's environment introduces into the process, a week later she and the veterinarian know no more about the drug's effect on Dandy than they did when they started.

Training Aid Environment Analysis

Review your notes about your own environment, and imagine yourself using the products you find acceptable on your new pet there. Note anything that might undermine their effect. If you live in an apartment, condominium, or suburban neighborhood, list the names of your neighbors.

Note whether they own any pets, and jot down any dog-related comments about them. If you anticipate needing an anti-barking device or sirens to keep your pet off the bed, make a note to schedule a friendly get-together with these folks before you get your new dog.

Aid-Assisted Leadership

"Why do I get the feeling that, for all your attempts to be non-judgmental, you really don't approve of most of these devices?" asks Marty accusingly. Actually, I have nothing against any of these approaches. It's how and why some people use them that I find troublesome. Recall your definition of what constitutes a good leader in your human-canine pack.

"That's easy," Helen declares. "It means that I set the standard for Dandy and my other dog and do everything in my power to help them achieve it in a safe and enjoyable way."

I certainly wouldn't argue with that definition, and I doubt any other dog lover would either. However, what exactly constitutes a *standard*?

"Not snapping at people is definitely one of my standards," Helen replies without hesitation.

No one would contest the legitimacy of this leadership policy. What's the next step?

"I find something that will stop the snapping in a manner I consider acceptable," Helen reports with equal confidence. "I wouldn't *want* to use a shock collar on Dandy, but if it was a case of using it or him biting someone, I'd certainly be tempted."

At this point, Helen succumbs to the kind of erroneous cause-and-effect logic often evoked by people who recommend and use various training aids. However, in order to resolve even the simplest behavioral problem using the most idiot-simple method, we need to know *why* the dog displayed the behavior. If, as it seems likely, Dandy snaps because he doesn't recognize Helen's leadership, she can zap, sound-blast, and drug him until Lassie gets a degree in theoretical physics and that won't change anything. True, if she shocks or sound-blasts him enough, he may eventually stop snapping at her; give him drugs, and he may appear perfectly normal.

However, suppose Helen does succeed in stopping Dandy's snapping using some gadget or drug.

Knowing what we know about the role a human-centered pack structure plays in the health and good behavior of every dog, exactly how does that shock or sound blast or pill treat the *human* leadership problem that caused the dog's negative behavior in the first place? The stated or implied answer to that claims that, once the dog stops snapping (barking, running away, etc.), the relationship between the owner and dog will become perfect.

Aside from its scientific inaccuracy, this explanation begs the issue on several fronts. First, just because Dandy no longer snaps at his owner doesn't automatically mean leadership status is conferred on Helen. He doesn't stop snapping at her because he recognizes her leadership; he stops snapping at her because he gets shocked or his ears hurt when he does or, thanks to the drug, he doesn't care enough to bother. Unless Helen does something to establish her authority based on her *presence*, the relationship between her and Dandy remains essentially unchanged, regardless of the outward changes in his behavior.

Second, because these approaches focus on eliminating symptoms rather than causes, Dandy may find it more difficult to internalize the necessary supporting behavioral changes. If so, he certainly would benefit from a strong leader who would take the pressure off of him during this difficult time. However, because Helen chooses these approaches to compensate for her *lack* of leadership skills, she can't give her dog the additional support he needs.

Finally, we've repeatedly seen that effective leaders possess knowledge: the more we know about the problem, the more we can select the method that will best treat it. As I scanned the literature for the various anti-barking collars, I recalled a Sherlock Holmes mystery whose solution hinged on the answer to the question, "Why did the dog bark during the night?"

Manufacturers of most of these products claim owners can use them to eliminate all but certain kinds of "acceptable" barking which they define as "alarm" or "protective" barking. However, nothing short of a full-sized computer strapped to the dog's neck could even begin to determine what constitutes alarm or protective barking for a particular owner of a particular dog in a particular environment. Country dwellers might want their dogs to sound an alarm anytime anyone comes within 100 feet of their front doors, a behavior that could make a high-rise dweller exceedingly jumpy, to say nothing of unpopular with the neighbors. "Protective" barking poses an even more troubling dilemma because we already noted that fear motivates far more so-called protective dogs than love or courage.

Some systems get around these annoying idiosyncrasies of normal canine behavior by not allowing *any* barking. However, the more sophisticated systems cleverly define acceptable barking as lasting for less than a certain period of *time*. If the dog exceeds that interval, it gets zapped. Thus, Dandy may bark the canine equivalent of "Help!" "Fire!" "Spider" "Dustball" "What?" "Cat" "Wind" or "e = mc²," provided he gets it out in the acceptable interval. The system does nothing to address his fears, acknowledge his brilliance or courage, or discipline his overreaction. Unless Helen does something to compensate for this deficiency, the dog will live with this skewed view of canine communication, and his owner will live with whatever right or wrong definition she assigns to those barks that occur within the approved period.

Why does the dog bark? A good leader will ask that question, just as a good leader will ask why the dog snaps or won't come when called. A good leader also will ask, "Why do I want to use *this* training aid to solve the problem?" and will accept as the only right answer, "Because I believe from my knowledge of myself, my dog, my environment, and our relationship that it's the best one."

Leadership/Training Aid Compatibility Check

Review your analysis of your leadership style from previous chapters. Apply what you learned to your list of acceptable training aids. Note any discrepancies between your ability and that required to properly use any devices you selected. If discrepancies exist, how can you rectify them? Would another aid work better for you? Should you develop additional skills before you try to use a particular aid? Which ones?

After two chapters of training-related soul-searching, let's now consider the amazing array of different ways you can play with and exercise your new dog.

7

The New Millennium Workout

Designing a Healthy Human-Canine Exercise Program

F ran Ruben, an intense, hardworking advertising executive, adopts a racing greyhound rescued from a local track. She names the sleek, silver dog Mercury and imagines him running at her side as she prepares for the Boston Marathon. However, Mercury completely vaporizes Fran's idyllic vision during their first run together. Every time a bird hops or a leaf flutters beside the path, the dog lunges after it, dragging his petite owner with him.

Fran's frustration and irritation turn into absolute disgust, though, when the exhausted dog sits down and refuses to budge five miles from her home just as a cold rain begins to fall.

All too often new owners give little, if any, consideration to the exercise component of the human-canine equation.

"Everyone knows dogs need exercise," Fran remarks as she laces up her running shoes and whistles for Mercury to join her on another seven-mile jaunt.

"Right," agrees jazz pianist Eric Olson with a yawn in the direction of his snoozing Border terrier, Digger. "You gotta walk 'em around the block at least twice a day."

Most of our ideas about what constitutes the proper amount of exercise for a dog fall somewhere between these two extremes. We know our dogs need more exercise than a short walk, but our schedules don't allow us much free time. Further complicating things, the less time we spend with our dogs, the greater their need for exercise because it confers so many other benefits on our canine companions. As a medical practitioner, I used to keep track of littermates in my ongoing quest to determine why one animal develops problems and another one doesn't. Among other factors, including the nature of the human-canine bond, I discovered that dogs whose owners exercised them regularly not only tended to maintain their optimal weight, but also succumbed to fewer health problems, a real plus for busy owners.

Beyond the health-related benefits, regularly exercised animals also experienced fewer behavioral problems such as barking, or chewing and digging at themselves and/or their environments. Given a dog's sense of self and function, exercise that challenges the dog to use its mind as well as body can yield the same postexercise sense of well-being and contentment that people enjoy under similar circumstances. This, in turn, greatly reduces the feelings of frustration and boredom that so often contribute to negative behaviors. When Mercury sinks into a deep sleep after a stimulating morning workout, Fran finds it much easier to leave him for the day than if he constantly paces with nervous energy while she makes her preparations.

"But why bother with a formal program?" Eric asks as he searches his chair for the remote control to turn on the television. "I'd much rather just take advantage of any opportunities that arise for some fun exercise with Digger."

Although that sounds good in theory, owners who choose this route often wind up exercising their pets haphazardly. Unlike those who implement a specific program, they may never stick to any activity long enough to make exercise an integral part of their relationship with their pets. Implementing a specific program doesn't mean you can't switch activities if they no longer meet your or your dog's needs somewhere along the line. It just makes it easier to incorporate some kind of meaningful human-canine exercise into your relationship from the beginning.

It definitely pays prospective owners to consider the many exercise options in terms of their own orientation and any financial, time, emotional, or physical limits; their dream dog; their environment; and their leadership style *before* they get a new pet. That way they can get off to a running start in this most rewarding of human-canine interactions.

A Feast of Canine Exercise Options

Many owners think of obedience-training their dogs as "work" and exercising them as "play." However, for our dogs, *any* activity that enables them to use their minds and bodies in a manner that fulfills their needs and pleases us constitutes play, and any activity that exceeds or doesn't fulfill their needs and/or makes us cross or irritable constitutes work for them. Above all, when we speak of a particular activity as meeting a dog's and owner's needs, it must meet those needs on three levels:

- physical
- mental
- emotional

Neither Fran nor Mercury gains anything when she takes the greyhound jogging and spends the whole time yanking him back on the trail or yelling at him because he's "ruining" her training schedule. Similarly, little Digger suffers more than gains in the long run if Eric's lethargy leads him to make all sorts of excuses for not learning the rules and regulations of canine agility after he enrolls his pet in such a program.

The following sampler of human-canine activities represents the rather mind-boggling array of options facing the new owner:

Obedience: traditional, freestyle, Canine Good Citizen

Formal activities: agility, carting, earthdog, fly ball, Frisbee, herding, hunting, lure coursing, pulling, retrieving, search and rescue, service dog, skijoring, sledding, tracking

Informal activities: backpacking, biking, boating/kayaking, massage, running, travel/sight-seeing, swimming, tricks

These activities can meet the needs of a broad spectrum of owners and dogs in every imaginable lifestyle and environment. Some owners opt to involve themselves and their pets in organized competitive obedience for sporting reasons, while others teach their pets the basics of herding, retrieving, tracking, or other "sporting" activities simply for their own personal enjoyment.

"I could never teach a dog to hunt or track some poor innocent creature!" Fran protests vehemently.

Perhaps not in the traditional sense, but surely anyone familiar with news reports of search-and-rescue dogs working the scene of a disaster or looking for a lost child must admire the dogs and owners willing to develop such "hunting and tracking" skills.

"I do admire them," Eric admits, "but they're a breed apart."

Yes and no. Although professional human-canine duos do perform some amazing feats, so do the dogs and owners engaged in all of the other activities listed. And although some of these skills enabled dogs to perform functions in the past that Fran and others might find unacceptable today, those same skills can contribute to the development of a mutually rewarding physical, mental, and emotional exercise program.

Many times owners select these activities as exercise options because they and their dogs find it easier to interact in a way that takes advantage of the dog's natural tendencies, rather than in a way that requires the dog to develop unfamiliar skills. In other words, they discover that sometimes it's easier and faster to teach a new dog old-breed tricks.

Let's consider one of the latest additions to the exercise repertoire, the terrier sport called "earthdog," to see how all the different factors come into play to create a total breed-based body, mind, and spirit canine exercise.

Until fairly recently, terriers didn't rate a specific classification like other breeds because Danish King Canute (who ruled England during 1016–1035) forbade the lower classes from owning any dogs except those used to rout "vermin" out of their lairs in the ground. Thus, while the noblemen and merchants hunted with their hounds and spaniels, the rest of the population bred scrappy little dogs willing to "go to ground" (the name "terrier" derives from *terra*, the Latin word for earth). Later, gentlemen foxhunters began carrying terriers in baskets as they followed the hounds. When the hounds ran the fox into its hole, the hunters released the terriers to locate it. With that elevation in status came the development of specific terrier breeds.

Now, whether we agree with breeding dogs for this function or not, all terriers—Australian, Bedlington, Border, cairn, Dandie Dinmont, fox, Lakeland, Norfolk, Norwich, Scottish, Sealyham, Skye, Welsh, and West Highland white terriers—as well as dachshunds claim this special heritage. Consequently, terrier owners can naturally exercise their dogs by:

- using them for this purpose
- training them for an activity that mimics this purpose
- training them for some completely different activity

The American Kennel Club designed a noncompetitive test, the Earthdog Event, that falls into the second category. This event creates a simulated hunting experience wherein owners can get a real workout constructing a course consisting of a roughly nine-inch-square wooden tunnel 30 feet long buried nine feet underground, sometimes with right-angle turns, a false exit, and false dens. Owners of beginning dogs release their pets 10 feet away to follow a scent trail into a sloped opening designed not to frighten the animal, and the animal must enter within 30 seconds.

Once inside the tunnel, the dog must follow the scent trail and locate the quarry—caged rats or artificial quarry—within another 30 seconds. Steel bars as well as cages protect the rats, and a judge oversees their feeding, watering, and welfare from a position above them on the course. (According to some reports, the rats quickly learn that the dogs can't get to them and sleep through the entire event.) Once the dog locates the quarry, it must begin "working" it (digging, barking, growling, or lunging at it) within 30 seconds and do so for a full minute.

In the Junior Earthdog test, the judge then signals the owner to retrieve the dog by lifting it through an opening in the tunnel above the quarry. In the Senior test, dogs must follow the scent for 20 feet above ground, then dive down a vertical entry, locate the quarry in a more complex maze faster, work the quarry longer, and then find their way out and return to their owners on command. Although earthdog is a relatively new sport, enthusiasts already plan a Master Earthdog course that would involve working two dogs started 100 feet from the tunnel, with false and hidden entries, distractions, obstacles, and constrictions in the path. Like many AKC performance tests, the Earthdog Event doesn't pit one dog against another, but rather strives to make the experience fun and rewarding for all involved. Although Eric Olson might find the mere thought of such strenuous activity exhausting, an awareness of such breed-related activities can give prospective owners a great deal of insight into their dream dogs' exercise needs and potential.

Other sports capitalize on the natural tendencies of other breeds. Although any dog can enjoy lure coursing, sight hounds take to it with a particular zeal. This event involves tieing several plastic bags to a line, then dragging them over a 600- to 800-yard zigzag course. The dogs run in groups of three and instinctively tend to work the plastic bag "prey" as a team rather than individually. Skijoring combines the dog's natural ability to pull (per pound of body weight, dogs can pull more than horses) with cross-country skiing. In competition pulling, dogs pull sleds carrying anywhere from 900 to more than 2,700 pounds to their owners standing 16 feet away. Although any breed can participate, the powerful musculature of the malamutes, Siberian huskies, Newfoundlands, Great Pyrenees, mastiffs, and rottweilers gives them a competitive edge. We previously mentioned that Bernese mountain dogs naturally enjoy carting, and who can think of a retriever without imagining a ball or stick in its mouth and a wet coat if it lives anywhere near the water?

At the opposite end of the formal-informal exercise spectrum, we see those dogs who get their exercise traveling and sight-seeing with their owners. Before you laugh, take a look at Maria Goodavage's more-than-*800*-page book, *The California Dog Lover's Companion* (Foghorn Press, 1994). In addition to rating hundreds of parks and accommodations from a dog owner's unique perspective, the book lists "diversions" such as railroad, carriage, cable car, surrey, or ferry rides; museums; concerts; restaurants; and even a laundromat that welcome dogs. Travel-dusty pooches can take advantage of one of the many self-service dog washes, too! Less-detailed but also useful guides to New York City, Los Angeles, New England, the West Coast, and the Mid-Atlantic and Southeast states, plus general pet-oriented travel guides are also available. A travel agency called Pet Cruzin' Travel will even arrange pet-friendly air travel and accommodations, in addition to providing information about pet-friendly restaurants and attractions along the way.

"You call that exercise?" puffs Fran as she jogs in place. "Sounds more like goofing off to me."

That depends on how you look at it. Most dogs will probably get more exercise if they travel with their owners than if their owners kennel them. More important, though, an increasing number of owners belong to the ranks of the self-employed who can take their pets with them when they travel. In addition to providing companionship and a feeling of security, those who travel a lot in their work find that their dogs inspire them to do more than eat junk food and stare at the television in their motel rooms at day's end. Books and other sources of dog-friendly travel information can help these folks find areas where they can safely and enjoyably exercise their pets as well as themselves.

Though the exercise options offer a wide range of opportunities that at least theoretically are capable of keeping every dog fit and trim, once again the problem becomes selecting the options that will work best for you and your new dog.

Personal Exercise Program Analysis

Review the list of exercise options at the beginning of this chapter. Jot down those that appeal to you. If none of them does, write a brief description of what you consider the ideal canine exercise program.

Anthropomorphic and Chattel Aerobics

Our views about our dogs' exercise needs can exert profound effects because, unless we just turn them loose to exercise on their own, they pretty much depend on us to fulfill this requirement. Fran Ruben approaches her running with the same passion she brings to her work. Given her more anthropomorphic orientation toward dogs, she automatically expects Mercury to share her view because, after all, he *is* a greyhound. However, Fran adopted Mercury from a greyhound group that rescues track dogs, and she harbors strong negative feelings about dog racing. These feelings lead her to spoil the dog indoors at the same time she ignores his sight hound breed qualities and his limited stamina outdoors (which made him unsuitable for racing to begin with). These two conflicting positions conspire to undermine their exercise program.

Coming from the opposite perspective, Eric got Digger because he wanted a "get it and forget it" pet.

"I know big dogs need a lot of exercise, so I got a little one instead," he explains as he stumbles through a sea of unused dog toys littering the floor. "A dog Digger's size can get plenty of exercise running around my condo."

Perhaps Digger could, but she most likely won't unless Eric deliberately involves her in some kind of activity. Considering what we know about the terrier's heritage, how likely does it seem that Digger will take a few laps around the house just for the heck of it? No doubt she'll exuberantly take off after anything she considers intriguing, probably barking like crazy and digging at the rug if she decides something lurks under that lump. However, unless Eric wants to turn a few vermin loose in his home—and get angry calls from his neighbors—he can't expect his dog to exercise on her own indoors.

Both anthropomorphic and chattel views also can undermine the quality of competitive exercise programs. Because Fran performs so well in her races, she won't even consider the possibility that Mercury won't excel in coursing. Many competitive activities also attract their share of "stage mothers" and "tennis dads" determined to force their canine "kids" to act out their owners' personal fantasies. Although these people's behavior dismays most dog lovers, they, themselves, appear oblivious to it. Some will even say they do it solely for the dog and that the dog loves it, even though the animal is frightened, miserable, or even in pain. In this situation, the owners project their own beliefs so strongly onto the dog that they lose all sight of the dog and its needs.

230   DogSmart

Owner Orientation Exercise Analysis

Before reading on, get out your trusty notes about your own orientation toward dogs and review them in terms of exercise. What options appeal to you? Does the appeal spring from knowledge (K) or emotion (E)? Does it come from an anthropomorphic (A) or from a chattel (C) orientation?

Fran's and Eric's lists look like this:

Fran	Eric
running (KA)	walking (KC)
skijoring (EC)	tricks (KC)
Frisbee (EC)	earthdog (KA)
lure coursing (KA)	travel/sight-seeing (EA)

Fran's interest in running and lure coursing comes from her own enjoyment of running and her knowledge of greyhounds as a racing breed. She loved playing Frisbee as a kid, and she thinks skijoring sounds much more exciting than cross-country skiing, about which she knows nothing. Eric automatically thinks of taking Digger for walks and teaching her tricks because "that's what you do with a dog." He adds earthdog because it seems like the right thing to do even though the idea of digging nine-foot-deep 30-foot-long trenches doesn't appeal to him any more than watching a dog disappear down a hole and reappear 90 seconds later does. However, he likes the idea of taking Digger with him when his band tours, for purely emotional reasons.

If a particular form of activity appeals to you but you don't know much about it, check out Direct Book Services' *Dog and Cat Book Catalog* (call 800-776-2665 or E-mail dgctbook@cascade.net for a copy) which lists books on competitive obedience, showing, agility, fly ball, Frisbee, backpacking, tricks, lure coursing, tracking, search and rescue, sledding (mushing), pulling, carting, herding, hunting, retrieving, and traveling—among other interesting subjects. Contact the AKC or your local kennel or breed club for additional information about Canine Good Citizen, earthdog, and other performance tests that you and your dog might enjoy as part of your healthy exercise program. Finally, don't forget the Internet. It seems as if every canine activity known to humankind can claim its own newsgroup. If you can't find what you're looking for, just ask. You'll find plenty of helpful people willing to steer you in the right direction.

Fitness Fees

All this talk of tunnels, agility obstacles, and lures flying around 600-yard courses might give the impression that it costs a great deal to exercise today's dog, but that's not true at all. If you opt to combine obedience with exercise, you need only invest in a collar and a leash to start. For owners and dogs who walk in cities with pooper-scooper laws, another $13 will get you a nylon pouch that holds 30 pickup bags and attaches to the leash. More and more towns set aside fenced areas in public parks specifically for dog use, which offers these municipalities the benefit of reducing the problem of dog waste in other areas. Owners love it because these areas often provide benches for humans, disposable cleanup kits, and a secure place for pets to exercise and interact with other dogs. If you can't find one in your area, talk to other dog owners, town officials, local veterinarians, groomers, pet store owners, and others in animal-related businesses: they might eagerly offer their support for such a project.

If you want your arms free to jog with your dog, add about $20 for a no-hands leash you can wear around your waist, or just loop the end of your dog's leash around your belt. Those who walk or jog early in the morning or evening can make their dogs more visible with a fluorescent orange vest for less than $10. If you prefer hiking and backpacking, you can outfit your dog with a backpack for $25–50 and let it carry its own inflatable bowl ($12) *after* you spend $9.95 for Charlene LaBelle's *Guide to Backpacking with Your Dog* (Alpine, 1993).

If you envision a Frisbee hound in your future, budget $5–15, depending on the quality and characteristics of the toy. These come in floppy, floating, and chewable forms, as well as fleece versions for indoor use, in addition to the standard hard plastic ones people use. Beware if you opt for a flavored chewable form and have a mouthy dog, though: the Frisbee may not remain aerodynamically sound enough for much exercise once your pet chews it.

If you picture your dog retrieving au naturel, you can teach it to retrieve sticks ($0), used tennis balls ($0), brand-new rubber balls ($1–20), or even Kong toys ($6–20), which offer the added advantage of bouncing unpredictably and honing your pets' coordination and focusing skills. Of course, you can also teach your pet to fetch your newspaper or slippers. Purists, however, can opt for AKC-regulation dumbbells ($6–10) or the plastic and canvas training dummies used to train bird dogs (around $10).

Although we normally think of dogs as natural swimmers, some dogs don't share that view—particularly if we take them kayaking in the ocean or white-water canoeing. If you plan to do more than just splash around in a placid pond with your new pet, allow $20–35 for a life preserver to keep your dog safe.

Bikers can keep their dogs safely next to them with a special bike leash for $35–60. Add another $295–350 if you want to give your new pup rides in a bicycle trailer until he's old enough to keep up with you on his own. (That trailer also will come in handy if you want to take him with you when he becomes a canine senior citizen.) Those who want their pets to accompany them in the car can protect the vehicle's doors and armrests from canine claws with special covers for about $35, and put protective denim or padded poplin covers on the seats for about $30–60. You can also convert the back portion of your sport utility vehicle, minivan, or station wagon to a cozy traveling area for your pet for $75–200.

If you think you'd like to participate in agility, carting, coursing, or any other human-canine activity that demands more elaborate equipment, your best *first* investment remains a good book or video on the subject, and these range in price from less than $10 to more than $50. That way you won't get carried away after watching some event and invest in a lot of equipment only to discover that you, your dog, and/or your lifestyle make this a poor choice. After reading an article about skijoring, native Southern Californian Fran invests a small fortune in cross-country boots, bindings, skis, poles, skijoring belt, line, and dog harness only to discover that she *hates* the cold.

Fortunately, many competitive activities spawn formal or informal groups that either split the cost of the equipment or raise money to pay for it some other way. Members also may provide information about used equipment or other low-cost options for those interested in the sport.

"What if you want to do something like agility but can't even afford the membership or entrance fee?" asks Eric, recalling those times when he had to squeeze pennies just to make ends meet.

Granted some of the agility obstacles can become quite costly or require a certain amount of know-how and tools to construct, but owners can create equally challenging low-cost, or even free, courses for their pets. Sometimes when we watch dogs negotiating the crisp white obstacles of an agility course, we forget that dog owners designed these to mimic the obstacles used in horse events which were designed to mimic those the animal *naturally* would encounter. You can build a ramp or find a steep embankment; a downed tree in the woods makes a wonderful jump; balancing on another downed tree over a brook or jumping from rock to rock through the water will sharpen your dog's skills just as effectively as any man-made balance beam. Cost? Nothing but the time it takes to ferret out these natural gems in your local area.

If you see only other houses when you look out your windows and still crave some variety in your pet's exercise program, fear not. Cardboard boxes make excellent tunnels, as do kids' plastic tunnels (for smaller dogs). A picnic bench becomes a balance beam, jump, or hurdle, depending on how you place it. Dogs enjoy small plastic kids' slides as much as kids do. Set up a line of smaller boxes or pound a row of stakes into the ground for your dog to weave through. Or put a bigger cardboard box on your own or your kids' heads and/or feet and play "Big Foot," stomping around the backyard with your new dog. Naturally, you want to ease the dog into any more exuberant games (and you might want to prepare your neighbors, too), but dogs do love games as much as kids do, and you can give yourself and your pet a good workout without spending a penny.

Exercise Financial Analysis

Review your dog owner's budget with an eye toward your dog's exercise program and ask yourself the following questions: What kind of equipment will I need? Can I afford it? If I can't, what other options are available?

Timely Exercise Limits

Without a doubt, the least time-consuming form of canine exercise involves merely opening the door and letting the dog out to do what it will on its own, followed by snapping on the dog's leash and walking or running it long enough to relieve itself. However, this holds true only if that limited amount of exercise suits both human and canine needs. If following such an excursion Digger comes home and bleeds all over the new rug because she cut herself on a piece of glass during her unsupervised romp, or tears through the house to burn off any excess energy after her brief walk, the resultant medical and/or behavioral problems may take a lot more time to treat than any exercise would. Although installing a dog door to a secure outdoor space would seem to offer Eric the best of all worlds, this works only if Digger uses it to do more than go outside long enough to relieve herself.

Regardless of the exercise approach owners use, the more time put into it, the more both owner and dog get out of it. Although some activities require that canine participants achieve a certain age before serious training or competition begins, pups of any age can master the basic obedience necessary to excel at any of these. Combining basic training with the rudimentary skills it takes to master the desired activity not only makes any obedience training more goal oriented—and hence more productive and fun—but it also saves time when the actual training begins.

Reading books describing this process before you get your new dog will save you a lot of time down the line. When slow-paced Eric decides his idea of exercising his prospective dog means sitting in his easy chair while the animal performs one trick after another at a brisk clip, he reads several books on the subject whose training methods appeal to him. When he gets Digger, he trains her to do tricks, all the while claiming he cares little about obedience and exercise.

"What a smart little dog, and so beautifully behaved!" Eric's mother marvels when she comes to visit. "You must spend hours working with her."

"Hardly any time at all," Eric boasts, completely forgetting about all those hours he did spend because he and Digger enjoyed them so much.

Also, don't forget to factor in travel time for any activities that require formal classes or equipment that you can't set up at home. It takes Fran an hour to drive to her agility class, another hour for the group to set up the obstacles and discuss upcoming events, and then an hour or more for the dogs to work. Some weekend events last all day. Because some of these activities serve as human social events as much as dog training/exercising ones, that can add more time, too.

If the skills involved in a certain activity appeal to you but formal participation doesn't interest you, you and your pet can develop and master many of these on your own. Knowledgeable proponents of even the most rigorous activities say the same thing as those who prefer a slower-paced workout: short (10-minute) sessions that the owner and dog both enjoy teach more skills faster than long ones. Although many owners who fail to develop a consistent exercise program with their dogs blame it on a lack of time, more often than not, a lack of owner commitment is the real culprit.

Exercise Time Check

Review the schedule you worked out for your new dog and compare it with the exercise options that appeal to you. Are the two compatible? Can you free more time to pursue them if necessary? If not, note any other programs that might meet your time needs better.

Emotional Exercise Limits

Owners should never adopt an exercise program that generates any negative emotion. If Eric finds earthdog events numbingly dull and goes only because his friends laid a guilt trip on him for not letting his terrier become one with her roots, his negative feelings will more than cancel out any benefits to his dog.

When you select an exercise program for your pet, ask yourself *why* you chose it. If you did so only to fulfill your dog's *or* your own needs, the chances that such a program will help you create a solid relationship with a healthy, well-behaved animal plummet. If hard-driving Fran sees Mercury's performance in coursing as evidence of her own superiority, she'll find anything less than perfection on his part intolerable. Consider all the negative effects this situation generates:

- The activity upsets the dog, stressing rather than enhancing his physical well-being.
- It undermines the human-canine relationship.
- It spoils the event for other owners and their pets.

Given that novices who abandon a certain activity most commonly cite the behavior of other *people* in the group as the reason, plan to observe a few events before making any final decision. If you find the people annoying or if the group espouses an anthropomorphic or chattel orientation or uses methods that bother you, consider another option.

Also evaluate any prospective exercise program in terms of your own social nature. Some of us are more social than others. I once shed 10 unwanted pounds on my own by promising a friend I'd attend aerobics class with her if I didn't. The mere thought of participating in such a group activity so appalled me that it spurred me to develop and religiously adhere to a diet and at-home exercise program religiously, and I incorporated my dogs into it. Between sit-ups and deep knee bends, I throw Violet's rubber bone and Watson's ball. When one of them steals the other's toy and initiates a mad-dog dash through the house, I get in a round of jumping jacks before they come charging back to me again.

Finally, never lose sight of the fact that any activity should exercise the animal's mind and spirit, as well as body.

"How can you tell?" asks Eric while Digger's eyes glitter in anticipation as he balances the matchbox on her nose for her to flip and catch.

You can tell by the dog's and owner's expressions and body language. Ask people who follow competitive canine sports, including the Westminster Dog Show, and they'll tell you that even though the rules dictate that a pair of human-canine winners always will emerge, every once in a while they see a pair of *Winners*. When they do, they never forget it. The dog who leaps into his handler's arms in delight whether he wins or not, the owner who calls off the pull because he knows his dog would injure herself to reach him, the agility duo who makes the sport exciting for everyone, the hunter who considers rubbing down his dog the best part of the day, the giggling child and the fuzzy, cheerful pup visiting the nursing home: these Winners and their dogs love what they're doing, and it shows.

Exercise Emotion Checkup

Imagine yourself and your ideal dog keeping fit in your chosen activity. What do you see? You and your dog learning and mastering the necessary skills together and working as a *unit*, or the judge handing you the blue ribbon?

If winning is everything to Fran, and especially if it's the *only* thing, she should let someone else exercise her dog while she runs alone.

Exercise and Physical Limits

Back in my medical practice days, one of my clients, 70-year-old Jake, adored black Labs and vice versa, to the point that I decided Jake carried a few Lab genes himself. Shortly after his last dog died, Jake fell and broke his hip. His loving but misguided out-of-town children met and decided he shouldn't own a big dog anymore and presented him with a sweet but grossly inappropriate Pomeranian. When I walked into the examination room and saw that dog on the table, I stood dumbfounded.

"Go ahead and laugh," Jake shrugged good-naturedly, and I did until tears ran down my face.

"She's adorable!" I gushed, cuddling the happy fur ball. "But what in the world . . ."

"You don't know the half of it!" he snorted. "That damn dog's gonna kill me!"

What Jake and I knew but his absentee offspring didn't was that over the years Jake had come up with all kinds of tricks that enabled him to exercise his beloved Labs even as his own ability to exercise waned considerably. He chose his pups wisely and rolled balls to them and taught them to fetch from day one. Although arthritis and then the broken hip slowed him down, he never lost his good throwing arm, and he could give even the most energetic dog a good workout without moving 10 feet from his cabin on the lake. However, he couldn't begin to keep up with the Pomeranian who couldn't care less about fetching balls.

"She's too quick," he complained. "I'm scared to death I'm gonna kick her or she's gonna trip me."

Fortunately, once I convinced Jake that his children wouldn't hate him if we told them the truth, Jake got another Lab, and the Pomeranian went off to live with one of the grandkids.

This case illustrates a basic truth about owner physical limits and canine companionship: owners who acknowledge their physical limits fare much better, and so do their pets. Moreover, that truism applies to the hale and hearty among us as well as people with physical problems like Jake. For example, let's compare Jake with Eric Olson.

"No comparison!" Eric exclaims. "I'm 27 and in great shape."

True, but Eric can attribute that to genetics far more than his environment or lifestyle. He personally hates to exercise. Thus, if we evaluate these two men's physical limits as they relate to exercising a dog, Jake's activity level far surpasses the younger man's.

Regardless of what the President's Council on Fitness may say about Eric's torpid view of life, it won't cause his dog problems nearly as much as his failure to *acknowledge* this reality. Until he does, he can't select an exercise program that will meet his or his dog's needs.

Ideally, fast-paced owners select fast-paced dogs and fast-paced exercise programs to go with them, and then routinely share that fast-paced exercise experience with their pets. In reality, it doesn't always work out that way. Sometimes a fast-paced spouse or kids select the fast-paced pup and corresponding exercise programs, then get so caught up in their own fast-paced lives that someone else gets stuck trying to fulfill the dog's exercise needs.

"Make sure you run him at least five miles a day," Fran reminds her sister when she drops Mercury off for the third time that month while she goes off on a business trip.

It never dawns on her that her sister, a self-employed couch potato with three kids and two cats, might not share her views that a five-mile run constitutes quality canine exercise. On the other hand, Fran's sister knows from sad experience that if she doesn't exercise Mercury, he'll drive her and the kids—and the cats—crazy. Needless to say, this does nothing to enhance her relationship with either Fran or the dog.

Physical Limits Self-Analysis

Think about your perfect exercise program in terms of your physical limits. Does it still seem so perfect? If not, what would you need to do to make it so?

The Dog Factor

Considering the merits of a variety of exercise options before getting a dog also gives prospective owners who are strongly attracted to a particular alternative the opportunity to select a dog who will enjoy that activity, too. Fran's disastrous foray into skijoring resulted as much from Mercury's unsuitability for the sport as it did from his owner's dislike of the cold. Certain breeds and lines do better in some activities than others. Dogs with powerful front ends do better at pulling, sledding, and carting; teaching many bird dogs to fetch balls, sticks, and Frisbees borders on child's play, while teaching that same activity to a scent hound may require a Herculean effort.

"Okay, so maybe skijoring was a mistake," Fran admits. "But how come Mercury refused to run when I first got him? That hardly seems normal for a greyhound."

While sight hounds and running theoretically go together like peanut butter and jelly, individual dogs can differ. Furthermore, when owners adopt older animals, two other factors come into play. First, as we noted in Mercury's case, the previous owner of a racing or working animal may have given the animal up for adoption because it couldn't or wouldn't perform that function for some reason. Second, many rescue groups and animal shelters lack the personnel and facilities to provide anything beyond the most minimal exercise opportunities for their charges.

Consequently, although the urge to atone immediately for the dog's past confinement may compel us to treat it to a real workout, an adopted dog will fare much better if we ease into any exercise program slowly, and constantly evaluate the animal's response. When Fran begins with relatively short walks, then gradually increases both their length and pace over time, Mercury soon comes up to speed.

Also, if you plan to buy or adopt a purebred older dog, don't forget to discuss any exercise plans with breeders or others familiar with the breed as well as with your veterinarian. Just as a person should get a complete physical examination before beginning a new and rigorous exercise program, so should our dogs.

Finally, the more complex an owner's lifestyle, the more he or she should look for an exercise program that will meet the dog's changing needs over its lifetime. Just as many schools now expose children to athletic activities that don't require a whole team to enjoy, so more and more dog owners look to performance events as a way to provide their pets with a meaningful, lifelong exercise opportunity. Given that shift in awareness, I suspect—or at least hope—that we'll see more of these programs evolve and expand to meet changing owner needs. Already some agility clubs and instructors willingly adapt their courses, not only for the inexperienced pup but also for older animals or those with problems, such as hip dysplasia, that might limit their mobility. This represents an exciting and welcome shift in the dog world's emphasis from winning to providing dogs with an opportunity to fulfill their needs in a safe and fun way, even in the midst of a bustling metropolis.

Because some programs remain firmly entrenched in the old tradition, and can't—or won't—expand to include older or physically limited dogs (or owners), be sure to ask about such provisions. Busy owners can't afford to discover that their pet's exercise program has come to a grinding halt because it doesn't accommodate "losers," those with special needs, or—ironic but possible—those who performed so *well* that they're no longer eligible to compete. Fortunately, the rumble for change grows louder daily as behavioral-medical links become harder to ignore and as breeders see their beloved lines plagued by chronic medical problems or labeled "dangerous" or "destructive," all for want of exercise that fulfills the dog's behavioral as well as physical needs.

Ideal Dog Exercise Analysis

Stop here and compare your profile of your ideal dog with your ideal exercise program. How well do they match? What could you do to make them more compatible?

For example, Eric's lists looked like this:

Dog	Exercise Program
terrier	low-keyed
intelligent	inexpensive
spirited	at-home
female	maintenance-free

At first glance, it appears that Eric's abhorrence of physical activity will doom his dog and any exercise program. However, recall that both he and his dog thrive on tricks. Digger races around the condo fetching this, that, and the other thing. She rolls over again and again when Eric gives her the signal as he sits on the couch. She does somersaults when the mail comes and before she gets her food; she picks up her leash and dances on her hind legs when it's time for her brief walks. On the command "play," she removes all 40 of her toys from the box and scatters them around the floor; the phrase "cleanup time" causes her to put them all away again. When Eric says, "Enough" she leaps into his arms and gives him a big, wet dog kiss.

Digger probably couldn't get much further from her terrier roots, and few observers would consider her joyful antics a "serious" exercise program. Nonetheless, based on his knowledge of the breed and its potential, Eric designed a unique exercise program that perfectly met his dog's and his own needs.

The Canine Gym

The wide range of human-canine exercise options includes activities that suit practically every environment. With a little forethought, couch potato Eric can give Digger a good workout in his home, or he can walk her to the nearby park with its enclosed dog court and lounge on a bench while she romps with the other dogs and kids. The entire city of Boston serves as the backdrop for Fran's runs with Mercury. Although 100 acres of woodland and fields surround Jake's lakeside cabin, he gives his black Labs a brisk workout that rarely exceeds the limits of the short stretch of land between his home and the water's edge.

Remember, though, that the fact that we can exercise our pets just about anywhere doesn't mean we don't need to take the environment into account. I do most of my indoor exercising with my dogs on the first floor of my home because it consists of one large room. If I toss their toys while I do sit-ups on the rag rug in the kitchen, the dogs get a decent workout as they charge into the living room area at the opposite end of the house. By tossing Watson's ball to the left and Violet's rubber bone to the right of the center chimney, I can even decrease the likelihood of their stealing each other's toys.

While that may sound rather idyllic as indoor human-canine exercise programs go, it's taken time for us to perfect the system. A functioning woodstove stands in front of that center chimney, a 55-gallon aquarium sits in one corner of the living room next to the television, VCR, and other electronic paraphernalia. Plants, birdcages, and the usual furnishings and accessories also dot the interior landscape. Given the layout, I had to develop a certain amount of coordination and skill, not only to throw the ball or bone while I did something else, but also to throw it to the right spot. While the system works very well for me, I shudder to think what would happen to my belongings if one of my twentysomething sons tried to duplicate it. Because of this, I invite visitors to *roll* toys for the dogs in my house, or ask them to take the dogs and toys outdoors to play. Outdoors, I direct them to the open area in front of the house—the space with only one, easily avoidable flower bed.

What I discovered from careening birdcages, bashed plants, and one near-death experience when Violet's bone slammed into that 55-gallon aquarium is that you must take the environment into account when you design an exercise program.

Interior Environment Check

Examine your home with an eye toward its human-canine exercise potential. Tossing a ball up or down the stairs does provide great exercise for your dog, but can you create a ball- and dog-safe zone at both ends of the stairwell? Will that time-saving in-house program you envision for your 10-pound pup still work when he becomes a 50-pound adult? How about when you add a roommate, a spouse, an infant, or another dog to your family?

Next, we need to consider the outside environments that may affect the choice of exercise activities. Many people look at Watson, whose utter joy and grace when he runs bring tears to my eyes, and ask, "Why don't you let him run? There's nothing around here but woods."

True, but that sylvan scene contains stone walls and barbed wire remnants of fences from long-gone fields. It contains deer that his most basic instincts would cause him to chase, and porcupines just waiting to slash him with a quilled tail for getting too close. And now, a silent killer awaits the unwary: rabies.

The Atlantic strain of rabies has swept through the state of New Hampshire—like all of New England—killing the majority of the raccoon population and turning every wild mammal and free-roaming domestic one into a potential time bomb. Thanks to the importation of some rabid raccoons from the South for hunting purposes in the mid-Atlantic states, this particular strain now constitutes part of our normal environment and slowly makes its way westward.

"So, you vaccinate the dog and turn him loose," Eric comments. "What's the big deal?"

Like a lot of people, Eric erroneously believes that vaccinating his dog for rabies somehow protects *him* and other people. It doesn't. If a rabid animal bites Digger, and Eric happens to have a cut on his hand and examines and cleans her wounds without taking proper precautions, he could expose himself to the disease. All of us living in areas with rabies know the rules about free-roaming pets, such as wearing gloves when we check them for wounds and properly caring for any wounds we find. But recall the dangers of carrying rules about our dogs around in our heads: we may know them cold, but because children or visitors may forget the rules when the lovable family pet comes bounding up after a romp in the woods, the most sensible solution means not letting the dog out without careful human supervision.

If organized outdoor activities appeal to you, don't forget to evaluate these activities in terms of their environments from your dog's as well as your own point of view. An environment you find too distracting to handle easily probably will confuse your new dog, too. When Fran attends an agility event after years of mostly solitary runs, the high level of activity completely disorients her. Even if Mercury's past experience at the racetrack could enable him to deal with this successfully, he'd still need to deal with his owner's discomfort. Conversely, we see owners thoroughly enjoying themselves at events while their pups cower or their older animals look utterly bored.

Exterior Environment Evaluation

Think about the environment of any outdoor canine activities that appeal to you. How much noise is there? How much motion? Is the area kept clean? Do the other dogs and people appear friendly and helpful? Is the area secure? If your dog got away from you, where could it go?

Tandem Exercise

Adding a second dog to the household can do wonders to help busy owners keep their pets fit and trim—provided the dog they add is the right one. Eric envisions his new Bedlington terrier, Simon, and Digger frolicking together for hours on end. In fact, the dominant male Bedlington hassles rather than plays with

Digger, and the once joyful trickster soon refuses to perform her tricks.

Although two dogs who enjoy each other's company offer both humans and canines many advantages, we can't forget that the difference between one dog and two dogs isn't one dog: it's the difference between one dog and a pack. Consequently, whatever time multiple-dog owners may save on exercise they initially may need to spend honing their leadership skills. Digger learned her boundaries and never thought about leaving the yard. However, high-energy Simon grew bored with the space in no time and soon charged across the road and into the woods, with Digger right behind him. Whether concern for the new addition or a desire to explore the unknown in the company of a braver companion motivates Digger, the fact remains that Eric now needs to train *two* dogs to stay in the yard.

We know from the bystander effect that we need to either train two dogs separately or use methods that the subordinate animal won't perceive as dominant. We also learned the importance of timing in training, and that goes for training a dog to retrieve a ball or do tricks, as well as to sit or stay. If you want to participate in competitive or group events with your dog, the presence of a second animal will more closely approximate those group conditions. On the other hand, this raises the question of what to do with one dog while the other develops the necessary skills for your exercise program. Eric gives Digger a command, but before she can respond, the Bedlington does something that captures Eric's attention.

"Stop that!" he shouts at Simon.

Digger freezes halfway through the proper response, while Simon completely ignores his owner's command.

Ideally, choose a second dog whose exercise needs complement your first's. My client, Jake, owned as many as four black Labs at one time, all of different ages, but all incredibly stable animals. When he got the fourth dog, I asked him how he'd ever manage to exercise them all.

"No problem," he assured me with a confident smile. "Just need to keep a bigger pile of sticks by the door."

If your dogs' exercise needs don't complement each other, then resign yourself to separate programs. Eric puts Digger through her tricks while Simon observes the display quietly from his bed. When Digger finishes with her grand finale, she snuggles next to Eric while he picks up Simon's ball and tosses it from the couch to the second-floor loft, and Simon charges up the stairs in hot pursuit. Although a somewhat unorthodox approach, this system provides both dogs with a quality workout and further cements their relationship with their owner.

Pack Structure Calisthenics

Even though obedience training may not teach a dog about agility, tracking, or retrieving, these activities can teach a dog a great deal about obedience. Owners who opt to jog or bike with their pets quickly discover that the dog needs to learn to walk properly and orient toward its owner first, and no amount of human or canine equipment can compensate for a dog who lacks that basic skill, or the owner who lacks the skill to teach it.

In other words, a quality human-canine pack structure must exist in order for the activity to succeed on all three required levels—physical, mental, and emotional. Even though Fran may think she teaches Mercury the nuances of jogging with someone who wears a hands-free leash, all that specialized training and exercise means nothing if she and Mercury don't work as a unit and the dog doesn't know he can count on her to assume the leadership position.

Without a doubt, the owner's knowledge of any activity and its suitability for that owner and that dog in that environment heads the list of leadership responsibilities. Consider that simplest of all exercises—walking the dog—as it relates to the owner's leadership style. Even though Eric loves Digger, he maintains the same lackadaisical concept of pack structure that he does about exercise. When he walks her, she yanks him out the door as soon as he opens it, races down the street, snarls at every dog she meets, and jumps up and tries to lick every person they encounter. Although some may consider the 12-pound dog a nuisance, most tolerate her because she's a *small* nuisance. If Eric and a 130-pound Newfoundland conducted their daily walks in that same manner, no one assaulted by the animal would view the behavior positively.

Through this relatively mundane, hardly physically challenging activity, Digger communicates loudly and clearly that she doesn't recognize Eric's leadership, and he loudly and clearly communicates that's fine with him. Worse, he may even define all this as "good exercise" for his dog. Given this kind of relationship, what do you suppose will happen if Eric decides to become involved in a more complex sport like agility or tracking with his pet? Can any event teach leadership skills to an owner who doesn't want to assume that position? Although in the past we liked to believe it would, such no longer appears true.

To be sure, peer pressure and quality instructors can do a great deal to get timid or lazy owners to accept the leadership role in organized activities. However, some instructors and participants may get so caught up in the process of the activity— the *right* command, the *right* hand signal, the *right* terminology— that they completely ignore their often stated purpose of promoting a quality relationship between owner and animal. Get close to the people intimately involved in showing or any competitive canine sport, and you'll soon hear tales of owners who wouldn't hesitate to do anything—including using techniques that would harm the dog—to win. Get a little closer, and you'll hear tales of Jekyll-and-Hyde dogs who perform flawlessly in the ring or on the course, then turn into unruly, destructive, and even dangerous monsters at home. Although the owners of these "winners" may choose to believe they communicate leadership to their pets, the dogs and a lot of other people don't share that opinion.

From this it seems obvious that owners who want the benefits of an exercise program to carry over 24 hours a day need to evaluate it based on their leadership style. Fran's more anthropomorphic views definitely could lead her to baby a slower-paced dog if she interacted with it in a slower-paced exercise program. However, when she runs with Mercury, she doesn't have time to give in to these feelings. At the same time, the fast pace and short leash force the greyhound to focus on his owner, a passive but very effective way to reinforce Fran's leadership position. If this not particularly assertive owner of a somewhat headstrong dog had opted for a slower-paced form of exercise or one that required her to stand and give Mercury commands, the exercise sessions could have resulted in power struggles rather than enjoyment for both of them.

Eric and Digger provide another interesting variation on the exercise-leadership theme. The more time Eric spends doing tricks with the terrier in the house, the better she behaves when he subsequently takes her for her brief walks outdoors. This occurs because performing tricks exercises her on all three levels, calming her down while building her confidence and giving her a sense of accomplishment.

Compare that with what happens when Digger goes for a walk with Eric first. Because Eric won't accept the leadership position, that puts the happy, nonaggressive spayed female in charge of their pack of two, leaving her no choice but to deal with any real or perceived threats. She becomes tense and uneasy, and can't wait to scurry back to the safety of her home.

A contemporary dog's version of the wild animal's confidence effect comes into play when Digger does her tricks with Eric first. That activity makes her feel like a "winner," and this enables her to relax and enjoy her walk more.

Exercise Leadership Analysis

Evaluate the exercise options that appeal to you in terms of your leadership style. Do any books or videos on the subject ask you to use training methods you find too harsh or otherwise unacceptable? If organized activities appeal to you, evaluate their leadership style when you go to check out their environments: Do those in charge appear too process oriented? Heavy-handed? Lax—with both the animals and the humans involved? Indecisive? Inflexible?

If you don't agree with the leadership style of those in charge of and/or participating in the program, do yourself and your dog a favor and eliminate it from your list of exercise options.

Above all, when considering exercise programs for your new dog, don't feel guilty if you don't have the time or interest to become involved in some formal endeavor. Every quality interaction with our dogs exercises them on some level, and usually on all three. I think about the hunter rubbing down his dog and telling her what a fine job she did that day; I think about the old German shepherd dog with hip problems whose owner learned the basics of canine massage and communicated love and support along with comfort to her dog via her hands. Neither activity ranks high on the physical scale, yet such quiet moments surely rank among the most healthy human-canine activities.

Now that you know how to sort all those different exercise programs into manageable components and analyze them, tackling all the different feeding options will be a piece of cake.

8

Nouveau Nutrition

Choosing a Canine Feeding Program You and Your Dog Can Both Enjoy

N
o one questioned Julie Newcomb's contention that her Pekingese, Silke Sue, was the best pup in the world. In fact, so many people loved the little dog, it seemed only natural to shower her with treats. When Silke fell ill from their dietary indiscretions and stopped eating, practically every cook in the neighborhood whipped up something special for her.

A year later, everyone still loves Silke, but now they shake their heads sadly when she waddles by.

"She'd be a perfect dog if she weren't such a fussy eater and didn't have that nervous stomach condition," they say with a sigh.

Meanwhile Julie's neighbor, Tim Pachinski, can't understand this food-related agony at all.

"Why do they make such a big deal about what the dog eats when the answer's so obvious?" he asks, beaming down proudly at his new Doberman pup, Tully, wolfing down his meal. "You just feed him whatever dog food's on sale."

As these two opposing views demonstrate, determining what to feed the dog can pose a challenge for prospective and new dog owners. Just stroll down the pet food aisle of any major supermarket, and you'll see an array of pet foods promising everything from fulfilling every imaginable canine bodily need to nourishing the fur-covered soul.

Moreover, and quite unlike sorting through all the training and exercise programs, trying to make sense of nutrition takes us into the often mind-boggling world of biochemistry and mathematics. Time and time again, various experts exhort pet owners to "Read the labels!" But as Julie Newcomb stands in the supermarket aisle staring at that list of tongue-twisting ingredient names and incomprehensible "max" and "min" percentages, her eyes blur and she feels totally lost. Even if she could sort out that one label, more than 200 others await her. And that's only the *dry* dog foods on the market!

Fortunately, others with far more knowledge and skill than the average pet owner have made this task easier. *Doc Z's Canine Nutrition Primer* (PigDog Press, 1995) packs the basics into less than 30 pages of readable text. In addition to discussing how to read a pet food label, the booklet provides the necessary mathematical formulas to enable so-inclined readers to compare foods more accurately, and it includes a handy glossary and bibliography. Those who seek more detailed information can turn to Weitzman and Becker's *Dog Food Book* (Good Dog Magazine, 1993) or Coffman's *The Dry Dog Food Reference* (PigDog Press, 1995), among others. Prospective owners can even choose from a growing collection of canine cookbooks ready to further enlighten—or confuse—them.

The majority of the numerous nutritional options fall into one of four basic diet categories:

- regular
- premium
- home-cooked
- therapeutic

Regular diets make up the bulk of the foods seen on grocery store shelves, which essentially fulfill the dog's basic nutritional needs. In theory, premium diets contain higher-quality ingredients than regular ones. I say "in theory" because that holds true only if the nature and proportion of those ingredients meet your particular dog's needs. If they don't, then your dog will fare no better on such a product. Most manufacturers of both regular and premium diets also offer life-stage diets specifically formulated to meet the needs of puppies, working, less active, or older dogs.

Although many experts take a dim view of owners who believe they can prepare a home-cooked diet that meets all of their dog's nutritional needs, owners who question the value or safety of the fertilizers, pesticides, preservatives, and other chemicals used in farming or food processing increasingly opt for this approach. A growing number of veterinarians, trainers, and behaviorists endorse this owner option too.

Owners also may choose from an increasing number of therapeutic diets designed to meet the needs of animals with specific medical problems such as heart, kidney, or intestinal ailments. However, because the wrong diet could undermine rather than benefit the animal's health, owners should feed these foods only under veterinary supervision and following a complete medical workup to determine the exact nature of the dog's problem. Even the best kidney-sparing diet could cause Tully problems if he didn't need it.

Basically all nontherapeutic diets strive to fulfill the dog's nutritional needs in a manner the animal's owner finds acceptable. However, sometimes a considerable gap exists between these two criteria. Judging by their comments about dog foods, quite a few people still envision wild dogs hunting down a rabbit or wild bird, skinning or plucking it, then eating only the large muscle masses of the thigh and breast.

In reality, though, wild dogs often will consume much, if not all, of their prey. While the idea of five feet of raw rabbit intestine served au naturel might strike few humans as gourmet fare, it provides a wild dog with a marvelous source of concentrated, predigested, nutritious plant matter. Any fur or feathers contribute roughage to maintain gut motility, the liver and other internal organs supply critical vitamins and proteins, and the bones serve as a ready source of minerals. Such predator/prey combinations represent exquisite dances of nature which evolved over time for the benefit of both species. While this definitely doesn't mean that we dog owners should turn our pets loose to hunt and forage for themselves, it does mean that we should take this heritage into account when we consider our dogs' nutritional needs.

However, properly feeding the dog requires more than a knowledge of canine evolution and nutrition. When you hear someone say, "I'm going to feed the dog," what image comes to mind?

"I see myself getting out Silke's special bowl and filling it with her special food plus a portion of whatever I'm fixing myself for dinner," Julie reports proudly. "Then I put it on her place mat by my chair. After she eats, I wipe her face off with a clean washcloth."

"Give me a break!" snorts Tim. "When I feed Tully, I grab a bowl from the cupboard, dump in however much dry food the label recommends, and that's it."

From Julie's and Tim's comments we can see that feeding the dog consists of two distinct parts:

- what we feed it
- how we feed it

And how we approach and accomplish each one of these goals depends a great deal on our awareness of our own needs and limits, our dogs' needs and limits, our particular environments, and our leadership styles.

As I peruse the number of different dog foods that stuff the shelves of my favorite grocery store, or tackle the dizzying display of diets offered by a pet superstore, the computer guru's phrase "drowning in data and starving for information" comes to mind. In spite of all the options, veterinarians still see dogs suffering from nutritional problems, with obese animals still leading the pack of the nutritionally impaired. Moreover, the majority of these problems arise much more from the owners' lack of knowledge than from a lack of sound canine diets.

Dream Dog Feeding Evaluation

Think about feeding your ideal dog. What kind of food would you feed it? Did you make this decision based on your feelings about and experience with your own food, or on your knowledge and experience of dogs and their nutritional needs? Then think about how, when, and where you intend to feed your new pet, and who will feed it if you live with others. How did you come to these conclusions? Do they result from feelings, personal experience with humans and/or animals, or solid knowledge?

Julie's ideas about what and how to feed Silke arise from her desire to accomplish this in the best possible manner. However, when she analyzes these ideas carefully, she discovers that most result from her feelings about what *should* work rather than any experience or knowledge that indicates her ideas would actually meet her new dog's needs.

Furry Baby Feeding Rituals

When it comes to feeding the dog, Julie Newcomb typifies the anthropomorphic owner. Not only does she project her own beliefs about food on her pet, she also automatically assumes that what she eats will benefit her dog, too. In addition, and like more than a few other working owners, Julie imagines Silke spending the entire day in agony awaiting her owner's return, even though the pup provides her with no evidence of this such as territorial marking or other destructive behaviors. Nonetheless, this vivid, if inaccurate, image causes Julie to place a tremendous emotional charge on the feeding process. It begins the instant she walks in the door.

"Baby Silke, Mommy missed you so much! What shall we fix for dinner? Do you feel in the mood for some of that lasagna we made last weekend? No, wait, I know!" Julie exclaims to the little dog whose big brown eyes gleam with anticipation. "I'll grill a chicken breast and make a salad, then we'll top it off with strawberry shortcake for dessert!"

This announcement—and Julie's movement toward the refrigerator—causes Silke to leap ecstatically. Throughout the meal preparation, Silke hovers around Julie waiting for the bits of chicken, lettuce, tomato, green pepper, or French bread her owner accidentally or intentionally drops for her.

When it comes time to prepare their plates, Julie looks at the contents of the can of therapeutic diet the veterinarian prescribed for Silke's digestive problems.

"Yuck!" she announces as she digs at the dull homogeneous mass with a spoon.

Her eyes drift toward the aromatic chicken, the brightly colored salad shimmering with raspberry vinaigrette, the crusty French bread she just picked up on her way home from work. Naturally, Julie drops a little dab of the special diet into the bottom of Silke's bowl and tops it with chicken, salad, and bread.

"It's all healthy stuff," she assures the dog, who races her to the table. "You eat it all, and you can have dessert, too."

Few observers would deny the warm fuzzy feeling this human-canine exchange generates. However, if we look at it in terms of anthropomorphism we can see how Julie created both a canine feeding ritual and a diet based on her own beliefs rather than knowledge of her dog. Then she used her dog's positive response to it to validate her decision.

"If Silke didn't like it, she wouldn't eat it," Julie explains confidently.

Yes and no. Like most dogs, Silke will eat just about anything her owner presents in an upbeat, positive way. By nature dogs tend to gulp their food, which allows little time for them to taste it. Because they do this, however, dogs also evolved a vomiting mechanism they can trigger much faster and more efficiently than any human. If Silke eats something that irritates her stomach, up the irritating substance comes. If it doesn't disagree with her until further along in the digestive process, she experiences diarrhea.

When we develop feeding rituals that convey "I love you very much" or "This dog food looks like ground chicken lips," these beliefs naturally affect how our dogs respond to that particular food. Given that obesity remains the number one canine nutritional problem and creates the same physical complications in dogs as people, every veterinarian in the country sees dogs like Silke whose owners are literally killing them with (human) kindness while the dogs wag their tails and bark, "More! More!" While Silke's behavior appears suicidal, it occurs because she doesn't associate the food with any aftereffects: she associates it with Julie's positive response to it, and her, during the feeding ritual.

In many human-canine relationships, the feeding ritual becomes a form of communion and the food becomes a symbol of the owner's love.

"You think that's *wrong?*" asks Julie, hugging Silke tightly to her body as if to shield the pudgy Pekingese from some very bad news.

Not at all—provided the offered food reflects solid knowledge of the dog's nutritional needs and not the owner's feelings about what she'd like to eat if she were a dog. With that knowledge, the food does become an offering of love as well as physical sustenance. Without it, laziness or disregard for the animal's needs rather than love serves as the primary motivator.

Anthropomorphic Feeding Evaluation

Review your ideal feeding plan with an eye toward spotting any aspects of it that reflect anthropomorphic views. Note whether these arise from emotion (E) or knowledge (K).

When Julie evaluates her feeding preferences, she realizes that she takes a very anthropomorphic view toward this part of pet ownership and that most of her ideas arise from emotion rather than knowledge.

Food as Dog Fuel

Taking the opposing view to Julie's, we see owners such as Tim Pachinski who couldn't care less about what and how he feeds his dog most of the time.

"When I got Tully, the breeder told me to feed him this special food that I only could get through a friend of hers," Tim reports. "Then the vet highly recommended this stuff he just happened to sell right there. Then I saw ads for other foods that claimed to be just as good. That's when I decided all the diets are so much alike, it didn't matter."

In this situation, Tim adopts a chattel view of what he feeds his dog when all the conflicting claims overwhelm him. Unfortunately, because pet food sales are now a multibillion-dollar industry, the competition more than consumer needs may determine the content of the advertising. This means that, although some ads may leave us with a warmer, fuzzier feeling than others, they really don't supply much concrete information. Similarly, while some breeders, veterinarians, and groomers may carry a particular line of food because they know from experience that it truly will meet the majority of their clients' and animals' needs better, the high-pressure selling techniques used by others make it clear that profit rather than providing quality nutrition and useful information preoccupies their minds.

Given a choice between slick promotional data with little solid information and the cryptic terminology of scientific nutritional presentations, many owners simply give up. While a lot of feeling and little knowledge leads anthropomorphic owners like Julie to select a particular canine diet, a lack of both emotion and knowledge characterizes the food choices of chattel-oriented owners like Tim.

It should come as no surprise that owners who don't care what they feed their pets usually don't care how they feed it. Tully leaps joyfully around his owner while Tim dumps a couple cups of kibble into a bowl, but his owner barely notices. Tim cares only about whether Tully eats the food and whether it makes the pup vomit or gives him diarrhea. If it doesn't, Tim probably will feed it to him again sometime.

Just as Julie's approach can create problems for her pet, so can Tim's practice of jumping from food to food. In addition to some diets' not meeting Tully's needs as well as others, the changes from one food to another almost invariably upset the pup's digestive system to some degree. Although Tim immediately eliminates the foods that make Tully vomit or give the pup diarrhea, he doesn't omit those that create more subtle signs of digestive distress such as a gurgling stomach or gassiness because he misses these clues.

As we noted before, even though we may lean more in the anthropomorphic or chattel direction, our orientation toward our pets comprises an incredibly dynamic aspect of the relationship. Julie's concept of the ideal food and feeding ritual may change drastically when Mr. Right enters her life and wants to take her out to dinner every night. Although Tim cares little about what and how he feeds Tully during the week, he may share his lunch or dinner with his pet on the weekends. If either or both of these owners should happen to share their living quarters with others, engage others to care for their pets in their absence, or kennel their dogs, the animals will encounter other people with still other ideas about the right food and right way to feed the dog.

Tim readily acknowledges that most of his views about feeding Tully arise from his chattel views.

"In a way it's emotional, but in a way it isn't," he concludes. "I got so frustrated by all the conflicting information out there, I just said the heck with it."

Chattel Feeding Orientation Evaluation

Examine your ideal feeding program for any signs of a chattel orientation. Once again make a note of whether these arise from emotion (E) or knowledge (K).

No Free Dog Lunches

Unlike obedience classes or event entry fees that are the same regardless of the dog's size, activity level, and age, the cost of dog foods varies tremendously. Canned food prices range from less than 50 cents to more than $1 per can. A 40-pound bag of kibble may cost less than $10 to well over $20.

Further complicating matters, we can't consistently apply the "You get what you pay for" rule to canine diets. Although warning bells definitely should go off when you see 40 pounds of dry dog food for $2.98, the opposite doesn't necessarily hold true at the higher end of the scale. At that end, the higher cost may reflect higher advertising expenses or the manufacturer's attempt to capitalize on a product's emotional appeal. If the national press reports on a study that found product A in dog foods harmful to laboratory rats or product B beneficial, the first brands to boast "Absolutely No Product A!" or "Twice as Much Product B as Other Brands!" may command a much higher price based more on consumer fear than any true nutritional value of the food.

Also, while many dog-loving, pooper-scooper–toting city dwellers quickly recognize the benefits of a premium food that results in fewer, smaller canine bowel movements, that doesn't necessarily mean you feed your dog less of these higher-priced diets. Moreover, a more concentrated diet ranks as the most cost-effective only if your pet can handle that form of food. If Silke becomes constipated when fed such a food, Julie must add the cost of treating this problem to the food bill.

Further complicating the picture, manufacturers routinely offer coupons or rebates, or promote their products by periodically adding a few extra pounds of kibble to the bag for the same price. Consequently, how much you pay for the same brand also may vary a great deal. While the pet superstores or chains may offer lower prices than the local supermarket, the latter may run sales with comparable prices and also sell cases of canned product at reduced rates.

In general, pet stores, veterinarians, and groomers charge more for premium diets than pet superstores or chains. Whether it's worth that additional cost depends on what the extra cost gets you. If it gets you solid information from someone you trust, not only about that particular food but also about your particular dog and its particular nutritional needs, then you'll save money in the long run. However, if the seller just hands you a manufacturer's pamphlet and says, "It's all in there," the lower-priced source offers the better deal.

The higher price should also get you service as well as information. This means someone to haul those 40-pound bags out to the car if you can't, someone to put in a special order for you, and someone to call the manufacturer's research and development folks and sort through the technobabble for you if your pet experiences problems with the food. If you don't get this service, you might as well cart that bag to the checkout counter and stand in line with everyone else.

Finally, don't forget to factor in the cost of your own time. In order to save a dollar on a 40-pound bag of dog food, Tim wastes half of a rare day off driving to a store in a distant mall, fighting for a parking space, standing in the checkout line for 20 minutes with the other bargain hunters, and driving back home again, time he could have spent hiking with Tully.

Regardless of where you buy your dog food, check the date of manufacture and the shelf life. Although most products maintain their stated nutritional values for a year, some of the most expensive ones expire in four to six months. (This typically occurs because these products don't contain the chemical preservatives found in other foods.) Those eight bags of top-of-the-line food that Tim got at a bargain price because the seller wanted to move them quickly won't benefit his dog much if the food has deteriorated by the time he gets to the last bag.

If you envision cooking for your dog, the cost here also can vary greatly. Owners who opt for this route tend to fall into two groups: those who question the quality or safety of commercially prepared pet foods, and those who question the quality and safety of pet *and* human foods. Julie feeds Silke the same foods she eats because she believes that the producers of human foods adhere to stricter standards. Other owners who cook for their dogs use less expensive cuts of meat or poultry than they eat themselves; the dog still eats home-cooked human food, but not the same quality as the owners.

Those who question the quality and safety of both human and pet foods also come in two varieties. Julie's brother eats only organically grown foods and can't believe Julie would actually eat standard supermarket fare, let alone feed it to her dog. He feeds his dog an organically grown chicken-based commercial canine diet which Julie finds "so dull looking, I can't imagine giving it to a dog I love as much as Silke." Meanwhile, another dog owner cooks organically for herself as well as for her dog.

Unless you raise your own food and know how to preserve it, organic ingredients will cost considerably more than nonorganic. Preparing food for your dog using nonorganic ingredients might actually cost less than feeding some commercially prepared foods, provided you know what you're doing and don't precipitate some food-related problem. The most complex and expensive feeding regimen I ever encountered was developed by a delightful Orthodox Jewish organic vegetarian. This woman went to an unbelievable effort to find the ingredients and prepare an organic kosher diet that met her pet's nutritional requirements as well as those of her religion.

Whatever kinds of ingredients appeal to you, don't forget to add the cost of a good canine nutrition text and cookbook ($10–75) if you want to cook for your new pet.

Pet food dishes can run anywhere from nothing (if you use one of your own bowls) to $75 for an automatic feeder whose two lids pop open to serve your pet at preset intervals. Between these extremes you can find stainless steel bowls from $3 to more than $20 depending on size and style. Wider, shallower (1½″ deep) bowls make it easier for pups to feed neatly; no-tip bowls with wider bases eliminate spilled water and food; flared "spaniel" bowls keep long ears from dragging through dinner.

Ceramic and stoneware pet feeding dishes range from less than $10 to more than $20. Here, weight rather than shape prevents tipping, so beware of bowls that might scratch your floors or slide all over the room while your pet tries to eat. Some ceramic bowls come with rubber bumpers to prevent this, or you can place the bowl on a rubberized mat to stabilize it. Also, unless you know exactly where that darling pottery bowl from Aunt Esther came from, don't feed the dog from it. Depending on its age and place of origin, it may contain harmful lead.

Colored anodized aluminum pet feeding dishes run less than $5, and unbreakable plastic (styrene or polypropylene) ones cost between $1 and $10, depending on size. Although brightly colored bowls may appeal to humans, some animals can develop allergies to both the dyes and some of the plastics. Because of this, I prefer stainless steel or ceramic food and water dishes.

Feeding Financial Analysis

Think about any financial limits as they may affect how and what you feed your new dog. How much can you reasonably afford to spend on dog food a week? Can you afford to feed your dog the food you want on that amount? If not, can you find a comparable diet that you can afford? What kinds of containers do you intend to serve your new pet its food and water in? Do these fit into your budget?

Feeding Time Limits

As previously noted, you can purchase an automatic feeder that will feed your dog when you go away for the weekend. Get your 4-pound Yorkshire terrier a bulk feeder/water combination that holds 25 pounds of dry food and five gallons of water and you can cut your feeding time even more.

Although the image of that little Yorkie daily working its way through 25 pounds of dog food off in a lonely corner might tug at our heartstrings, many dog owners do spend the absolute minimum time feeding their pets. A fair number provide food free-choice, or ad libitum, which means the dog can nibble its food anytime it feels the urge, with the owner refilling the bowl as needed. While this approach might fit Tim's schedule, it can wreak havoc with a pup's house-training. Random input means random output which the young pup's not fully developed bladder and rectal sphincters can't control. Consequently, whatever time this feeding method saves Tim pales compared with how much longer it takes him to clean up and house-train Tully.

Other busy owners feed their dogs on-the-fly one, two, or three times a day, depending on a wide variety of human and canine circumstances, including the owner's schedule and the dog's age. Some may feed the dog while they get the kids ready for school, others while they wait for the coffee to brew, and still others while they prepare their own meals.

"It's a matter of necessity, not a case of not caring about the dog," Tim explains as he rushes from his office in the insurance company where he works full time.

On a typical weekday, Tim feeds and walks Tully between 7:20 and 7:30 A.M. before rushing off to work from 9:00 to 5:00. At 5:00 he rushes home, feeds Tully and gulps down his own dinner, walks the pup, and then either attends classes (three nights a week) or studies. Fearing accidents in the house during his absence, he urges his pet to eat as quickly as possible so he can spend more time walking him.

"Geez, Tully, get a move on!" he yells at the eating pup as he taps his foot and looks at his watch every 15 seconds. "I gotta take you out and get to class!"

In this situation, the owner's anxiety greatly undermines whatever nutritional and emotional benefit the pup might have gained from the meal. Like those parents who chauffeur kids to gymnastics classes, soccer games, swimming lessons, choir practice, and/or softball games after work, Tim may find that it makes more sense to feed Tully when he gets home at night rather than try to cram feeding into those few hectic moments that occur between work and class. Not only does consistently feeding the dog at regular times avoid all the behavioral tension associated with random or rushed feedings, but it also enhances digestion.

Other owners develop more intimate feeding rituals with their pets, which require proportionately more time. Julie spends as much time preparing and serving Silke's food as her own because they eat the same food together. Others who feed their pets dog food may consciously or subconsciously develop rituals that include taking out the pet's bowl (or picking it up off the floor), measuring the kibble and pouring it into the bowl and/or opening the can and spooning out its contents, perhaps adding warm water or microwaving the end product, and then offering this to the dog. More often than not, owners talk to their pets during this process, frequently using a tone of voice quite different from the one they use to communicate with the dog at other times.

Given the human social precedent inherent in "breaking bread" and our inclination to include our pets in food-oriented rituals, incorporating feeding into our quality time with our dogs saves time, too. We need to feed them, so it makes sense to interact positively with them during that interval rather than run the risk of not finding the time later.

A drawback is that the more complex and lengthy the feeding ritual, the more it becomes part of the animal's life; if we can't find the time to fulfill it for some reason, the dog will miss it. Suppose Julie goes on vacation for a week. Suddenly Silke's world crumbles. Even if Julie leaves portions of the same foods she always feeds her pet with the dog-sitter, the fact that the owner no longer shares the ritual so confuses Silke that she can't eat. When Julie returns from her vacation, her best friend and dog-sitter starts yelling at her the instant she comes through the door.

"Do you have any idea how much time I spent trying to get that dog to eat!" she rages. "Don't you *ever* ask me to dog-sit for you again!"

While food-related rituals can add a wonderful dimension to our relationship with our pets, that holds true only if we can perform them consistently. If not, we run the risk of our pets not only missing us in our absence, but also not eating and drinking.

Feeding Time Analysis

Summon an image of yourself feeding your new dog and analyze it in terms of any time limits. Pay particular attention to how your weekday and weekend schedules differ. If you plan to feed and walk your new pup at 6:30 A.M. and P.M. Monday through Friday, can you do that Saturday and Sunday also, at least until you get your new pet housebroken? Because consistency is critical in the young animal's training, imagine your *busiest* day: Does your feeding plan fit into it? If it does, then it will probably work for all the other days, too. If you plan to adopt an older dog, don't forget to find out its feeding schedule so you can incorporate it into your own. If you plan to add a second dog, how will its proposed feeding schedule fit into the other dog's?

When Tim evaluates the feeding schedule supplied by Tully's breeder in terms of his own hectic lifestyle, he realizes that he can't consistently meet it on a day-to-day basis. Because of this, he rearranges the pup's meals so he can guarantee Tully a serene mealtime.

Emotional Dog Crunchies

Food-related love and guilt can cause the most trouble with canine feeding programs. Although feeding our pets in a loving manner definitely benefits them, our definition of love must incorporate our awareness of the animal's physical and behavioral well-being. No amount of love can counter the negative effects of feeding the dog too much or the wrong diet.

From experience, I know that the vast majority of obese dogs belong to people who love them very much. Because these owners often come from a long tradition that equates food with love, they feel they're showing their dogs more love by feeding than by hugging or exercising them.

This conviction remains so firmly entrenched in our society that it makes me wonder if it represents the human emotional corollary of the impulses that compel animals to establish and protect their territory, find food and water, and then reproduce. In the human emotional version, we claim a dog as our own "territory" (whether we treat it as child or chattel), feed and water it, and then intimately interact with it on some deeper, emotional level.

Viewed in that light, it appears that a lot of people get stuck on level two: they get the pet, vaccinate, neuter, train, and license it in order to establish ownership, then use food as the *means* to establish the deeper bond. The busier we become, the easier we find it to make the food-love connection, to the point that we never even think about moving beyond it to commune with the animal in other ways.

Consider the not at all uncommon case of Silke Sue, undoubtedly one of the world's most beloved dogs. We already saw how her owner loves her so much, she shares everything she eats with the dog. All the neighbors love Silke, too, and offer her bits of cookie or dog treats when they see her out for her evening strolls with Julie. Visitors to Julie's home also participate in the feeding ritual. When Silke periodically succumbs to digestive problems and goes off-feed, it so upsets Julie and everyone else that they prepare special foods to tempt the Pekingese because "everyone knows that a dog with a good appetite is a healthy dog." Later, when Silke's problems became so serious that her veterinarian prescribes a therapeutic diet, Julie finds it extremely difficult to feed her pet the food for three strictly emotional reasons:

- She believes all dog food inferior to people food.
- The idea that Silke *needs* a therapeutic diet violates her image of her dog as healthy and happy and upsets her very much.
- She interprets Silke's reluctance to eat the less palatable fare to mean that the veterinarian prescribed the wrong "cure."

Given these beliefs and her strong food-equals-love connection, we can see why Julie begins adding table food to the therapeutic diet, citing Silke's greater eagerness to eat the combination as evidence of the dog's improved health.

Because as many as a third of our dogs suffer from obesity and all its related medical and behavioral problems, and because so many owners experience enormous difficulty breaking the food-equals-love connection, I strongly discourage using food treats for training. Unlike wild animals, our dogs come to us primed for the higher communion of companionship and often preprogrammed with functions whose fulfillment, in and of themselves, gives the animals a feeling of purpose and joy. In so many cases, our pets don't need the food rewards nearly as much as we need to give these to them.

This brings us to guilt. In addition to substituting food for love because it saves time, many busy owners do it because they feel guilty for some reason. Even though Tully may spend as much as 19 hours a day sleeping, Tim imagines the pup pining away for him in his absence. This occurs even though Tim can see how much time Tully spends sleeping during the weekends that they spend together. Nonetheless, in order to atone for leaving the pup home alone, he shares part of his pizza with Tully, or includes the pup in his weekend feeding binges to make up for his absence.

Owners who can't find time for elaborate feeding rituals also may feel guilty. They, too, often will attempt to assuage their negative feelings with food. After class, Tim unwinds watching television with a bowl of popcorn in his lap and Tully beside him. Every time Tim takes a handful from the bowl, he gives half of it to Tully.

Finally, and thanks to all those feeding options and their promoters, contemporary dog owners also may succumb to guilt about *what* they feed the dog as well as how.

"I really think Tully's coat would look shinier if you put him on a premium food," Tim's veterinarian earnestly suggests.

"You feed him something that uses BHT as a preservative?" fumes a co-worker. "Are you tying to kill him?"

"How can you feed him *dog food*?" asks another. "Don't you love him?"

It may be an indicator of how strongly our beliefs affect what we feed our dogs that loving owners who feed their pets regular pet food for financial reasons often feel much guiltier about not feeding premium foods than owners who feed their pets table food without considering whether it fulfills their pet's nutritional needs. However, even though a certain amount of guilt may stimulate pet owners to initiate needed changes, it often quickly gives way to resentment of both the person who recommended the change and the dog. Because of this, I always urge owners to eliminate guilt from the feeding process.

"Does that mean I shouldn't feel guilty about feeding Silke table food and rewarding her with treats?" Julie asks hopefully.

Yes. Even worse than a poor diet is a poor diet presented in a negative emotional environment. This recognition now leads me to recommend that owners who attach a strong emotional charge to their pet's food and feeding make any dietary changes very gradually, even if the existing diet contributes to serious health problems. I know from sad experience that rushing the process for strictly medical reasons can lead to even greater owner guilt, upsetting both dog and owner at a time when the animal needs positive emotional support the most.

Feeding Emotions Checkup

Summon an image of yourself selecting food for your dog and feeding it, and any loving or guilty feelings that go with it, now, before you get your dog. Then ask yourself why you feel that way. Do such feelings arise from solid knowledge or propaganda of one sort or another? Now imagine noticing that your year-old dog doesn't eat as much as it used to: How do you feel about that? Does it make you want to rush to the fridge for a piece of cheese or meatloaf to tempt it to eat? Did you automatically assume your pet's appetite waned because it misses you so much when you're gone? How do you feel about that? What can you do to eliminate any negative feelings? What's the best food and feeding process for you and your dog, given your emotions about food and feeding?

"I feel like I'm going through psychoanalysis!" Julie laughs after she examines her feelings and completes the exercise. "I never realized how much I allowed my feelings to affect what and how I fed my dog!"

Because recognizing the problem is a major step toward solving it, Julie now finds herself in a position to look at her feeding practices more objectively.

Kibble Push-Ups

Aside from needing strength to lug bags of dog food home from the store, it wouldn't seem that owner physical limits play much of a role in what and how we feed the dog. However, recall that dogs often act as four-legged, fur-covered mirrors of ourselves. Even though how we feed our dogs may arise from deep cultural roots, what we feed them often reflects our awareness about the quality and safety of our own food. Although Julie may blanch at the thought of Silke's wild ancestors attacking and slaughtering a wildebeest, the idea of Silke attacking a commercial diet made from hormone- and antibiotic-injected, insecticide-dipped, pesticide-treated, and fertilized-hay-and-grain-fed cattle that didn't pass inspection for human consumption bothers her even more. Based on that belief about her own well-being, Julie opts to feed her dog human-grade food.

If you find yourself feeling at all guilty about wanting to feed your dog a commercial food, bear in mind that feeding our dogs what we eat doesn't mean we feed them *better*, for two other, purely physical reasons. First, a lot of people don't eat food that's healthy for humans, let alone for dogs. Second, because dogs aren't humans, even the most balanced, healthiest human diet won't meet a dog's nutritional needs.

On a positive note, owners who eat healthy diets themselves do tend to take a healthier view about what they feed and, equally if not more important, offer as treats for their dogs. If we can summon the will power to pick a carrot instead of a piece of pie for ourselves without feeling like self-righteous martyrs, we can do the same when we give treats to our pets. Owners who treat their pups with carrot slices report the same positive responses as those who use cookies; those who use broiled skinless chicken breast get the same positive canine result as those who feed their dogs fried hamburger.

Owner Dietary Fitness Exam

Because even the most determined owners find themselves slipping their pets a bit of food from their plates every now and then, pause here and think about what you eat. If you live on fast food or takeout, do thoughts of your new dog and its health spur you to upgrade your own diet before you get your new pet? If not, how can you keep your dog from succumbing to your own bad eating habits? Are you the kind of person who can enforce a strict "No table food" rule?

When Tim realizes how much his own eating habits can affect Tully, he decides to keep a small bowl of the dog's regular food or carrot pennies on the table so that he—and others—can feed his new pet a healthy treat when the urge occurs.

Canine Food Fetishes

Given all the different kinds of diets and all the different feeding strategies owners design to meet their own needs, sometimes the dog can get lost in the shuffle. Obviously, any diet or feeding ritual that fails to meet the dog's physical and behavioral needs inevitably will cause problems. Although we want and need to feel good about the food and feeding ritual, we can't lose sight of the main goal: to inspire the dog to eat a well-balanced diet. But what, exactly, stimulates the dog's appetite?

Summon the image of that wild dog hunting its dinner with the pack. Unlike humans, dogs really don't care much about their food's appearance. However, they do care a great deal about how it moves because their vision recognizes motion much more than detail. The sound and scent of their prey also draws them closer and further triggers the predatory response. Finally, when they pounce on a potential meal, the texture and taste of the food stimulates the canine appetite center, too. Such sensitivities serve the wild dog perfectly, alerting it to the most subtle motion, sound, or scent of its prey and causing it to stalk, then move in for the kill as the amount of incoming data increases.

Because most of the time the domestic dog receives no such sensory cues from its food, it tries to fill the void as best it can. Maybe Silke's food doesn't make any noise, but the bag and can opener do, as does Julie who cheerfully talks to the dog as she prepares the food. If Julie adds a bit of warm water or microwaves the cold canned food to room (not hot) temperature, that will increase the amount of odors the food emits.

While most contemporary dogs don't routinely need such primitive triggers to stimulate their appetites, they do play an important role in two situations. First, dogs who stop eating because of illness may need extra stimulation to start eating again. By selecting foods with more odor and texture, warming cold foods slightly, and offering them in an animated upbeat manner, owners can help trigger a sluggish appetite.

Second, the downside of canine appetite stimulation occurs when Silke stares morosely at the dry food in her bowl while Julie eats, then eagerly leaps to gulp down whatever Julie offers regardless of its nutritional value. Consider Silke's dilemma in terms of appetite stimulation: She can focus on her nutritionally complete but silent, unmoving, and minimally scented dry food, or she can concentrate on Julie's warm, aromatic food moving from plate to mouth with clanking dinnerware, cheerful chatter, and a riot of other sounds, motions, and odors that stimulate the canine appetite.

Because of this, Julie must guard against the temptation to convince herself that Silke prefers people food over her own because "dogs know what's good for them." The fact that the food meets the dog's psychological needs in no way guarantees it will meet the animal's physical needs. If you've ever over-indulged with rich food and drink because your "eyes were bigger than your stomach" and paid the price the morning after, you know how easily the mind can trick the body!

Because both canine physical and behavioral factors can trigger food and feeding problems, we need to consider both the dog's body and its mind when selecting a food and feeding method. Physical factors that can trigger feeding problems primarily arise from three sources:

- extrinsic: parasites, poor-quality food, failure to provide the proper amount of food
- intrinsic: breed or individual idiosyncrasies
- food allergies

You know a problem exists if you feed your pup 2 cups of food and it produces 1½ cups of stool. Regardless of your new pet's age, take along a stool sample that your veterinarian can check for worms when you take your dog for its first examination. Not only can intestinal parasites consume nutrients meant for the dog, they also can burrow into the intestinal lining, further interfering with the animal's ability to digest and utilize its food. If your pet does play host to these unsavory characters, safe and gentle medication will solve the problem. At such times, you'll also greatly appreciate that decision to train your new dog to eliminate in one corner of the yard before you take it for its daily jaunts. That way you can easily obtain a sample and clean up all of your dog's stool during the worming process so your pet doesn't reinfect itself.

How much food a dog requires to fulfill its needs also varies from breed to breed and among individuals, as well as over the life span of a specific animal. Always bear in mind that the amounts indicated on any can or bag of dog food serve only as a rough guide, and you may need to adjust these up or down to meet your own pet's needs. Old-time sportsmen refer to some sporting dogs as "easy keepers," meaning they don't require as much food as other dogs. If you feed these dogs more *and* make house pets out of them, they soon may resemble four-legged blimps.

Even in this day and age, you'll still hear people say they don't want to neuter their pets because it makes them fat, as if part of the operation involved brain surgery to teach the dog how to open a can or cupboard and prepare its own meals. In reality, such owners overlook the fact that both neutering and maturity decrease a dog's caloric needs. If Julie keeps feeding one-year-old neutered Silke the same amount she fed the unspayed pup, her older pet will gain weight. If Julie continues feeding that same amount through middle age when Silke's caloric requirements drop again, the excess weight will make the Pekingese's final years less than golden.

Although a lot of dog owners maintain strong ideas about what constitutes a poor-quality food, their views often constitute an arbitrary judgment at best. Some dogs do remarkably well on diets that would horrify a canine nutritionist. On the other hand, some dogs on these same diets look sickly and malnourished and show almost immediate improvement when fed a different food.

Unfortunately, though, sorting through and solving diet-related problems with their nonspecific and intermittent vomiting, diarrhea, and skin conditions can take a great deal of time and cost a great deal of money. Because of this, it behooves prospective owners to know as much as possible about their particular dog's food and feeding habits. W. D. Cusick devoted an entire book, *Canine Nutrition: Choosing the Best Food for Your Breed of Dog* (Doral, 1995), on how breed affects diet. Although the book focuses on helping owners create diets similar to those these animals ate in their countries of origin, some breeds or lines of dogs may handle one particular brand of commercial food better than others, too. While suspicious prospective buyers or those with strong dog food preferences that exclude a particular brand may dismiss this as brainwashing by the pet food industry, such idiosyncrasies do occur, and busy owners ignore them at their peril.

After Tim's habit of feeding Tully the weekly special costs him more in veterinary bills than he saves on food, he decides to put the Doberman on the food recommended by the breeder. However, because he knows from sad experience that, even though food A or food B might not cause the dog any problems at all, a sudden change from A to B can cause diarrhea, he makes the change very gradually. First he replaces a quarter of Tully's current diet with a quarter of the new for a week, then he feeds half old and half new the second week, followed by a quarter of the old and three-quarters of the new the third. Finally, he feeds all of the new diet the fourth. If at any time during this process the dog had shown signs of digestive problems, Tim's veterinarian recommended he feed Tully the previous week's proportions for another week.

"Once I got Tully on one food, both of our lives became much simpler," Tim confessed. "Plus, after he'd been on the recommended diet for a while, I could see that it did make a difference. His coat's much shinier, his bowel movements are consistently firm, and I don't hear his stomach gurgling like I used to when I fed him some of the other foods."

You may have noticed an increase of lamb-containing dog foods dotting the shelves of your grocery store. These reflect the dog-owning public's increased concern about canine food allergies. Notice I didn't say, "These reflect an increased number of canine food allergies." I didn't say that because specifically identifying a food allergy requires a long and tedious process few owners desire to undertake. Instead, some owners put their dogs on a commercial lamb-based diet or a nonallergenic therapeutic one with the idea that, if the dog gets better, that proves a food allergy caused the problem.

Keep a few points in mind about these diets. First, there's nothing magical about lamb. Allergies occur after an animal eats a food for a while, and "nonallergenic" products simply consist of foods not normally part of the typical canine diet. After lamb-based pet foods established themselves in the market, allergies to lamb began to appear, too.

Second, the fact that the product name includes the words "lamb" or "lamb meal" doesn't rule out the possibility that these diets contain poultry, beef by-products, or other ingredients found in other canine diets. Naturally, an animal allergic to one of these other ingredients still will exhibit signs of a food allergy if fed one of the lamb-based foods. This in no way means you should avoid these products. It simply means that they don't *prevent* or necessarily *treat* dogs with food allergies.

Dogs also may refuse to eat for behavioral reasons. Chapter 1 described how some animals may experience separation anxiety and refuse to eat anything when separated from their owners. Other animals experience feeding problems related to their territorial natures. When Julie leaves sweet little Silke home alone all day with a full bowl of food, Silke wouldn't dream of touching it. However, the instant Julie comes home, Silke dives into the food and wolfs it down so fast that it comes right back up a few minutes later.

Remember: establishing and protecting the territory takes precedence over eating and drinking. When left alone, Silke spends most of her time patrolling Julie's home and worrying about various real or imagined intruders, and cares nothing about food. As soon as Julie returns, that takes the pressure off the dog, who then tackles her food with gusto. If Silke's insides still churn from the sound of the delivery man pounding on the door, even if her mind says, "I'm hungry," her gut needs time to settle down before she eats.

If your new dog exhibits this pattern, put it on twice-daily feedings, and delay the evening meal until after the household quiets down. At the same time, consider free-access crate-training and also recall what we said about the benefits of downplaying those joyous homecomings. After Silke's tense day on patrol, Julie's screeches of joy and hugs and kisses further excite rather than calm her pet. Now Silke must deal not only with the tension generated by her territorial duties, but also with that generated by the impending and actual joyous reunion with her owner.

Dream Dog Nutritional Checkup

Review your description of your dream dog, then jot down questions regarding its specific food and feeding rituals to ask the breeder or previous owner. What kind of food did the dog eat? How much? Where? When? Why did that person feed that particular food? Determine if this diet and feeding ritual fit your needs. If they don't, what can you change and how?

Unlike Tully's breeder, Silke's original owner fed the dog almost all table food, an approach that initially appealed to Julie, too. However, because this caused Silke so many problems, like Tim she decided to trade her dog over to a diet that met her pet's needs better.

"The first three months, I had to work really hard at accepting that the new diet really was the best food for Silke," Julie recounted six months later as she tossed a ball for her slim and trim pet. "But as she lost the excess weight, she gained so much energy, I couldn't believe it. It was like she was a pup again."

Candlelight Canine Cuisine

The environment also influences what and how we feed the dog. Even the highest-quality dog food won't benefit Tully if Tim leaves the bag open and the food becomes contaminated or loses vital nutrients due to exposure. Nor will it help either owner or dog if Tim stores the food in an easily opened closet and Tully consumes half a bag and develops explosive diarrhea.

If you intend to feed dry food and buy it in large quantities, you need the space to store it. Although many dried products now come in bags with protective liners to preserve their nutritional value, these don't protect the food from curious or hungry pets and the occasional stray mouse. Investing in a plastic container with a secure lid for storing your dry dog food, and buying only the amount of food you can store properly and use before its expiration date will prevent this problem. Canned food also requires proper storage, which means refrigerating any unused contents.

Dry food mixed with water, canned, or home-cooked diets all will spoil more quickly than plain dry food. That means Julie shouldn't leave a big bowlful of moist food for Silke when she heads out for a long day at the beach. By the time Silke feels like eating hours later when the sun goes down, the meal could do the little dog more harm than good.

Although we previously discussed the value of passively training a dog to tolerate the presence of people around its food, that doesn't mean we should routinely feed our pets in the midst of a three-ring circus. Sensory input that threatens or even simply alerts the dog can either speed up or slow down normal gut activity, neither of which enhances digestion. You don't need to keep the kids away from the dog when it's eating, but you do need to teach them not to run wild at such times.

Some owners find that putting the pet's food down just before they sit down to eat their own meal works best for human and dog alike for several reasons. First, the dog spends part of the owner's mealtime engrossed in its own food. Second, because just-fed dogs don't pester their owners for food as much, owners find it much easier not to offer scraps from the table. Finally, dispatching someone to walk the dog after the family dinner while others clean up reduces the temptation to feed the dog any leftovers.

Whether or not such combined human-canine mealtimes work depends on the humans far more than the canines involved. As noted before, owners who routinely fly into the house at 5:30, throw something in the microwave, and wolf it down while trying to find bathing suits, soccer balls, grocery lists, class notes, or the minutes from the last planning board meeting don't do themselves or their pets any favors by feeding them under those circumstances.

Always feeding the dog in the same place within your home also enhances the feeding process by conferring three advantages. First, such consistency makes it easier to keep the area clean, which cuts down on odors, flies, and the chance of food contamination. Obviously, if we routinely wipe off the table after we eat because even the most well-mannered diner may drop a few crumbs or drip soup occasionally, it seems likely our dogs may do likewise. Granted they do tend to clean up after themselves with their tongues, but still, it's a lot easier to clean up that one corner of the kitchen and/or that plastic place mat under the dog's bowls than police the entire house for evidence of far-flung slurped dog food.

In addition to choosing your pet's feeding area with an eye toward cleanability, also evaluate it in terms of traffic flow. Practically everyone who visits Julie comes to the kitchen door. If she feeds Silke near that door, not only does she increase the probability that people will barge in on the feeding dog, but she also increases the likelihood that a visitor will kick Silke's food and water bowls—or even the little dog herself!—across the floor.

Finally, feeding the dog in the same clean and serene location lends a certain dignity to the event. While some owners may enjoy watching their pets work themselves into a frenzy at mealtimes trying to determine where and when the owner intends to put the food down, such activities promote neither canine stability nor efficient digestion. Compare that with Tim's calmly expecting Tully to sit or lie down throughout the meal preparation and until the bowl of food hits the floor. While Tully initially sits like a tightly wound spring, Tim's calm approach does a great deal to calm his pet and eventually make mealtimes a more mellow experience for them both. Not only that, Tim saves time by incorporating Tully's training into his meal preparation.

If you intend to get an adult dog, find out what, when, and how the previous owners fed the dog. I recall one old dog who lived with an elderly shut-in who always sat on a kitchen chair next to the dog and talked to him as he ate. When the owner died and a young couple with children adopted him, the animal refused to eat. The new owners tried every food on the market and even home cooking to no avail. Finally one day the young woman became so overcome with frustration that she sat on the floor, put the dog's bowl down next to her instead of in the corner where she usually placed it, and began pouring out her soul to her new pet—whereupon he began gobbling up his food. When the new owner later recounted this strange miracle to a friend of the original owner, the friend immediately recalled how the former owner always sat and talked to the dog while he ate.

Feeding Environment Evaluation

Consider your home as it relates to your new dog's food and feeding: Where do you intend to store your new pet's food? Can your dog or any other animal get into that area? How much food can you store at one time in that space? Where do you plan to feed your dog? Can you clean that area easily? Is it outside any areas of heavy traffic flow or household activity?

Tim discovers that he covered all of the environmental bases except one.

"I'm not too good about cleaning up the area where Tully eats," he says, grinning sheepishly as he hastily stacks last night's dishes in the sink. "I think I'll get a place mat to put his bowls on to remind me to do this."

Of course, we can't expect a young, fast-track tiger like Tim to change his sloppy stripes overnight, but his awareness of the problem will make it easier for him to remember this part of the feeding ritual.

Multiple Dog Table Manners

Feeding problems related to the introduction of a second dog almost always involve social eating among animals given free access to dry food. Suppose Tim feeds Tully free-choice and decides to get a pup when Tully reaches adulthood. What will he do with Tully while the new pup eats? How will he keep the new pup from getting into Tully's free-choice adult food and keep Tully out of the pup's nutritionally different puppy fare? In this situation, Tim discovers that switching Tully to twice-daily feedings before he brings home his new pup saves him a lot of time.

We know from Chapter 4 that one dog will assume the dominant role with respect to protecting the territory in the owner's absence, and that that dog often won't eat or drink anything during that time. That leaves the second dog with nothing to do *but* eat. Consequently, in some two-dog households, one dog may maintain its optimum weight while the other puts on extra pounds. When the owner comes home, however, the dominant dog—who cared nothing about food a minute before—suddenly growls at the chow hound. Owners who don't understand the pack dynamics may erroneously discipline the dominant dog or, worse, grab a slice of bologna out of the fridge to "treat" the overweight one driven away from the food because they feel sorry for it.

A more insidious version of this occurs with two evenly matched dogs. Here, the tension between the two animals may reach such proportions that neither feels comfortable eating at any time. Some dogs may develop diarrhea which may even become explosive and bloody in some cases. Unless owners recognize the role the animals' behavior plays in their health, they might put themselves and their dogs through an extensive and expensive medical workup to determine the cause of the "digestive" problem.

Although I like free-choice feeding in single-dog households for animals who are capable of regulating their own weight and who belong to owners willing to interact positively with the animal in other ways, this approach can create more problems than it solves in multiple-dog households. Although tensions will still run high in canine packs in which closely matched animals vie for the top slot, removing the food from the competition will prevent nervous eating and all the problems it creates.

Owners of such animals also should deemphasize homecomings and delay feeding until after the animals settle down. Putting the dogs through a few rounds of obedience commands to remind them that human rather than dog rules now apply also can help relieve the tension.

Top Chef at the Canine Café

Throughout this discussion of canine foods and feeding methods, we've seen the need to select diets and formulate feeding procedures that decrease any food-related tension. Review the following list of recommendations which hold true whether owners opt to feed regular, premium, home-cooked, or organic home-cooked foods.

- Don't force your food preferences on your dog.
- Avoid making problematic food-equals-love connections.
- Avoid implementing feeding rituals to which you can't adhere consistently.

- Feed the dog in a serene environment.
- Don't rush the feeding process.
- Provide tension-relieving, confidence-building training and free-access crates for the stay-at-home pet.
- Address the special needs of a multiple-dog household.

All of these recommendations fall under the umbrella of human leadership. Even owners who take the most chained-to-the-doghouse chattel view of their dogs can't avoid the fact that dogs depend solely on their owners to fulfill their nutritional needs. If the owner doesn't give the dog a food that meets its needs in an environment where it can comfortably eat and digest it, the animal will sicken and maybe even die. The same applies to the most beloved household pet in the most beautiful home.

Lately I've encountered more overweight aggressive dogs, which would seem to fly in the face of territorial behavior taking precedence over eating and drinking. However, as a group, these animals experience very close, often highly anthropomorphic relationships with their owners who usually maintain strong food-equals-love beliefs. Under these circumstances, a lack of human leadership adds a major wrinkle to the problem. Because overweight Silke can't protect her territory as well, she responds much more quickly—and strongly—to perceived threats in her territory, setting a vicious cycle in motion. The stressed dog eats more to relieve her tension, gobbling down not food but love and attention; she gains weight which increases her feelings of vulnerability and aggression. How much healthier and happier she'd be if her owner assumed the leadership position!

Put another way, good human leaders provide their pets with two food-related advantages: They willingly

- gain the necessary knowledge to select a diet that meets their particular animal's needs
- train and interact with the animal in such a way that it recognizes their authority, thereby freeing the dog to relax and enjoy its food

Good leaders also realize that the two must go together. All the wonderful training and quality human-canine interaction in the world won't correct the digestive problems that erupt every time Tim switches Tully from one on-sale dog food to another. By the same token, even consistently feeding Tully the best diet in the world won't benefit the pup if he lacks the physiological wherewithal to properly digest it, or the training that gives him the confidence to eat under a wide variety of circumstances. While something from the oven may say "lovin'" to some folks and even some dogs, the most lovingly prepared and served home-cooked meal does nothing to build the confidence of a timid animal.

We always come back to the same basic truth. People who share mutually rewarding relationships with their pets share one quality in common: knowledge of themselves, their pets, and their environments, and the willingness to gain more knowledge and make changes if needed.

"But I don't have time to go through all those diets and figure out which one will work best!" Julie insists as she flips Silke a piece of doughnut.

She doesn't need to. Consider this alternate scenario. Julie decides she wants a Pekingese because she finds them irresistibly cute. She reads up on the breed and talks to breeders, her veterinarian (or one recommended by a friend, if she doesn't have one), and people who own the kind of Pekes she likes. She discovers that a lot of people baby these dogs. Balancing that, both the breeder and the veterinarian remind her that the adorable squashed nose, prominent eyes, and squat little body can increase the dog's susceptibility to respiratory, eye, and knee problems, and both strongly recommend maintaining Silke on a quality diet to keep her fit and trim. The breeder recommends one diet, the veterinarian another. When Julie contacts other Pekingese owners, she hears both diets touted repeatedly, as well as several others that she should avoid because the breed doesn't do well on them.

When Julie mentions her desire to cook for her dog herself, the veterinarian gives her the name of a colleague knowledgeable in holistic health and canine nutrition. After discussing her plans with that person, Julie realizes that cooking for a dog means more than feeding her pet what she eats. She then evaluates her options in terms of her own orientation toward dogs and her financial, time, emotional, and physical limits, and chooses the diet that best meets her needs. If it differs from what her new pet has been eating before she got it, she gradually changes the diet after the dog settles comfortably into her home. If the new diet doesn't work for some reason, Julie goes back to the old one, or tries another after discussing it with her veterinarian.

"Sounds like a lot of work," Julie remarks dubiously.

Perhaps, but it involves only a small fraction of the time and effort—and money—Julie currently spends treating Silke's "nervous stomach." If it sounds like a lot of work to you, too, you might reconsider getting a new dog at this time. Acquiring all this dog-related new knowledge should delight, not discourage you. Preparing for a new pup should elicit all the positive feelings of preparing for the arrival of a special friend. Zeroing in on *the* perfect breed, *the* perfect breeder or source, *the* perfect pup or dog, and *the* perfect feeding and other programs to go with it over a period of weeks or months may take time, but you should enjoy it.

Prospective owners willing to assume the leadership position and arm themselves with knowledge of canine foods and feeding programs offer their pets a distinct advantage. Those who make this effort experience fewer food-related problems with their pets than less knowledgeable owners. However, and in a way I don't completely understand but believe relates to *presence*, these owners also can make mistakes—sometimes horrendous ones—and the animal and the relationship will survive.

I recall one owner who forgot to put away a large bag of a very poor-quality dog food left by a visiting friend. Her ancient dog wolfed down about 10 pounds of it plus part of the bag before the owner returned home from work that evening and discovered her error. In purely biological terms, the food should have made that old dog incredibly ill, if not worse. However, aside from passing a little gas, the dog did just fine. It was as if this owner's knowledge and relationship with the dog somehow protected him.

Leadership Feeding Test

Review your notes regarding your own leadership style, and apply them to your preferred canine food and feeding ritual. Do they complement each other? If not, what changes can you make in one or the other that will make them compatible?

When Tim performs this exercise and reviews his notes, he discovers that his casual approach to nutrition reflects his casual approach to leadership.

"Tully's such a smart pup," Tim claimed when he first got the Doberman. "He can take care of himself."

When this approach leads to nutritional and behavioral problems, Tim decides to assume the leadership role consistently to take the pressure off of his new pet. When he does this, he automatically seeks out the knowledge necessary to design a feeding program that meets Tully's needs as well as his own.

For many owners, feeding the dog ultimately takes about 10 minutes a day at most. By taking a little time to consider your feeding options before you get your new dog, you can imbue those few minutes with a quality that can add years to your pet's life.

Just as a training, exercise, and feeding program that optimally suits your and your dog's needs will do a great deal to ensure your pet's health, in the next chapter we'll see how the selection of a compatible health-care program will help ensure the best handling of those few problems that arise.

9

Well and Good

Selecting the Best Health-Care Program for You and Your Dog

When Dori Liu gets her new Akita pup, Kiley, she vows to do everything right.

"I love you so much, I'll never let anything bad happen to you," she promises the pup as she adjusts his brand-new red collar. "I'm going to do everything I can to keep you healthy, but if you do get sick, I'll use the herbs and other alternatives I use myself."

However, when Kiley develops diarrhea that evening, the new dog owner panics. She grabs a guide to the use of herbal remedies in people and frantically leafs through it, seeking a reference to something that would help her pet. Fortunately, Dori has some of the herbs suggested for diarrhea on hand. Unfortunately, when she gets up the next morning she realizes that her haphazard combination made Kiley's problem worse rather than better. That realization causes her to hurriedly flip through the phone book for the number of the nearest veterinary clinic.

"I'm sorry, we don't have evening or weekend hours," the receptionist announces after Dori describes her schedule.

Because Dori truly cares about her pet, she takes time off from work to take Kiley in for an examination. That experience leaves both owner and dog feeling more frazzled than ever. Not an empty seat remains in the crowded waiting room when they arrive for their appointment, and when they finally see Dr. Drennan, the veterinarian, he asks Dori a million technical questions that so intimidate her, she doesn't dare tell him about the herbs she gave the pup.

"Got a lot of hip dysplasia in the breed," Dr. Drennan comments as he pokes and prods Kiley. "Definitely ought to x-ray him."

Then Dori stands at the counter in the waiting room again, gaping at the bill she holds in her hand.

"When can you bring him in for those x-rays?" the receptionist asks while Dori struggles to make sense of what she and her dog have just experienced.

———————

As soon as they hear the phrase "responsible pet ownership," most people think of veterinary care. You get a new pup, you get it examined, vaccinated, and checked for worms. When it gets old enough, you get it neutered. As in human medicine, however, changes now occur so steadily in veterinary medicine that owners encounter ever more health-care choices, all of which can confuse even the most knowledgeable owner.

To put some order into this seeming chaos, let's begin with a few definitions, starting with the two broad categories of health-care options currently available:

- traditional medicine
- alternative medicine

Traditional health-care embodies the "team in white" concept, with scores of trained professionals and technicians using the latest science and technology to diagnose and treat disease or injury. Although referred to as "traditional," in reality this approach represents one of the most recent additions to the treatment lineup. Prior to the French Revolution surgeons ranked on a par with butchers, and the use of antibiotics to treat disease gained popularity only after World War II. Many of the techniques currently used in veterinary practice didn't even exist 50 years ago.

The "alternative" category essentially contains all other health-care options, including homeopathy, chiropractic, acupuncture, herbal remedies, and massage, among others. Although some traditional caregivers scoff at these approaches, many others have come to appreciate their value. Veterinarians who previously spoke only in hushed tones about their use of homeopathy now mention it in their ads in the yellow pages. For others, acupuncture now plays such an important role in the treatment of certain conditions that they no longer think of it as an "alternative."

Within these two categories, we find veterinarians and pet owners with two distinct orientations:

- problem-oriented
- prevention- or wellness-oriented

Problem-oriented veterinarians and owners focus their efforts on the treatment of diseases or injuries as they arise. Problem-oriented veterinarians keep track of the latest diseases and the latest tests and treatments, while owners with this orientation seek out the most qualified person to treat their animal's specific problem. When Dori brought her new pup home, she didn't give a thought to how their activities that first day might affect his health. However, as soon as she saw that he had diarrhea—a problem—his health became her overriding concern.

On the other hand, veterinarians and owners who take a preventive or wellness approach focus the majority of their efforts on practices they feel will protect the animal from illness and injury. Had Dori taken this approach, she would have realized how the excitement of a new environment can stimulate the canine gastrointestinal tract and paid closer attention to what she and her friends fed Kiley that first day.

Owners who want to understand more about their pet's health can find a variety of books that address the basics of both orientations. More-traditional, problem-oriented books range from general texts such as Carlson's *Dog Owners Home Vet Handbook* (Howell, 1992) and Bamberger's *Help! Quick Guide to First Aid for Dogs* (Howell, 1993), to those discussing specific problems of specific dogs, such as Wilcox and Walkowicz's *Old Dogs, Old Friends: Enjoying Your Older Dog* (Howell, 1991) and Brown's *Cocker Spaniel Owners' Medical Manual* and *Poodle Owners' Medical Manual* (Breed Manual Publications, 1989 and 1987). Books that take a traditional preventive view include Terri McGinnis's *Well Dog Book* (Random House, 1991) and the American Animal Hospital Association's *Encyclopedia of Dog Health and Care* (AAHA Publications, 1994).

Problem-oriented texts such as *The Doctors Book of Home Remedies for Dogs and Cats* (1996) and preventive ones such as Marder's *Your Healthy Pet* (1994), both published by the Rodale Press of *Prevention* magazine fame, bridge the gap between traditional and alternative medicine.

Both Dori and Kiley would have fared much better had she purchased a book that discussed the use of alternatives in animals rather than relying on the information in the guide she uses for herself. Schoen's *Love, Miracles, and Animal Healing* (Simon & Schuster, 1995) provides a general overview of the field. Prospective owners seeking more specific information can turn to Stein's *Natural Remedies for Dogs and Cats* (Crossing Press, 1994) or the classic, *Dr. Pitcairn's Complete Guide to Natural Health for Dogs and Cats* (Rodale Press, updated in 1995). Although some alternative texts tackle only one kind of problem, such as Pleichner and Zuker's *Pet Allergies: Remedies for an Epidemic* (Very Healthy Enterprises, 1986), most books focus on a specific alternative method such as homeopathy, herbal remedies, massage, or acupuncture which the authors apply to a broad range of problems.

Within the alternative preventive realm, Wolhard and Brown's *Holistic Guide for a Healthy Dog* (Howell, 1995) or the monthly holistic newsletter "Love of Animals" (call 800-861-5969 for further information) will introduce people considering this approach to the full spectrum of alternative options.

Health-Care Preference Evaluation

Before going on to the next section, think about what kind of health care would best meet your needs. Do you prefer traditional approaches, or do some of the new alternatives appeal to you? Do you see prevention and wellness as a viable concern, or do you prefer to treat problems as they arise?

Finding Dr. Right

In addition to all of those treatment options and styles, new owners can choose from an expanding pool of veterinarians maintaining a variety of views. Although many times tight schedules cause us to look for the closest clinic as Dori did, owners who consciously select the best practitioner to meet their and their new pet's needs will discover that caregivers break down into three main categories:

- god-player
- best friend
- facilitator

As the name implies, the god-players basically call all the shots. They see their job as diagnosing the animal's problem and determining the best way to treat it. In return for this service, they expect the owner to do exactly as directed and pay for all of this, willingly if not cheerfully. While some god-players such as Dr. Drennan can act pompous or overbearing, others radiate genuine warmth and concern. Exclusion of the owner from the treatment process, not the veterinarian's personality, is the distinguishing characteristic of this approach.

Best-friend practitioners express concern not only about your dog, but also about your kids, your home, your job, the local school board, and likely contenders for the World Series. While some of this may relate to your pet's health, much of it falls under the heading of "friendly conversation." Even so, a genuine concern for their clients as well as their patients usually motivates these veterinarians. Where Dr. Drennan couldn't care less where Dori works, his associate Dr. Stoner routinely asks about occupation to help put her clients at ease.

Facilitators offer their clients a wide range of options. A display of pet food, collars, and flea products may greet you in the waiting room. These practitioners may offer grooming, kenneling, and training in addition to a full range of treatment options designed to fit every budget and lifestyle. Although some owners find this approach confusing, those with changing needs often appreciate the wide range of choices provided.

While most veterinarians feel more comfortable in one particular role, any caregiver may adopt a different approach if he or she feels that doing so will better meet a particular owner's needs. Whether this works depends on that person's ability to determine the owner's needs accurately as well as the owner's willingness and ability to communicate his or her needs clearly. Dr. Drennan opted for the god-player approach when Dori plopped Kiley down on the examination table, then glanced at her watch when the veterinarian asked if she had any questions. He thought that glance at her watch indicated disinterest in the process. In reality Dori had many questions buzzing in her mind, but her concern about her boss's reaction to her extended absence drove them out of her head. While Dr. Drennan viewed her as disinterested, she felt exactly the same way about him.

Regardless of what they bring to the party, three equal partners participate in the health-care dance:

- the veterinarian
- the owner
- the animal

If Dr. Drennan and Dori agree on the purpose and form of any health-care program, but it doesn't meet Kiley's needs (for instance, he's allergic to the drug Dr. Drennan and Dori agree would help him the most), it won't keep the pup any healthier than if Dr. Drennan prescribes a treatment in which Dori doesn't believe and therefore gives her pet erratically, if at all. By the same token, if Dori asks Dr. Drennan to prescribe a treatment for Kiley with which the veterinarian disagrees (such as an herb or homeopathic remedy), this, too, could undermine the treatment process. Because of this, prospective owners need to evaluate any health-care package to ensure that it balances the needs of all three partners.

"Kiley's my first dog," Dori points out. "How can I possibly know whether a particular vet would work for us?"

Granted owners can't know this for sure until they get in that examination room with that particular veterinarian and that particular dog, but you can avoid unhappy surprises if you accumulate some basic information beforehand. Talk to pet-owning co-workers and friends, breeders, groomers, and animal shelter personnel. If a holistic or another alternative approach appeals to you, contact the American Holistic Veterinary Medical Association (2214 Old Emmorton Rd., Bel Air, MD 21015) for the names of practitioners in your area. While nonveterinarians skilled in the use of certain alternatives in animals do exist, their success depends on their ability to diagnose as well as treat a particular problem correctly. Given the differences between human and canine anatomy and physiology, and because a more *natural* remedy isn't always necessarily a *safer* one, veterinarians trained in both traditional and alternative medicine usually offer their patients the best blend of knowledge and experience.

The plethora of options available makes it tempting for the new owner to grab the phone book and pick the closest veterinary clinic and be done with it. However, the success of both the most sophisticated, advanced treatment and the humblest folk remedy depends, more than anything else, on the owner's faith in it. Because of this, the smart owner will select a form of health care and a practitioner most likely to strengthen rather than undermine that faith. Before you can do that, of course, you need to understand your own and your new dog's needs.

Dr. Right Want List

Envision your ideal Dr. Right. What kind of orientation does that person adopt toward you and your dog? Are there any times when you would prefer that person to use a different orientation? Ask your neighbors, your co-workers, and other pet owners about their veterinarians. Jot down any names that come up more than once for good or bad reasons, and list those reasons as well. The more specific your information, the fewer the surprises for you and your new dog.

Dori decides that under normal conditions she prefers the options routinely presented by facilitators.

"But if Kiley ever got really sick or hurt, I couldn't deal with it," she admits candidly. "Then I'd much prefer a god-player to take the matter out of my hands."

Or consider the Dr. Right criterion preferred by Dori's neighbor, Henry Woeshack, a somewhat reclusive writer who works at home. Henry wants his veterinarian to make all the minor decisions concerning the needs of his miniature poodle, Icy, but when it comes to something serious, he wants to know everything about the treatment process.

Owner Orientation Checkup

In addition to the concern that the vast majority of pet owners feel for the well-being of their pets, owners who lean more toward the anthropomorphic or chattel end of the orientation spectrum often respond the most erratically to canine health problems because they find the number, and often conflicting nature, of animal health-care programs so bewildering.

Consider what happened to Dori. Her company offers employees a managed health-care plan that essentially gives participants little choice. She doesn't like her assigned physician but doesn't want to go through all the paperwork necessary to switch to another who might not meet her needs any better. Because she doesn't trust the system she must use if she becomes ill, she develops an interest in alternatives as a means of protecting her health. When Dori got Kiley, she fully intended to find a veterinarian who shared her interest in wellness and the use of alternatives. But when the pup developed diarrhea so soon after she got him, her concern caused her to dash to the closest clinic.

"Who would drive right by a hospital looking for the 'right' one if they were critically ill?" Dori challenges.

Dori's question embodies two common errors. First, people who *know* about the kind of care they would get at a particular hospital and whether it fits their needs probably *would* drive by one, two, or even three facilities to get to one at which they felt they would receive proper attention. Second, while emotion undoubtedly comes into play, such a choice also arises from concrete knowledge: truly sick or injured individuals can't afford to waste time with health-care providers they don't trust to treat their problems effectively.

The key phrase here is "truly sick or injured." As I often tell students and owners, only knowledge separates an abnormal situation from a critical one. The less Dori knows, the more critical even Kiley's most minor ailment appears to her. Worse, the resultant fear for her pup's well-being drives her to focus on what little she does know: how *she* would feel if that happened to her; how *she* would treat *herself*. In other words, ignorance often forces us to respond anthropomorphically.

"Does that mean I can't apply the same preventive alternative approach to my dog?" Dori wants to know.

In this particular case, not at all. In fact, had Dori actually done that, she never would have made that first, disastrous appointment with Dr. Drennan.

Consider this alternate scenario: When Dori notices the diarrhea, she evaluates the situation objectively rather than emotionally. She remembers how excited Kiley acted when she brought him home, how he wolfed down his food, and all the snacks she and her friends couldn't resist giving the sweet little fuzzball. Then she takes his temperature and discovers it's within normal ($101°$–$102.5°F$) range and also notices his clear eyes, his nice pink, healthy gums, and his bright alert response to his surroundings. Finally, she recalls that the breeder had just wormed the pup and that the veterinarian gave him a clean bill of health two days before she took him home. Armed with that information, Dori decides to give Kiley's excited system a chance to settle down, so she takes up his water and doesn't feed him his evening meal.

"The hardest part was not to give in to the urge to medicate him with something. *Anything*," Dori admits later.

Although we might condemn owners who do nothing when their animals become ill as the worst examples of chattel orientation, always remember that the validity of any treatment rests on the amount of knowledge that underlies it. Giving the wrong treatment, or the right one at the wrong time, can cause our pets far more problems than doing "nothing" but offering them our emotional support based on concrete knowledge that this comprises the best approach.

Once Dori withholds food and water for 18 to 24 hours to give Kiley's gut time to settle down, *then* she can begin giving him small amounts of water (or ice cubes), then small amounts of a bland diet (such as boiled rice flavored with a little chicken breast), then gradually trade him over to the full ration of his regular food. On the other hand, if she immediately begins feeding him the bland food and water to make herself feel better, that diet could irritate his system and perpetuate his problem every bit as much as a less medically sound treatment.

Just to prove how easily owners can flip-flop between anthropomorphic and chattel views when it comes to health care, let's see what happens when Dori wakes up to Kiley's diarrhea the day she must make an important presentation at work.

"Just part of owning a puppy," she assures herself as she quickly cleans up the mess, her mind so engrossed with the impending presentation that she forgets to feed and water her new pet.

In this situation, Dori's blatantly chattel view of her pet leads her to treat him in a manner far superior to any anthropomorphic one which would compel her to force food and water on Kiley to prove himself "healthy" for her benefit.

"So, what's better?" asks the now confused new dog owner. "Doing the wrong thing for the right reason or the right thing for the wrong reason?"

Neither. The best solution means gaining sufficient knowledge to always make the right decision for the right reason.

Owner Orientation Health-Care Check

Take a few minutes to think about any health-care preferences you have for your new dog. Then imagine yourself encountering these three common animal health situations:

• routine care: vaccinations; flea control; heartworm preventative

- acute problems: sudden, explosive bloody diarrhea; broken leg

- chronic problems: recurrent ear infections; epilepsy; diabetes

Notice your response to them. Do you take a more objective, almost chattel view to routine care but become more anthropomorphic in times of emergency? Or vice versa: Do you act cool as a cucumber in an emergency but find that the idea of treating those chronic ear infections drives you up the wall? Once again, note whether your views arise from solid knowledge, pure emotion, or a combination of the two.

Health-Care Costs

How much will it cost to keep your new dog healthy? That depends on what you mean by *healthy* and where you live. The charge for a veterinary visit averages about $52 (and roughly double that for house calls) nationwide, with veterinarians in some areas charging anywhere from half to twice that amount. In addition, the definition of what owners must do to ensure their pet's basic health changes almost daily.

Take, for example, something as seemingly necessary and mundane as vaccinating the dog. Everyone knows that new pups need "puppy shots," but what does this mean? Kiley's breeder tells Dori to vaccinate her 8-week-old pup at 10, 12, 14, 16, and 18 weeks of age, then annually thereafter, and gives her the name of a mail-order company that sells vaccine to the general public.

"It's the same stuff the vets use and costs a fraction of what they'll charge you," the breeder informs the new owner.

Dori feels a little squeamish about sticking needles into her pet, so she calls Dr. Drennan's office to find out how much he charges.

"That'd be $28 for the examination and $14 for the vaccination," Dr. Drennan's receptionist informs her.

"What a rip-off!" Dori later tells Kiley. "I can get you a dose of vaccine for less than $10 from this mail-order place, and the more I buy, the less I pay for each dose. Now, let me see. Should I get you the one that protects you from distempter, hepatitis, adenovirus, and parainfluenza, or the one that also protects you from all that plus parvovirus, or the one that covers those five diseases plus leptospirosis, or this one that protects you from leptospirosis but not parvovirus? It's all Greek to me."

Dori interprets Kiley's inquisitive look to mean he doesn't have a clue, either.

"Well, since I can buy five doses of the most expensive vaccine that covers seven diseases and it'll cost me less than seeing Dr. Drennan once, that's the one I'll get you."

Several problems can disrupt this financially rosy picture. First, more and more veterinarians and scientists question the need for all those vaccinations. Not only do they see them as a waste of the pet owner's money, but some also question whether the stress placed on the animal's immune response by all those vaccinations may cause certain individuals to develop other problems as they get older.

Second, what kind of vaccinations a dog needs may vary greatly from area to area. While Kiley might need protection from all seven of those diseases, he might not. Or he might require protection from others that don't occur in the mail-order mixture Dori chose.

"But it won't hurt him to give him all seven, will it?" asks Dori. "Better safe than sorry, I say. Especially for that price."

When it comes to vaccinating your new dog, that particular truism doesn't necessarily apply. The more, different kinds of vaccine in a mixture, the more other additives and the greater the chance for an individual animal to experience an allergic reaction. A vaccine that makes Kiley's head swell up like a basketball and necessitates another frantic trip to Dr. Drennan's office doesn't save Dori any money. Or suppose that when Dr. Drennan examines Kiley, he discovers that the pup has ear mites, a condition Dori could treat with an over-the-counter or mail-order antibiotic ointment for months to no effect. During that same visit Dr. Drennan also tells Dori that two more doses of the vaccine he uses extensively in his practice will protect Kiley from the diseases in their area with no side effects.

Given all that, if you plan to self-vaccinate and self-medicate your new dog, you need to know all the basics of canine health as well as all the related idiosyncrasies of your particular locale, breed, and dog. So, put aside at least $50–150 for a canine medical library that includes books on canine anatomy and physiology in addition to canine medicine, and read and understand them before you get your new dog.

If you get your new pet from a shelter, the adoption fee may include a free or reduced-fee veterinary examination and a voucher that may cut the cost of neutering considerably, so don't forget to ask. Many veterinarians also offer discounts to senior citizens and, as the awareness of the value of the human-animal bond continues to grow, to people with special needs or on limited incomes.

In general, alternative and traditional options cost about the same when we take all the different factors into account. Although one acupuncture treatment for hip dysplasia definitely costs less than a total hip replacement, the dog may require the former on a regular basis for the rest of its life—and both treatments require the same preliminary workup and x-rays to determine the extent of the problem. The best approach remains to call the office of any potential Dr. Right and ask the charges for routine puppy vaccinations, worming, neutering, heartworm preventative, flea control, and anything else considered necessary in your area. Don't feel embarrassed; pet owners call for this information every day.

When the receptionist or office manager gives you those charges, make sure you understand what they include. Dori assumes that the price quoted for neutering Kiley covers every-thing. Imagine her surprise when she sees the additional charges for the examination, anesthesia, and hospitalization!

Also, don't forget to ask about any payment policies (cash, credit card) or payment options. When Dr. Right recommends a particular treatment for your pet, bring up the cost if he or she doesn't, and if you can't afford it or would need to make special payment arrangements in order to afford it, say so and make those arrangements *before* you agree to the treatment. If you can't afford it, ask Dr. Right to describe your other options. And don't feel guilty about doing this, either. Although some god-players might look askance at you for your concern about cost, and some truly insensitive clods might even imply that you don't love your dog, agreeing to a treatment you can't afford definitely will undermine your relationship with your pet as well as your veterinarian.

"What about those one-stop pet superstores with the vet right on the premises?" asks freelance writer Henry, thinking of his wildly fluctuating bank balance. "I hear they charge a lot less."

Whether this option will save Henry money depends on the veterinarian and the parent company's philosophy. If the veteri-narian meets Henry's and Icy's needs, then he can save some money. However, if the facility experiences a rapid turnover of veterinarians, if these practitioners perform only the most basic services, or if they spend a great deal of time trying to get Henry to purchase other products sold in the store, he might wind up spending more. When Icy suffers from a severe heart problem, a veterinarian Henry's never seen before tells him to take his pet somewhere else. Now Henry needs to locate and establish a working relationship with a new veterinarian under trying conditions.

Pet health insurance offers another financial option for contemporary dog owners. Although those unfamiliar with the concept may laugh, many who subscribe to the service swear by it. Annual premiums may run less than $50, with a $20–40 deductible, for coverage of everything from skin rashes to cancer.

If this interests you, check for ads in dog magazines (such as *Dog Fancy*) and discuss the option with your veterinarian. Because of the relative newness of pet insurance, some practitioners may not be familiar with the required paperwork. Others simply hate to do any kind of paperwork at all, so you may need to go to extra lengths to make sure the veterinarian or a competent staff member submits any claims on time. Theoretically, if the insurance company pays the veterinarian directly rather than reimbursing you, that's not your problem. Nevertheless, if paperwork-hating Dr. Drennan perceives Dori and her insured pet as needlessly complicating his life, that could undermine their working relationship. The last thing Dori needs when Kiley suffers from a serious illness or injury is a veterinarian who thinks of her and her dog as a pain in the neck.

Finally, it should go without saying that prevention costs less than treatment. Even at the high end of the scale, proper vaccination for a disease such as parvovirus can save you hundreds of dollars compared with the cost of treating your new pup for this devastating, life-threatening virus. A routine heartworm check ($15–20) and preventative ($20–50) definitely costs less than the $300-and-up to treat the disease. If Dori keeps Kiley on a leash ($10) and carefully monitors his path, she doesn't need to worry about his cutting a footpad ($75 and up) or getting hit by a car ($150 and up). If she picks up his waste in the yard ($0) and keeps him away from areas where other dogs soil ($0), she needn't worry about treating him for recurrent worm problems ($50–75). She can daily comb him with a flea comb ($5–10) and vacuum her home ($0), or regularly use some sort of chemical flea protection ($10–50) on her pet. If she does nothing, a flea infestation on her premises will cost her at least twice the latter amount to eradicate. She can buy Kiley tartar-control toys ($10–25) and brush his teeth (roughly $10 for a canine toothbrush and toothpaste) or spend $150 or more for anesthesia and professional cleaning when Kiley develops a gum infection.

A young woman I know lost her heart to a pet store pup, paid an exorbitant price for it and numerous accessories, and took advantage of the store's convenient financing plan to pay for it all. By the time she made those monthly payments, though, she could afford only the most minimal health care for her new pet. Because of this, her dog wound up suffering from one costly and preventable problem after another.

Health-Care Financial Analysis

Review any financial limits you determined for your new dog. Deduct the amounts you already allotted for any training, exercise, and feeding programs, and related paraphernalia. Determine how much it will cost for any initial vaccinations, neutering, and other medical care for your new pup or dog. Can you afford this? Then determine what health care your pet will require on an annual basis after that and see if that fits within your budget. Does your prospective Dr. Right offer different payment options to owners of new pups or in cases of serious illness or injury? Talk to other veterinarians, dog owners, breeders, and shelter personnel: Can you find less-expensive health-care options that would meet your needs? If not, could you free up the money from another area (such as by training your dog yourself rather than sending it to a professional)?

No Time to Get Sick

During the late '60s when more women began working, more families found themselves pressed for time, and with each successive decade the time crunch has gotten worse, even for single people.

"Why did you get a dog?" asks Dori's mother. "You're never home. What if he gets sick?"

All busy dog owners who know how much their dogs mean to them in spite of—or maybe because of—their hectic lives *hate* those questions. We barely have time to worry about what we'll do if we get sick ourselves, let alone if the dog does. That being the case, it makes good sense to consider how your schedule can affect your new pet's health.

First, recall that recurrent theme: it takes less time to prevent a problem than treat it. Every busy owner who could never find the time to initiate some form of flea control in the early spring lives to rue that decision when the demonically prolific parasites take over their pets and their homes in late summer. A more sensible course is to talk to the breeder, other pet owners, and veterinarians in your area to identify the potential health hot spots and learn how to prevent them.

Also think of any potential Dr. Right in terms of your time limits. It does Dori no good that Dr. Drennan ranks as one of the most highly qualified veterinarians in the world if she becomes so upset waiting to see him that she can't remember anything he says when she finally gets into the examination room. If she truly wants to make use of his services, then she must decide if and how she can alter her time limits to accommodate his style of practice. For starters, Dori could request the first appointment of the day. Not only would Dr. Drennan more likely be running on time then than at the end of the day, but also Dori and Kiley wouldn't need to cope with a crowded waiting room.

Dori also could ask if Dr. Drennan offers drop-off service. More and more practitioners invite busy owners to leave their pets at the clinic on their way to work, then pick them up at noon or at the end of the workday. While convenient, the success of this approach depends on the quality of the communication between the owner and veterinarian. Some practitioners provide preprinted forms for owners to complete with any necessary history, plus descriptions of any problems or services the owner wants to have addressed.

Obviously, the more information the owner provides, the more efficiently and effectively the veterinarian can treat the animal in the owner's absence. If Dori drops Kiley off with a hastily scrawled note requesting a "puppy shot" and "something for worms," she may get called out of a business meeting to describe exactly what puppy shot she had in mind and what kinds of worms she thinks Kiley has. If Dr. Drennan can't reach her, he may opt not to treat Kiley at all rather than treat him improperly; then Dori will need to take her pet back another time, or wait until Dr. Drennan can squeeze her in at the end of the day.

Day care also can benefit owners whose animals succumb to medical problems. When Kiley develops diarrhea, Dori keeps him at Dr. Drennan's while she works. That way she avoids two equally troublesome alternatives: crating her pup with diarrhea, or giving Kiley the run of a room in her newly carpeted apartment. She also uses the day-care option when Kiley develops an eye problem that requires medication more often than she can fit into her schedule. Dori relies on Dr. Drennan's technicians to medicate her pet for her while she works, then takes over the task herself during evenings and weekends. While Dori definitely will pay for this service, it will cost far less in both time and money than treating her pet under less than optimum conditions.

This raises another time consideration about health care: the most perfect treatment in the world won't work if your pet doesn't get it as directed, and it could actually make the animal worse rather than better.

"Isn't *some* treatment better than none?" Dori asks.

No. Suppose instead of taking Kiley in for day care or telling Dr. Drennan she can't medicate the pup three times a day for a urinary tract infection, Dori tries to tough it out. During the seven-day medication period, she treats Kiley three times Saturday and Sunday, then once or twice a day during the week, sometimes giving him two of his three daily pills at the same time.

At the end of the seven days, the pup seems a lot better but hasn't fully recovered. At this point, Dori faces two equally problematic options:

- finish out the medication
- do nothing and hope the problem gets better

Not only does giving pets antibiotics at a dose lower than that prescribed run the risk of prolonging the problem, disease-causing microorganisms can become resistant to drugs administered in low or irregular doses. Kiley's infection appears to respond to the first course of antibiotics, but then the problem recurs. When the veterinarian prescribes the same drug, it doesn't work at all.

If Dr. Drennan announces, "Here, give Kiley one of these every eight hours," but Dori leaves home at 7:30 A.M. and doesn't get home until 5:30 P.M., she needs to know whether her schedule will hamper the drug's effectiveness. While some of the newer drugs requiring only twice-daily administration may cost more, they may make sense because time does mean money for many owners. If Dori accepts a treatment she can't fit into her schedule and Kiley gets worse, she'll spend even more time caring for and worrying about her pet.

Owners also should view any alternative approaches with their own time limits in mind. Sometimes people maintain a mistaken impression that so-called natural approaches don't require the same conscientious attention as traditional ones. But just because the homeopathic remedy prescribed doesn't possess the potential to cause the same problems as an improperly used antibiotic, that doesn't mean it can't cause *any* problems. Any treatment not given properly can prolong rather than cure an animal's illness.

Finally, many owners who work in their homes appreciate veterinarians who make house calls. Because reclusive writer Henry dreads the thought of taking Icy to Dr. Drennan's bustling clinic, he arranges for Dr. Drennan's associate, Dr. Stoner, to come to his home. That way he can work right up to the time the doorbell rings, then go back to work as soon as he bids the veterinarian farewell.

Timely Health-Care Analysis

Review any time limits that might affect your choice of a health-care option. Can you fit your desired program into your schedule? Evaluate any prospective Dr. Right in relation to time: Does this person offer options that fit into your schedule? Talk to other dog owners whose relationships with their pets you admire and ask them for any time-saving health-care hints.

Emotionally Charged Health Care

Of all the emotional factors that can undermine canine health care, strong feelings about a problem or its treatment take the lead. Some owners can't bear the thought of medicating eyes or vaginas, seeing or smelling any kind of discharge (pus or blood), or using medication they find offensive in any way (color, odor, texture). In the latter case, we also see owners who don't want to give a certain medication to their animals because they experienced a negative response to it themselves, or read something about it that makes them distrust it. Steroids such as prednisolone and prednisone often fall into this category.

For certain, owners should never give their pets any form of treatment they don't support wholeheartedly or at least feel neutral about.

"What difference does it make?" asks Henry as he tosses a chewable heartworm preventative pill to Icy.

It can make a great deal of difference. More and more studies of the mind-body effect indicate that faith in the treatment greatly affects its success. Even owners who find that hard to swallow readily admit that if anything about the problem or the treatment bothers them, they don't pursue it nearly as conscientiously.

Henry agrees.

"I just don't feel good about giving Icy that cortisone for her itching, plus it makes her drink and urinate too much. I always cut the dosage back sooner than I'm supposed to and don't give the pills as long as directed because it bothers me."

Although Henry might get away with that when using cortisone for itching, we already know that administering other drugs, such as antibiotics, that way can precipitate disaster.

"But what can I do?" asks Henry.

Simple. Tell the veterinarian you don't want to use that drug, or that the thought of medicating your dog's eyes makes you faint, or that the stench of the medication prescribed makes you want to throw up. Insist on learning about your other options. If the veterinarian won't respect your needs, find another who will.

By the same token, don't choose a form of health care for your pet in which you don't believe. If Dori truly believes in alternative approaches and considers many traditional medical treatments detrimental, those negative feelings will affect her relationship with a traditional veterinarian and, subsequently, her pet's health. Even if Dr. Drennan's office sits right next door to Dori's apartment building, she never needed to wait, and he practically gives his services away, Kiley won't benefit from his care if Dori believes the veterinarian practices what she considers an inferior form of medicine.

A second emotional aspect of canine health care occurs in human health care, too. Parents and pediatricians—and caregivers who treat adults—often comment that illness causes many people to revert to more childlike, even infantile behavior. However, some fail to realize that sick individuals may act that way because the health-care professional or caregiver *treats* them that way.

To see how this works in the canine arena, let's look at a common scenario. Dori feels guilty about leaving Kiley alone all day while she works, but because she didn't take the time to establish a routine exercise program, her "quality" time with him usually consists of watching television with him after she gets home. One day when Dori comes home, she notices Kiley limping.

"Oh, you poor baby!" she cries.

When Dr. Drennan diagnoses a sprain, Dori fusses over the Akita and gives him more treats than usual during the following week until he recovers.

While this seems like a completely caring owner response, it misses the mark on two counts. First, Dori acts out of guilt. Second, her overly solicitous response actually rewards Kiley for his injury. The smart pup who wants attention quickly realizes that illness and/or injury wins him a lot more of that than acting healthy. Soon every time Dori gets ready to spend an evening or Saturday afternoon with friends, Kiley starts limping.

Remember that emotions tend to rule when we lack knowledge. If Dori feels comfortable about her lifestyle and her ability to provide a quality life for her dog, and if she knows the basics of canine health, then she won't allow her pup to manipulate her. By the same token, the fact that Kiley tries to do so should inspire her to teach her pet a few tricks, roll his ball, or put him through a few rounds of obedience while she watches television.

"But isn't that the same as giving in to him?" Dori asks as she lounges on the couch after a long day.

Not really, because we know that such activities build the dog's confidence. The more confidence Kiley possesses, the more adaptable he becomes. Given that, if Dori can't play with her pet, he curls up and goes to sleep rather than limps.

Finally, if you're one of those folks who can't bear the thought of your pet getting any kind of shot, let alone succumbing to a serious illness or injury, work through your options before you get your pet. Given an owner's ability to undermine as well as enhance a pet's health simply by virtue of his or her feelings about it, the last thing a timid owner needs is a timid pet.

In addition to choosing a stable animal, a timid owner should ask the veterinarian to examine and treat the dog in his or her absence if he or she can't handle it. Although ideally we should offer our pets emotional support at such times, an owner who can't should leave this to others who can. Any time Icy requires treatment that Dr. Stoner can't accomplish during a house call, Henry asks a friend to take the dog to the clinic for him.

"But what will he do if Icy gets really sick?" Dori wants to know.

Such a possibility should spur prospective owners to deal with their fears beforehand. Almost invariably they discover that their fears spring from a lack of knowledge. Because of this, such owners need health-care providers with whom they can communicate freely. When Henry somewhat ashamedly admits his fears to Dr. Stoner, she invites him to the clinic for a personal tour and explains exactly what will happen to Icy there and what he can expect. Many veterinarians will gladly give new owners tours of their facilities and/or explain what they intend to do to the animal during the examination before they begin, answering any questions the owner may pose. The catch is that if Henry doesn't recognize his emotional limits, he won't ask.

Another owner stress-relieving addition to canine health care takes the form of formal and informal support groups. While the formal ones almost exclusively help owners deal with the loss of a pet, informal collections of owners whose pets experience a wide variety of problems (epilepsy, diabetes, chronic skin problems) often form for the purpose of mutual support. If your new pet develops such a problem, ask your veterinarian for the names of others dealing with similar conditions, and contact them. I remain amazed at the ingenious ways busy owners find to cope with even the most serious problems, and I admire their willingness to share their experiences with others. Those with access to the Internet can find such support worldwide.

While knowing our emotional limits always plays a vital role, it's particularly beneficial when it comes to health care. The more worst-case scenarios you run, the less likely they'll occur, and the more likely you'll respond confidently when they do.

Health-Care Emotional Evaluation

Imagine your dog receiving routine vaccinations or other health care. Note any aspects of that process that bother you. If you don't know anything about the process, arrange to accompany a dog-owning friend on a veterinary visit, or call any prospective Dr. Right's facility to see if you could visit and ask some questions.

Next, think about how you would feel if your dog became ill. Jot down any kinds of ailments you feel you couldn't deal with and note why you feel this way. Then note what, if anything, could change your mind, and if you see that as a viable alternative. If not, what will you do under these circumstances?

Owner Physical Limits and Dream Dog Health

Stuffing a pill in a dog's mouth, medicating an eye, ear, or paw, lifting a dog up and putting it into a tub for a medicated bath, and many of the other activities that fall under the heading of "treating the dog" involve physical interactions that communicate dominance. When Dori gives Kiley a pill, she wraps her hand over his muzzle, curls his upper lips over his upper teeth, opens his mouth, tilts his head back, shoves the pill as far back into his mouth as she can get it, then holds his mouth shut until he swallows it. If she practices this beforehand, she accomplishes it quickly and with minimal stress to either herself or her pet.

However, what if Kiley doesn't recognize Dori's dominance? In that case, as soon as she wraps her hand around his muzzle to open his mouth, a power struggle ensues, and Dori can medicate her pet only if she can physically subdue him. Although she might succeed with the 15-pound pup, she probably won't with the 85-pound adult.

"No problem," Dori shrugs. "I'll just put the pills in his food or get some kind of chewable tablets."

Although many owners who can't handle their pets take this approach, it begs the issue rather than resolves it. Also, not eating ranks as one of the most common signs of illness in dogs, which pretty much rules out medicating the food. In addition to posing that same problem, chewable or flavored medications usually cost more and come in limited forms. Back in the days when both an unflavored and flavored daily heartworm preventative were more widely available, I'd ask new owners to give the unflavored one for the first year. By the time that period ended, not only did they feel comfortable physically handling their pets, the dogs also recognized their owner's authority.

If you're physically unable to administer any treatment for any reason and no family or friend can do it for you, tell your veterinarian immediately. Some clinicians may suggest day care during the treatment period; others may switch to an injectable form of medication which the animal receives in once- or twice-daily visits to the clinic. When a broken wrist makes it impossible for Henry to give Icy the necessary medicated baths, he asks Dr. Drennan's staff to do it for him.

Another aspect of owner physical limits concerns what will happen to the dog if something happens to the owner. One unexpected benefit of selecting a stable, social animal and providing even the most basic training is that any number of folks will often volunteer to take the animal if the owner can no longer care for it. It's a standing joke among my friends to ask, "Can I have Violet if you die?" Nonetheless, people who live alone or those with medical problems especially should give this some thought for their animal's sake. What if Dori becomes involved in a car accident on her way home from work and no one even thinks of Kiley until two days later when she regains consciousness and asks, "How's my dog?"

By federal law, anyone admitted to a hospital must now provide an advanced directive (a living will), and many people prepare this document beforehand, picking up the necessary forms at the local hospital or library. They then give copies of it to trusted family members and friends, in addition to keeping one on file at the local hospital and carrying a card in their wallets indicating its existence. Caring owners also include any pets in this process, noting whom to call to care for the animal(s) in the event they can't.

"That's gruesome!" exclaims Dori. "I don't even want to think about it!"

Perhaps not, but prevention always paves the better path. By making advance provisions for her pet, Dori saves herself from all the worry involved if she becomes incapacitated. While some more enlightened hospital admissions clerks do ask about any animals at home, and some areas even provide volunteers to attend these animals' needs if the owner can't, the more responsibility owners assume for this themselves, the more likely their pets will receive quality care in their absence.

One final note: Several veterinary colleges now provide special facilities to care for animals in the event their owners predecease them. For those who desire top-notch, state-of-the-art care and treatment for their pets but don't want to burden friends or family members with this responsibility, this option offers a great deal of comfort. If such a program interests you, ask your veterinarian for the name of the school nearest you. Even if that particular school doesn't offer such a program, they should be able to give you the names of those who do.

"I gotta admit, thinking about that made me feel pretty spooky at the time," Henry confesses later. "But when I broke my wrist, it was a tremendous relief knowing I had a friend ready and willing to care for Icy."

Physical Limits Evaluation

Review any physical limits you noted previously as they relate to your new dog's health, imagining yourself giving your new pet pills, bandaging a foot, bathing it, and so on. Jot down any problems you see occurring. Next, think about what will happen to your new pet if something happens to you. Who will take care of it? Talk to the person or persons you have in mind. Do they share your feelings?

Environmental Health-Care Concerns

The familiar statement "Cleanliness is next to godliness" goes back to ancient Hebrew law and arises from an awareness that basic cleanliness can do a great deal to prevent many health problems that curse human and beast alike. Dr. Drennan can know more about veterinary medicine than anyone in the world, but if he's lax about the cleanliness of his instruments and his facility, he can do Kiley more harm than good. If Dori becomes so enthralled by her veterinarian's equipment and technical jargon that she misses the odors and the dirty cotton balls and used syringes strewn about the counter, Kiley may pay for this oversight later. Granted cleanliness doesn't guarantee competence, and vice versa, but prospective owners should strive to find a practitioner with both qualities rather than one or the other.

If your dream dog will need professional grooming, evaluate the groomer's facilities for cleanliness, too. When Dori can't keep up with Kiley's thick coat and it gets matted, she selects the closest groomer sight unseen.

"Why didn't you ask me first?" Henry chides her later when she tells him about the skin infection Kiley developed after the groomer clipped him. "I know for a fact that woman never disinfects or cleans her clipper blades except when they're so dull they don't cut anymore."

Health-Care Professionals' Environmental Check

When you collect pertinent data about the health-care professionals you want to treat your dog, don't forget to evaluate their environments, too. Does the facility appear clean and odor free? If you tour the facility, notice the cages where the animals are kept. Although animals in strange surroundings do soil their quarters, their caregivers should routinely check for this and replace any soiled bedding.

Granted, if Dori doesn't keep Kiley and his quarters clean at home, even the cleanest veterinary facility and the best antibiotics won't prevent him from becoming sick. Nor will the best grooming job keep Kiley's skin healthy if he spends most of his time lying in a filthy crate or pen in Dori's home, or if she never grooms him.

Nevertheless, despite the best of care dogs occasionally get sick or injured, so it makes sense for prospective owners to run environmental "what-if" scenarios, too. For example, let's ask Henry and Dori what they'd do if their dogs came down with a gastrointestinal virus and experienced a few episodes of vomiting or diarrhea. Where would they keep them?

"That's easy," Henry pipes up. "I'd put Icy in the bathroom with her crate. That way if she did mess, she'd still have a clean place to sleep, and I could clean it up easily."

The brand-new wall-to-wall carpeting in Dori's apartment rules that out, so she gets a heavy 9' × 12' plastic tarpaulin for just such emergencies, and uses it to cover the entire floor in the small room to which she confines Kiley in her absence. If the problem proves more than she can handle, she takes advantage of Dr. Drennan's day-care service.

What-if scenarios also should take into account that, just like ill or injured people, ill or injured animals need a certain amount of peace and quiet. For our dogs, that means an environment in which they feel secure. Obviously, if something threatens Icy under the best of circumstances, she may well feel more threatened by it when her stomach churns or her leg aches. This brings us back to private space. Because Henry free-access crate-trained Icy, the poodle can retreat to her crate next to his bed when she feels stressed. Henry also uses this behavior as an early-warning system.

"She only goes into her crate when my nieces and nephews come for a visit or if she's not feeling well, so I pay particularly close attention to her when she does," he explains. "A few times I know I picked up a problem much earlier than I normally would have because I noticed her doing this."

Home Environment Health Check

Recall those areas in your home you thought would meet your dream dog's needs for a personal space. Now imagine your pet suffering from an illness or injury in that same environment. Could you keep this space clean? Would it provide the necessary security for your sick pet under these circumstances? If not, how could you improve it when such conditions arise?

Finally, evaluate your environment for disaster preparedness. All the recent devastating hurricanes, tornados, earthquakes, floods, and fires nationwide make this a legitimate concern. Heartbreaking stories abound of owners whose pets took off during a disaster or were turned away from crowded human shelters.

"That's terrible!" exclaims Dori. "I don't even want to think about it!"

Few people do, but once again, prevention can save the day. Consider the following contents of a typical do-it-yourself disaster kit:

- two days' supply of the dog's usual dry and/or canned dog food plus a can opener
- gallon jug of water
- plastic bowls for food and water
- leash
- copies of your pet's vaccination records
- a photo of your pet
- a week's supply of any medications your pet needs
- first aid kit including:
  rectal thermometer
  clean washcloths or gauze sponges
  1" adhesive tape
  2" elastic bandage
  Kaopectate or Pepto-Bismol
  hydrogen peroxide
  muzzle
  first aid manual

In our worst-case scenario, a major hurricane heads right for Dori's small coastal town. While other pet owners race around frantically, she picks up the large plastic bag containing the disaster kit and Kiley's crate and heads out the door with her pet. Some disaster shelters now accept animals provided they're in crates. If they don't, emergency facilities set up by animal shelters certainly do. Naturally, people maintaining shelters want and need to know the vaccination history of any animal guests, and Dori can provide this immediately.

If Kiley did happen to get loose, the photo will help others identify him. More and more owners also now have their pets injected (in a simple procedure) with an identifying microchip whose numbers animal shelter personnel or others armed with scanners can read. They then call a national registry for the owner's name and address. Still other owners tattoo their pets and enroll them in similar national registries.

In both cases, however, the person who finds the dog must know to look for such identifiers, and the dog must allow that person to do this. Consequently, in addition to selecting stable animals, training them well, and identifying them with microchips or tattoos, pet owners in disaster-prone areas often use distinctive collars to further help distinguish their dogs. Although most of Dori's neighbors couldn't tell the difference between an Akita and a malamute, they all remember the fuzzy dog wearing the bright red-and-blue collar with the sequins on it.

The photo also helps because, although it seems hard to believe, a lot of owners really can't describe their pets in much detail, especially amid the chaos of a natural disaster.

"She's a little gray, poodly sort of a thing," a flustered Henry tells the overworked shelter volunteer. "Black nose. Looks like a button."

Granted the emergency food and water supply in the disaster kit won't last forever, but at least it will provide some nourishment in a form familiar to the dog. Kiley's excited gastrointestinal tract doesn't need a new brand of dog food as he copes with all the other changes.

"Why the muzzle?" Dori asks apprehensively.

Every first aid kit should contain one because a frightened or injured dog may bite; even if it wouldn't, owners who fear this will respond in a less than confident manner when the animal needs the owner's assurance the most. A lightweight nylon muzzle works well, as does an old nylon stocking or strip of gauze bandage long enough to loop around the dog's muzzle and then tie behind its ears.

By replacing the food and water and updating their kits routinely (some owners do this when they move their clocks forward and backward in the spring and fall), owners can take some of the worry out of a worrisome situation. Such kits are also a boon to people who travel with their pets. Rather than packing for Kiley as well as for herself when she goes to visit her folks, Dori simply takes the disaster kit and then replenishes anything she used when she returns.

Disaster-Preparedness and Travel Check

Imagine you and your dream dog needing to make a sudden and unexpected trip away from your home, possibly to a strange and limited environment. What would your pet need? How easily could you pack and transport this?

When Dori ran this scenario, she made two major changes in her dream dog programs.

"First, I decided not to cook for Kiley myself," she recalls. "The weather's so iffy around here during hurricane season, we could be evacuated at any time. I couldn't see lugging an ice chest with his food in it, plus worrying about spoilage in addition to everything else. Second, I decided to take a mixed traditional and alternative approach to health care. That way, if Kiley needs help, I'll feel comfortable with whatever kind of care we can get."

Had Dori lived in a home with an auxiliary power source and/or a woodstove in an area where natural disasters primarily took the form of snowstorms that trap dog owners in their homes, she would have stayed with her original programs.

Breed Health-Care Considerations

Thanks to the increased numbers of purebred dogs and the increased capacity to study them in detail, we now have a much clearer picture of breed-related problems than in the past. Thirty years ago, a pamphlet could contain a description of all the known genetically transmitted canine problems. Today that same information requires volumes, and even those volumes address only medical problems. It seems reasonable to expect that a comparable amount of data will result when scientists begin seriously studying the genetics of canine behavior, too.

Because breeding and judging primarily for looks can create health problems, it behooves prospective dog owners to evaluate their dream dogs from this perspective. Although ideally the breeder serves as the most reliable source of the most specific information, that's not always the case. Some breeders and breed books naively insist that their dogs possess no faults—a nice thought, but not a particularly realistic one. If you make the effort to get the names of others who own animals from a particular breeder and ask those folks about any health problems their pets may have experienced, that will give you a much broader view.

Depending on the author, breed profiles in magazines such as *Dog World* or *Dog Fancy* can be brutally frank or suspiciously vague about any physical or behavioral problems in a particular breed. Puppy selection books that explore a wide variety of breeds tend to offer general but more objective information. Do bear in mind one phenomenon as you peruse such texts: the more you've set your heart on a particular breed, the less likely you'll pay attention to any negative information about it. I can't tell you how many times owners say, "I never would've gotten this dog if I'd known the breed had hip (eye, skin, liver, allergy, biting) problems," even though they had the information right in front of them.

Aim for a solid mental image of a physically and behaviorally healthy animal, and then select the breed and individual that match that image, rather than try to impose that image on a breed or line that may lack those particular qualities. Henry maintained some vague image that he wanted a "happy dog" which he decided Icy fit the instant he saw her. She's definitely a happy dog, a good thing because any nastiness on her part would make her bum knees, epilepsy, and heart, skin, and ear problems even more of a chore for Henry to treat.

One way to get valid information and meet any potential Dr. Right is to make an appointment to discuss getting a new dog. That way you can evaluate Dr. Right as well as his or her facility, and get valuable information about specific breeds and individuals from breeders and shelters in your area all at the same time. Some veterinarians even maintain computer databases with the latest breed-related information. After Dori narrows her dream dog breed to Akitas, golden retrievers, and malamutes, she makes an appointment to discuss the merits of these three breeds with Dr. Drennan. He calls up each breed on his computer and points out relevant health issues for her consideration. Then he discusses the local sources of such dogs—breeders, rescue groups, pet stores—and provides her with information based on his experience with animals from these sources over the years. By the time her appointment ends, Dori possesses solid information not only about her dream dog's physical soundness but also about Dr. Drennan and his facility.

Dream Dog Physical Soundness Check

Think about your dream dog's physical and behavioral health. How much do you really know about it? Where does this information come from? Once again note whether it comes from solid knowledge or emotion.

Like many other prospective owners, Dori fell in love with Akitas when she met a happy, well-behaved one belonging to someone she found equally attractive. This created such a positive image in her mind that she projected it onto the entire breed, not unlike the McKelveys in Chapter 2 when they began their frustrating quest for the perfect golden retriever to match a fond childhood image. The same can happen with any breed of dog. Just as a blue ribbon in the showring doesn't guarantee physical soundness and good behavior, a stable temperament doesn't guarantee good health, and vice versa. What we see in one dog in no way holds true for an entire breed.

Healthy Leadership

So often when we think about getting a dog, we think about what the dog will do for us. What we must do for the dog often occurs as an afterthought and usually focuses on fulfilling the animal's physical needs. However, nowhere does human leadership with our pets come into play so critically as it does in health care.

Returning to the recurrent theme that good leaders claim their leadership position by virtue of knowledge, what kinds of health-related knowledge do good leaders accrue for their dogs' benefit?

Above all, good leaders recognize what's normal for their breed of dog as well as for their individual animal. Because Dori knew that Akitas can experience hip, leg, thyroid, and eye problems, she selected a breeder who addresses these conditions in his breeding program. She also realized that other factors besides genetics contribute to these conditions, so when Kiley developed hip problems as he got older, she didn't rant and rave about it, but rather focused all of her attention on the best treatment.

On an individual level, Henry knows exactly how much Icy normally eats and drinks, her normal schedule of urination, the consistency and frequency of her bowel movements, her normal temperature, and the normal color of her gums. Because of this, he can spot changes in his pet much more quickly than an owner who lacks this knowledge.

Because both of these owners took the time to locate and establish a good relationship with a veterinarian they trust, they convey confidence rather than apprehension to their pets during any veterinary examination. Even though it hurts Icy when Dr. Stoner examines her swollen paw, the poodle sits calmly in Henry's lap because she senses his calmness. Whereas her response arises from her trust in him as the leader of their human-canine pack, Henry's calmness arises from his knowledge that Dr. Stoner always will treat his pet with the utmost concern for both man and beast. In this way, dog, owner, and veterinarian form a unit based on knowledge and the trust that results from knowledge. This, in turn, literally creates a healing environment.

"You're kidding!" Henry laughs. "It sounds nice enough, but . . ."

Recall how we and our animals affect each other's physiology as well as behavior. Imagine two scenarios. In the first one, Henry takes Icy to the veterinary clinic where he sits in the waiting room, two activities that make him irritable. Finally he sees Dr. Drennan, whom he doesn't particularly like. In the second scenario, Henry asks Dr. Stoner, whom he likes very much, to examine Icy in his home. In the first situation, the sensitive little poodle easily could experience a purely stress-related elevation in heart rate, pulse, and temperature, and maybe even some vomiting or diarrhea as a result of the negative feelings she picks up from her owner. Not only can this compound any other physical problems she might possess, but it also clouds the issue for Dr. Drennan as he tries to sort out what symptoms denote a serious threat to the dog.

In the second scenario, Henry communicates his positive feelings about both his environment and Dr. Stoner to his pet. As a consequence, any changes the veterinarian detects in Icy most likely relate to a specific medical problem.

Realizing how his feelings increased the pressure on his pet, Henry saw switching to a veterinarian who makes house calls as the best way to meet his own and his dog's needs. On the other hand, because Dori's budget didn't allow her to do this, she did everything in her power to make her visits to Dr. Drennan's as stress-free for herself and Kiley as possible. She asked for those first appointments in the morning to avoid waiting, took advantage of Dr. Drennan's drop-off and day-care services, and got over her fear of him enough to raise the issue of using alternatives on her pet. Much to her surprise, he openly shared his views on the subject with her.

Whether Dr. Drennan agrees or disagrees with Dori, the fact that she overcame her fear and raised an aspect of her pet's health that concerns her enables her to make a decision based on knowledge rather than emotion regarding the person she chooses to help ensure Kiley's health. If Dr. Drennan agrees with her views, then she gains a valuable ally; if he doesn't, she either can find a veterinarian who does or change her views so they don't undermine Kiley's health.

In addition to this, Dori trains and interacts with her dog in such a way that he always recognizes her authority. That both helps preserve his health by relieving him of all the stress associated with leading a human pack, and enables him to relax and concentrate on getting well when illness or injury occurs.

Compare Kiley's calm response with that displayed by dogs who are forced to lead their human packs and who become nervous and edgy when illness strikes because of their increased sense of vulnerability. Instead of just barking at the meter reader, the dog-leader with the intestinal virus feels obligated to bite him, too. Sadly, a lot of unknowledgeable owners will *excuse* such behavior, saying, "He's not feeling well." Worse, some of these dogs won't even let anyone medicate them, including their owners. Medical problems that should resolve in a week drag on and on and even grow worse because the same lack of human leadership that predisposes the dog to many health problems thwarts their treatment when they arise.

Although a lack of human leadership invariably creates problems for our dogs, when it rears its ugly head in the health-care arena, it acts like a cancer, eating away at what could and should have been a healthy relationship.

Health-Care Leadership Analysis

Review all the notes you made about the different aspects of health care for your new dog. Then review your notes about your dream dog and your leadership style in the preceding chapters. Are your views about canine health care compatible with your dream dog and leadership style? If not, what can you change to make them so?

Dori considers herself a relatively anthropomorphic owner with limited time and money who leans strongly toward alternatives and prevention, gets easily upset when something goes wrong with her dog, and finds it difficult to ask her canine best friend to do much of anything. However, she also discovers that her dream dog belongs to a powerful, independent breed that requires firm and patient handling and can develop specific breed-related medical problems. When she realizes the essential role her relationship with the dog plays in any wellness program, as well as in the successful treatment of any health problem, she trades in her more passive leadership style for a more active one.

The magic formula that underlies other programs in the preceding chapters still applies: the more you know about yourself, your dog, your environment, and your leadership style, the more likely you'll be to select a program that will work for you. The more you know about all the health-related problems that could occur and how to avoid them, the less likely your dog is to experience them.

Congratulations! You now know, or know how to find out about, a great deal more than the average dog owner. Not only that, you've learned enough about yourself and your dream dog, environment, and leadership style to give form and substance to that once hazy vision that began with the thought, "I want a dog." Given this foundation, let's close with a consideration of what you can do throughout your pet's lifetime to maintain the wonder of that special relationship.

10

A Dog to Keep Forever

Maintaining a Lifelong Living and Learning Program for You and Your Dog

L
enny Lacota, a top-notch auto mechanic, owns one of the
healthiest, best-behaved dogs in Holderness County.
       "I treat Nika the same way I treat my car," he admits
with a twinkle in his eye whenever anyone compliments him on the
magnificent Samoyed. Then he laughs and tells them about the
"1,000-mile checkups" he's given Nika ever since she was a pup.
       "Don't want her breaking down or losing her control
on some tight curve, do I?" he chuckles as he rubs the furry
snowball's ears.

Throughout this book, we've examined the greatest influences on the human-canine relationship, and how to use your
specific knowledge of these variables to select the best training,
exercise, feeding, and medical programs for you and your new
dog. At the same time, we observed many different owners con-
fronting a range of situations with an assortment of dogs under
a variety of common and not-so-common circumstances.
Throughout, we've seen the dynamic nature of contemporary
dog ownership.

"I learned a lot," agrees Lenny's neighbor Libby Faulkner as she stares at her collie, Ryan, and her collection of lists and notes, "but what if Ryan's or my needs change? I teach preschool full time and can't imagine I'll be able to find the time to go through all this whenever that happens."

Certainly situations may arise—moving from an apartment to a house, divorce, illness—when rereading sections of this book may help you analyze your options more clearly. However, once you master the basics, you can incorporate them into your relationship with your dog in such a way that they hardly take any time at all. To help owners do that, I like to use a simple, at-home monthly health, behavior, and bond checkup that takes less than five minutes.

"No way!" laughs Libby waving her stack of notes.

In spite of Libby's skepticism, it does work. Although you can wait until you get your new dog to try the following exercises, you may want to borrow a friend's dog to practice these skills beforehand. That way when you check out any possible dream dog candidates, you can examine them then and there and gain valuable information about the animal.

The At-Home Checkup Basics

We'll begin with a description of the mechanics of the checkup and the components of particular medical significance, then we'll move on to what the examination tells us about an animal's behavior and the human-canine bond.

As soon as Lenny got Nika, he started giving her regular at-home physical and behavioral checkups for several reasons.

"First, after I read up on the breed and talked to breeders and others who own Samoyeds, I knew I couldn't let an active, intelligent, vocal, independent dog with a thick coat like that get ahead of me," he explains, signaling to Nika to jump up onto the picnic table in the backyard while he picks up her brush. "Second, I wanted a dog I could take to work with me, and that meant one whose behavior I could trust completely. And third, since I don't have much time to treat medical or behavioral problems, I needed to pick up any signs of change as early as possible before things got out of hand."

Because of this, Lenny routinely and systematically examines Nika from head to tail. To do this, he places her on a solid table, keeps his hands on her at all times to prevent her from jumping off, and talks to her in a soft, reassuring (not whimpering!) tone to alleviate any apprehension she may feel. Next, he steadies her head and looks in her ears, noticing their color and checking for any odor or discharge. Depending on the breed and individual, the color of the inside of the ear flap and ear canal ranges from almost white to pink, and you'll detect a slight odor—which I personally don't mind, but which does bother some people—and usually no discharge.

Though this description may sound a bit vague, it points up the need to know normal for your own dog. Perfectly healthy dog ears do emit different odors; my own dog Watson's almost-white, hound dog ears smell much doggier than Violet's pinker corgi ones. Violet produces a small amount of ear wax, whereas Watson's ears remain spotlessly clean. The outer ear canals of some other breeds, such as poodles, may naturally sport a fair amount of hair.

Dream Dog Ear Check

Put your new pet or a friend's dog on the floor or a solid table, and look in both of its ears. Notice the color, odor, and any discharge. Make notes about what you see if necessary. Do *not* probe the ears with swabs. If you see something that strikes you as unusual, look it up in your breed book, or ask the breeder and/or your veterinarian about it. Also note how you feel about performing this examination and how the dog responds.

Next, Lenny cups Nika's chin in his hand and raises her head slowly until he looks directly into her eyes. When he does, he checks for any discharge. He doesn't see any, but owners of dogs with protruding eyes such as poodles and some brachycephalic (squashed-nosed) breeds such as Pekingese may notice discharge, as may owners of shar-peis, Saint Bernards, and some hounds with droopy lower eyelids. This doesn't occur because these animals necessarily produce more tears, but rather because their conformation interferes with normal tear drainage.

If the tearing appears excessive or if the dog squints, don't accept the breeder's explanation that "all these dogs do that." Protruding eyes may obstruct the tiny drainage ducts in the inner corners of the upper and lower lids, while the ducts in droopy lower lids may lie too far away from the eye itself to do much good. Exactly the opposite condition may occur in these same and other breeds, too: the eyelid may roll inward, not only blocking the tear duct, but also irritating the eye itself. In dolichocephalic breeds (those with long noses and deep-set eyes such as collies and Shetland sheepdogs), any discharge may collect in the corner of the eye next to the nose. Libby's new collie, Ryan, normally wakes up with a small amount of a clear grayish, gelatinous substance in the corner of each eye.

As long as the amount and appearance of the secretion in Ryan's eyes remain the same, it poses no problem. However, if Libby notices a change in color and consistency—to a cream- or greenish-colored pus—that condition requires medical attention. Obviously, if you notice anything that strikes you as out of the ordinary in a dream dog candidate, have your veterinarian examine the animal before you buy it. If you're considering a breed prone to eye problems, check with owners of other animals from that breeder so you'll know what to expect.

To complete the eye check, Lenny steadies Nika's head and pulls down her lower eyelids with his thumb, once again taking note of color as well as any evidence of swelling. In addition to telling us about the eye's health, this soft tissue (the conjunctiva) that lines the inner surface of the lids can provide other valuable clues. Normally it appears pink and relatively smooth; a swollen one would definitely indicate conjunctivitis (inflammation) which could be caused by an infection or an irritant. On the other hand, a relatively smooth conjunctiva with a yellowish or very pale pink to white color could indicate serious problems that run the gamut from liver disease to shock and blood loss associated with injury.

Dream Dog Eye Check

Follow the process described for checking your or a friend's dog's eyes to determine normal for the animal. Don't forget to jot down any notes about anything you consider unusual, then consult the proper sources to find out more about it.

Next, Lenny examines Nika's mouth. To do this, he wraps his hand over her muzzle and lifts her upper lips to expose her teeth and gums without opening her jaws. He checks the color of her gums because, just like the conjunctiva, this serves as an excellent indicator of general body health. To determine Nika's normal color, Lenny presses his index finger firmly on the gum just above her upper canine tooth (fang). This forces all the blood out of that area, and, when he releases the pressure, he can see a distinct difference between this whiteness and the natural pink of the rest of her gums. Some dog gums normally contain areas of pigmentation that form dark spots or streaks. If you see a chow chow in your future, however, you can forget the gum color test: the tongue and gums of this breed appear uniformly black rather than pink. Regardless of color, healthy gums also appear smooth and evenly moist—neither sloppy wet nor dry to the touch.

Once Lenny checks Nika's gums, he examines all of her teeth on the outside, making sure to pull the corner of her lips all the way back so he can see the upper and lower molars tucked in the area where the lower and upper jaws converge. He also notices the normal color of the gums immediately above the teeth because any redness or swelling in this area could indicate periodontal disease.

To examine the inside of the Samoyed's mouth, Lenny curls Nika's upper lips over her upper teeth, places the index finger of his other hand in her mouth, and gently but firmly presses downward until she opens her mouth. Once she does, he slides his finger farther back, pressing down on her tongue to give himself a clearer view of her throat and the inside of her mouth.

Once again, what you'll see depends on your dog's breed. Because the squashed-nosed brachycephalics must cram all their teeth into a relatively small space, the soft palate that forms the back part of the roof of the mouth often hangs down and blocks inspection of everything else. On the other hand, put that same number of teeth in Ryan's long jaws, and we see gaps between some of his teeth. However, even though the collie's soft palate doesn't occlude the opening to his throat, the narrowness and length of his muzzle make it as difficult for Libby as it was for Lenny to see much in that area.

Although some people feel queasy about smelling a dog's breath, don't forget to take a whiff while you're conducting your canine oral examination. Puppy breath definitely smells different from adult dog breath, and if you don't know what your pet's breath normally smells like, you'll miss the change in odor that can signal liver, kidney, or digestive problems, as well as those involving the teeth and gums.

Dream Dog Mouth Check

Examine your dog's mouth. Note anything that strikes you as unusual. Also note your dog's behavior and your feelings about performing this part of the examination. Consult the usual sources if anything strikes you as unusual.

Next, Lenny repeatedly runs his hands over Nika's body from head to tail and down all four legs, ending his sweep by picking up each foot to get a feel for her coat and general body condition. During his first pass, he checks her coat, including its odor. Her thick coat feels and smells quite different from that of a smooth-coated greyhound or even Libby's full-coated collie.

If Lenny feels anything abnormal in Nika's coat, he examines it more closely. Longer haired dogs may develop tiny tangles under their ears which, if not removed, may become large mats that not only bother the dog, but also may lead to skin infections. Smart dog owners also pay particular attention to the coat and skin around the base of the tail. Little dark specks in this area could mean fleas, a common cause of allergic reactions in dogs.

"How can you tell it's not just dirt?" asks Libby as she parts Ryan's fur and scrutinizes the area.

If any doubt exists, sprinkle some of the specks onto a wet paper towel, and let them sit for a minute or two. Because fleas feed on blood, their waste (also called "flea dirt") contains dried blood products. When dampened, flea dirt dissolves and turns red, while dirt remains black.

The second time Lenny runs his hands over Nika's body, he focuses on her skin and anything he can feel within or beneath it. With a little practice, he can feel the lymph nodes where the lower jaw meets the neck, those in the axillary ("armpit") area, and those on the back surface of the lower hind legs. Whether he feels lymph nodes, cysts, or tumors, the basic questions remain the same:

- What's normal for my dog?
- What does this lump feel like: Is it smooth, lumpy, attached (to muscle or bone?) or freely moving, within or under the skin?
- What does this lump look like: Is it the same color as the skin, or does it appear darker or lighter?

During the third pass, Lenny does a weight check by placing both hands flat on the sides of Nika's chest, then sliding them slowly forward and backward. He should be able to feel her ribs, but not any great dips and valleys between them.

"How can you tell fat from fur?" asks Libby as she sinks her hands into Ryan's thick coat.

Although owners of all but the smoothest-coated overweight dogs may dismiss their pets' pudginess with an "Oh, that's not fat; that's just fur!" the two feel quite different. As long as you work your fingers through the coat to the skin before conducting the test, you should experience no difficulty determining how much fat underlies the skin.

Some people say optimum-weight dogs possess a definite "waist" area behind the ribs, too. Looking down on the dog from above, the body should curve inward on either side. When viewed from the side, the body wall should curve upward from the end of the chest toward the tail. While this serves as a good indicator in some breeds and individuals, bear in mind that pups don't develop these contours until they get older, and also that poor conformation on some dogs—a barrel-chested rottweiler with poor hips, for example—may obliterate it.

Dream Dog Coat, Skin, and Weight Check

Evaluate your dog's coat, skin, and weight as described. Once again, note anything you discover that requires explanation. Also note your dog's behavior during this part of the examination, and your feelings while you conducted it.

In the final part of the physical examination, you palpate your dog's abdomen to feel what's going on inside.

"Be serious!" laughs Libby. "I'm not a veterinarian!"

That's what Lenny said, too, when he started giving Nika checkups as a pup, but now he can feel all sorts of things during the exam.

"It's easy," he encourages Libby. "Just close your eyes and imagine you're trying to guess what's inside a soft bag. Put your hand flat against your dog's belly, press firmly and gently upward as far as you can, then bring your fingers and thumb together and let things slowly slide through them as you move your hand from the backbone down."

Libby looks at Lenny in awe as she struggles to palpate her wriggling pup.

"You really can feel something? I thought I felt something hard and kind of round up near the chest, but it pretty much feels the same everywhere else."

In fact, Libby felt a kidney that first time, and soon she can feel Ryan's stomach and bladder. Even more important, she learns what a relaxed, neither painful nor tense canine abdomen feels like, and how her dog looks and acts while she palpates him. If she wants to know the exact names of the various structures, she can refer to a canine anatomy text, or ask her veterinarian or veterinary technician to help her.

Establishing a solid mental image of a relaxed normal abdomen so that you can pick up any signs of distension or discomfort is the primary goal. Owners who don't know what their dog's abdomen normally looks like, let alone feels like, will miss early signs of problems.

Dream Dog Abdominal Check

Palpate your dog's abdomen as outlined in this section. Note anything you feel and its location. Notice how your dog responds to this part of the examination as well as your own feelings while doing it.

Finish your health check by lifting your dog an inch or so off the floor or off the table before you return it to the floor.

It may seem hard to believe but once you get used to handling your dog in this manner, you can accomplish the entire examination in one smooth motion that takes about two minutes. Even more amazing, we've discussed only a third of the information you eventually can collect in those few minutes.

The Behavioral and Bond Tune-Up

Another advantage of the at-home physical examination lies in its ability to incorporate the behavior and bond facets of the human-canine relationship. Consider this list of ways in which owners physically interact with their dogs during a routine at-home examination:

- placing hands on the dog's head, neck, or shoulders
- establishing eye contact
- wrapping hand around the dog's muzzle
- opening the mouth
- holding the paws
- lifting slightly

Virtually all of these displays communicate dominance to the dog. Because Lenny knows this, when he gives Nika those first examinations and the Samoyed turns around and tries to push his hands off her head and shoulders, resists ear examination and establishing eye contact, and tries to pull away when he examines her feet and lifts her off the table, he suspects that his happy-go-lucky pup wouldn't hesitate to take over their human-canine pack if given a chance.

"The way I saw it, I couldn't take a bossy dog to work with me every day," he later recounted. "Nor did I have any intention of fighting with her to keep that heavy coat in shape."

In addition to selecting training and exercise programs that utilize Nika's high energy level and intelligence, Lenny gives her the at-home examination daily at first, then twice-weekly, then weekly for the first year. Although he does look for any physical changes, he performs the examination this often primarily for behavioral reasons. By the end of the first year, Nika stands

patiently for her checkup, even when a visiting five-year-old performs it. Needless to say, her veterinarian and all the vet techs
can handle her effortlessly, too.

Compare this with Libby's experience. After she gets Ryan,
she never finds the time in her busy schedule to master the basic
skills of the at-home checkup.

"That's what we have vets for," she explains as she rushes
off to her aerobics class.

To Libby's disappointment, her failure to make this initial
investment and take the few minutes necessary to maintain it
produce the following results:

- Ryan develops all the problems associated with a lack of
  human leadership.
- Libby misses the early signs of medical problems.
- She can't properly groom her dog.
- She can't properly medicate him when he becomes ill.

As if all this weren't bad enough, Libby's veterinarian dreads
seeing Ryan because he knows he'll need to ask his technician
to restrain the dog. Worse, the collie sets up such a fuss that it
upsets Libby and affects all of his body functions, making it difficult to give him a decent examination. To put it mildly, this
owner's lack of time during this critical period will cost her
dearly throughout her dog's life!

During the examination I asked you to note the dog's behavior and your own feelings as you conducted each part of it.
Those notes will give you valuable insights about your owner orientation and leadership style. Let's see what Libby's comments
reveal about her and her relationship with her new pet.

Ears

Ryan: no problems
Me: a little queasy about sniffing them

Eyes

Ryan:	wouldn't let me pull his lower lids down
Me:	afraid I was hurting him; made me feel *really* queasy

Teeth and gums

Ryan:	kept pulling his head away; once I thought he wanted to snap
Me:	very uncomfortable and a little scared; I'm positive wrapping lips over his teeth hurt him

Coat, skin, weight

Ryan:	kept trying to get off the table; tried to pull away when I touched his feet
Me:	got frustrated and angry when he wouldn't hold still; yelled at him and almost smacked him when he pulled his feet away; then I felt guilty and gave him a treat

Abdomen

Ryan:	no problems
Me:	got very frustrated because I couldn't feel anything

Based on our discussions in the previous pages, I'm sure you can identify the comments that spell trouble for Libby and Ryan just as easily as I can. Not only does Libby approach the task emotionally, she also lets those emotions rather than any solid knowledge guide her. Because she doesn't feel comfortable examining Ryan's eyes and mouth, she sees discomfort rather than the dog's reluctance to accept her leadership as the reason he resists handling. However, when she does something she considers innocuous, such as checking his coat and lifting his feet, she becomes angry and frustrated when her pet doesn't share her view. Instead of asking herself what she and her dog communicate to one another via this behavior, she yells at him and then feels guilty about it and gives him a treat, essentially *rewarding* him for acting up.

The practice of giving ill-mannered dogs treats deserves further discussion. Sometimes out of ignorance, but almost invariably because they feel bad about the experience, some animal care folks as well as owners will give treats to dogs who misbehave when they try to work on them. Somehow these people assume that the treat will make the dog realize it had nothing to get upset about and decide to act better the next time. Unfortunately, such thinking flies in the face of everything we know about conditioned responses in all animals, including people. In reality, the treat reinforces the behavior that preceded it. Therefore, giving an unruly or obnoxious dog a treat loudly and clearly communicates, "I simply *adored* the way you leaped off the table and tried to bite the veterinarian and peed all over me. Please do it again the next time, too!"

So, if your groomer, veterinarian, or some member of the clinic staff offers you a treat for your dog, think twice before you give it to your pet. If Ryan didn't do anything *extraordinarily* good during his visit, Libby should save the treat until he does.

Dream Dog Behavioral Checkup

Review the notes you made regarding your dog's behavior during the examination. Designate the behaviors (ears back, trembling, cowering, urinating, rolling over during abdominal palpation) that express subordination with an "S" and those that express dominance with a "D." Then consider what these behaviors tell you about this animal.

We already saw how Lenny realized that Nika would require some extra effort on his part when he examined her. Suppose when Libby examines a pup she's considering, the animal trembles and cowers, then rolls over and urinates.

"I'd just *have* to take the poor thing home!" she exclaims.

No, she'd just *have* to read Chapters 1 through 4 again. Given her anthropomorphic orientation, limited time, hectic lifestyle, and environment, plus her tendency to make emotional rather than knowledge-based decisions, the last thing she needs is a submissive pup for which she feels sorry. Not only will the animal not provide her with the stable human-canine relationship she needs, but her orientation and lifestyle will make such an animal's problems worse, not better.

Bond Checkup

Review your notes about your own feelings as you examined your dog. Note whether each arises from emotion (E) or knowledge (K).

When Libby recognizes that most of the feelings she experienced during Ryan's checkup not only arose from emotion rather than knowledge, but also contributed to his negative behavior, she takes a two-pronged approach to the problem. First, she reviews her orientation and leadership style as it affects her pet.

"I realize now that I can't afford to be as anthropomorphic and laid back with him as I thought I could," she remarks as she makes Ryan hold a long down before she feeds him.

In addition, Libby employs a very useful self-help technique alluded to in previous chapters called *imaging*, used in areas as diverse as medicine and sports. Basically, while Libby sits stuck in traffic or at a boring faculty meeting, or as she lies in bed last thing at night or first thing in the morning, she imagines herself giving Ryan his examination in a confident and deliberate manner. As with imaging golfers who improve their scores almost as much as their friends who practice every day, all of Libby's mental training pays off. Using this approach, she can preview every step of the process in detail and focus on potential trouble spots. She can also imagine herself conducting the examination at a slower or faster pace to determine the rate that will enable her to do her part most naturally.

"But what if Ryan doesn't respond as perfectly as he does in my images?" Libby asks as the collie races around the yard like a furry tornado.

This question raises two points. First, because imaging occurs within the safety of your mind, you can easily cover all the worst-case scenarios—and I strongly recommend you do. The more probabilities you anticipate, the better you prepare yourself to respond in a positive and knowledgeable rather than emotional manner. Second, the very act of doing this generates confidence, and that enhances your presence. The more you envision yourself confidently examining your pet in one fluid, almost effortless motion that you both enjoy, the more confidently you'll approach your dog and the task.

When it comes time to examine Ryan, rather than worrying about how she and the dog will react to every step of the process, Libby simply recreates the scene she's experienced so many times in her mind's eye. She smoothly and confidently picks up her pet and puts him on the table, talks to him soothingly (but not submissively!), looks in his ears and eyes, examines his teeth and gums, calmly runs her hands over him, palpates his abdomen, gives him a hug, and puts him down on the floor. Just like that. The very smoothness of her actions communicates leadership to her dog, and he responds by standing quietly for a process he previously viewed as a power struggle he easily could win.

Some trainers like to say it's all in the hands, but it isn't really. So much of enjoying a solid relationship with a healthy, well-behaved animal begins in our minds.

Puppy Checkups

We already noted the advantages of giving pups more frequent checkups during the first year—daily to once or twice a week depending on the animal's behavior and the owner's confidence level. Now we need to look at any special challenges a particular canine life stage may present and incorporate them into the routine examination.

In addition to experiencing a great many physical changes, puppies undergo significant behavioral changes. In general, pups accept human and other animals most readily between the ages of three and fourteen weeks, with a period of optimum socialization occurring at six to eight weeks of age. However, right smack in the middle of this, the fear-imprint period occurs between the pup's eighth and tenth week. Memories of frightening events that happened during this period tend to persist longer—and even permanently—compared with those of similar events occurring at other times.

Further complicating matters, and yet another reason to take the time to find a qualified breeder if you desire a purebred dog, is the fact that different breeds and even pups from the same litter may mature at different rates. I recall one line of miniature poodles that could no sooner leave their mother at six weeks than fly. They barely grasped the concept of eating and drinking, let alone making it on their own in a human household.

Unfortunately, these variations in canine development can destroy the unprepared owner's schedule. Libby gets her new pup at eight weeks of age, which sounds right because this age group falls well within the socialization range and even takes advantage of a week of the optimum period.

"He'll have plenty of time to adapt to me and my friends and their dogs," the excited new owner explains.

However, though the socialization period may extend to week fourteen, two of these following six weeks paradoxically can produce exaggerated fear for the eight-week-old pup as well as the socialization responses. As soon as Libby gets her new pup, she takes him to the veterinary clinic for an examination, a disastrous experience because she knows nothing about what to expect, and she communicates her fears to her dog. Then she takes him to visit all of her friends and their pets, and even throws a "Welcome, Ryan" party for the pup, "to get him used to everything at once." By the time the fear-imprint stage ends, Ryan carries the imprint of more than enough fears to last him a lifetime.

So, what to do? Some experts advocate avoiding the fear-imprint stage completely by getting a pup younger than eight or older than ten weeks. However, lifestyle and environment play a big role here. It doesn't benefit Libby to get a new pup during the maximum socialization period if she can spend only evenings and weekends with him. Under those circumstances, the pup will fare much better if he stays with his littermates, the breeder and her three kids, eight dogs, two cats, and assorted neighbors, repairmen, and other distractions of everyday life, including that trip to the veterinarian's. If Libby doesn't know this, or if she chooses a breeder whose lifestyle offers the pup as restricted an environment as her own, then Ryan will miss this valuable socialization opportunity.

"What if the pup's living conditions are so bad that even my erratic lifestyle would be an improvement?" Libby asks.

Although I know Libby doesn't want to hear this, she should look for a more reputable breeder. No matter how much she may love her new pup, she doesn't have the necessary time and lifestyle to get a poorly socialized animal happily through the fear-imprint stage. Lacking these, she surely will lack the time and lifestyle necessary to deal with all the medical and behavioral problems this kind of early experience can precipitate.

Delaying getting that new pup until after the fear-imprint stage also may result in some benefits relative to the dog's sense of self. Although puppies lacking human contact during their early days don't make good pets, those lacking a sense of their "dogness" don't fare too well, either. Because so many busy owners feel guilty about their relationships with their dogs, this immediately places an anthropomorphic overlay on the relationship. In an attempt to make up for all the time she spends at work. Libby takes Ryan everywhere with her when she's home and spoils "her little baby" rotten. This kind of experience at this age could leave Ryan feeling as confused about his identity as his owner, and that can set him up for all of the function-related problems discussed earlier. If he gets a good start in a solid environment instead, his owner's behavior won't undermine his sense of self as much.

Making a successful transition, then, relies on a thorough knowledge of the breeder's and your own lifestyles. While the breeder's interactions with his or her animals should closely approximate that which you envision for yourself and your new dog, don't look just at your life now. Think about it over the next 10 to 15 years. True, single Libby rarely interacts with any young children *now*, but she does see marriage and a family in her future. Therefore, she should put interactions with children on her dream dog's list of early puppyhood experiences and also ask children to conduct at-home examinations on her new pet.

"What if I leave my new pup at the day-care center run by a local trainer?" Libby wonders. "Will that give him the right kind of early experiences?"

It depends on the center. Some of these offer excellent socialization programs, while others consist of little more than organized dog packs with minimal human supervision. Though the idea of their dogs gamboling with other dogs strikes a responsive chord in the heart of guilt-plagued working owners, spending eight hours a day playing by dog rules with other dogs could create more problems for the pet than it solves. Because of this, if you see doggy day care in your new dog's future, use the same process you used to evaluate a potential breeder or veterinarian.

Another ingredient to add to the puppyhood stew takes the form of early neutering programs. Some shelters now neuter young pups before they place them. So far this appears to cause no problems, but the newness of the programs means there's no long-term data available to evaluate. At this time, your best course is to select only the most stable animal under these circumstances, and pay particular attention to the cleanliness of the facility and the handling of the animals. Surgery at a young age, even under the best of conditions, creates a major stress. Consequently, these animals need a clean, stress-free environment to minimize any ill effects.

Early Socialization Check

Think about your lifestyle and environment as they relate to a pup's early socialization and the fear-imprint stage. What can you do to maximize the former and minimize the latter in your situation?

Because Lenny could take his new dog to work with him, he got Nika at six weeks of age and exposed her to a wide variety of sights, sounds, people, and animals during their first two weeks together. However, Libby didn't pick up Ryan until after the fear-imprint stage because the breeder could expose the dog to a much more varied but still controlled environment.

Finally, do yourself and your new dog a big favor during this period by not ever letting the words "He'll (She'll) outgrow it" fall from your lips. Busy owners can't afford to waste this wonderful period in hopes that some miracle will occur to cure any problem later. True, it might happen. As Ryan's breeder claimed, he might actually stop chewing the instant all of his permanent teeth come in and he "gets used to them" at 6.27 months. On the other hand, think of what all those negative feelings related to the destroyed objects (including hands!) can do to the relationship during that same period. Think about how much more time it will take Libby to teach Ryan not to chew her shoes after she tolerated the behavior for months in hopes he'd outgrow it.

If your new dog does something that bothers you, don't make excuses. Deal with it then and there.

Puppy Checkup

When you talk to people who own dogs belonging to your dream dog's breed, ask them about the dog's puppyhood experiences. Note any remarks about house soiling, chewing, and other environmentally destructive behaviors, as well as whining, barking, and other displays that you or your neighbors might find troublesome. Also take notes regarding the kinds of lifestyle, environment, leadership style, and training programs of owners whose dogs' good behavior impressed you. Can you duplicate these in your own household? If not, can you meet your dream pup's special needs some other way?

Growing Pains

Like children, dogs also go through adolescence, and it can complicate the busy pet owner's life as much as a parent's. Once again, different animals may experience this stage of development at different times. If backed into a corner and threatened with bodily harm, I'd probably define adolescence as the period between five months and two years of age. My great reluctance arises from the awareness of three canine realities. One, a tremendous amount of variation can exist among breeds, lines, and individuals. Two, the nature of the owner's relationship with the animal can affect how long this period lasts. Just as babying sick individuals can cause them to act babyish, routinely treating dogs as little babies can stunt their behavioral development. Three, the absolute necessity to rectify any behavioral problems during this period looms so large that I don't want to provide busy owners with any excuse to delay dealing with these *immediately*. I find nothing more disheartening than to face an unruly, growling, snarling year-old dog and its distraught owner who keeps murmuring, "I'm sure he'll settle down when he gets older."

Because these owners often chose to believe this because they didn't take the time to develop the leadership skills necessary to handle the unruly pup, they now face the much more difficult and time-consuming problem of handling an unruly teen. Obviously, if Lenny backs off from a 15-pound Nika when she growls, he'll find it extremely difficult to confront this same behavior in a 55-pound one-year-old.

Like parents of teenagers, often the first sign owners of adolescent dogs notice takes the form of selective amnesia. One day Nika, who always obeyed the "come" command, looks at Lenny, grins, and heads off in the opposite direction. During this period, that puppyhood basic comes into play even more: Don't make excuses; deal with it.

Above all, don't fall into the trap of thinking the dog does this to make you angry or to spite you or to get even with you for leaving it alone, or to punish you for paying attention to the new boyfriend (baby, job, home, etc.). Many times young pups respond very well to training because it fills their needs for function plus enables them to stay close to us. As their confidence grows, they begin to test the limits, a period that provides owners with a good time to test their own limits, too.

If the apparent loss of civilized behavior represents a transitory canine developmental phase, a little brush-up training may do the trick. However, if the problem arises because of boredom or frustration, then you need to reevaluate your lifestyle and environment in terms of your dog's needs. I remain amazed at the number of people who get a new pup, go through several months of intense at-home training and interaction with it, and then expect the animal to take it from there. This basically amounts to toilet training a child, teaching the child to eat with a fork, and saying, "You're on your own, kid. I gotta go to work."

When canine behavior deteriorates during adolescence, an interesting phenomenon may come into play. Because a fair number of people don't even think about "formal" training (i.e., obedience classes) until their dogs reach six months of age or older or until problems arise, many adolescent dogs populate formal training programs. In this situation, the following sequence occurs: the dog gets a function (learning the commands), the owner now interacts with it in a meaningful way on a daily basis (giving the commands, correcting and praising the animal), and the dog's behavior improves, all of which build dog and owner confidence and positively affect the relationship.

If the dog remains well behaved following the end of the course, a temptation exists to say the dog merely needed to learn those particular commands. And that may be true. However, if the dog reverts to problem behavior following the end of the class, the relationship and the environment deserve further scrutiny. In my experience, the vast majority of owners who experience ongoing or recurrent problems with their pets don't set aside enough time for tri-level (physical, mental, and emotional) exercise with their dogs. Because of this, their "exercise" consists of the diagnosis and treatment of one behavioral and/or physical problem after another.

Sexual maturity also occurs during adolescence and raises the question, "To breed or not to breed?" It would take an entire book to discuss all the reasons why people want to breed their dogs—and possibly a degree in psychiatry to evaluate all those reasons properly. Suffice it to say that breeding requires a tremendous amount of time, energy, and knowledge to do well, and the world already has more than enough dogs with genetically transmitted medical problems and breed-related behavioral problems.

Statements such as "He comes from a line of champions," "She's such a wonderful dog," and (most telling) "I've always wanted to have puppies" simply don't support breeding. Rather, the decision to breed should result from a thorough knowledge of that breed's physiological and behavioral genetic background as well as that of the two individuals you intend to breed, the types of environments where the resultant pups will go, and a willingness to accept the responsibility for those animals, no matter what happens. So, before Lenny thinks about breeding Nika, he should ask himself what he would do with eight more dogs if he can't sell all the pups, or if their owners return them for any reason at any time.

A discussion of breeding and neutering may automatically elicit images of pregnant females, but we also must include males in this component of the adolescent equation. If Lenny can't decide whether he wants to breed Nika, he'll have two or three heat cycles over the next 18 months to think about it. In Lenny's case, coping with one heat cycle with its 7 to 10 days of spotting and three weeks of dealing with every free-roaming male dog in the county quickly changes his feelings about pet parenthood. Granted neutering a female after her first heat increases her chances of developing mammary (breast) cancer, but it doesn't usually negatively affect her behavior.

On the other hand, when Libby postpones neutering Ryan until after he reaches sexual maturity at seven months, no surgery short of a frontal lobotomy will alter the leg-lifting and other territorial displays that kick in with that adolescent surge of male hormones. Because of this, and because it requires so much knowledge to breed properly, make this decision well *before* you get your new dog.

Also, because establishing and protecting the territory takes precedence over reproduction, adolescence may precipitate an increase in territorial behavior. During this period untrained "protective" dogs can become more so, and naturally more territorial animals or those who feel threatened by their environments may produce more anal gland secretions in an attempt to respond to the deeply rooted instinct to mark their territories. However, because many dogs lack the necessary wherewithal to empty these glands (most likely thanks to selective breeding to make sure they *wouldn't* secrete the foul-smelling substance), the contents may build up, causing the dog to drag its rear end on the ground or lick its anus and the area around it. Although tapeworms can cause a similar display, in my experience anal gland problems occur much more commonly. Because these glands can become impacted and infected, ask your veterinarian to check them if your dog develops this behavior. If the problem recurs, evaluate both your environment and leadership style, looking for ways to take some of the territorial pressure off your pet.

Finally, both neutering and the attainment of sexual maturity can decrease your dog's caloric requirements. Rather than blaming your pooch's pudginess on the veterinarian who spayed or castrated it, cut back on the amount you feed it. It really is that simple—provided you don't equate food with love. If you do, this aspect of your relationship will begin to haunt you at this stage of your dog's life and pursue you throughout your relationship.

Adolescent Checkup

Pause here and imagine your dream dog as an adolescent dog in your home. How do your views of leadership, training, and breeding hold up given the changes that occur during this period? Update your list of questions for the breeder, shelter personnel, or your veterinarian, if necessary, to reflect your concerns.

After thinking it over, Libby decides to take advantage of a local puppy kindergarten class rather than wait to attend the obedience class for dogs six months of age or older. Lenny makes a note always to ask the veterinarian to check Nika's anal glands, and incorporates more commands into her interactions with him and others at work to increase her sense of function.

The Age of Fulfillment

Between the ages of two and four, most dogs achieve their maximum in terms of their physiology and psychology, a good-news/bad-news period depending on the owner's orientation and leadership skills. Dogs who enter this period in the leadership role can become extremely resistant to change. After all, they got away with it before when they were smaller and inexperienced: why shouldn't they get away with it now? Owners of dominant leader animals who delude themselves that their pets in this age group will outgrow the problem live in a dream world. Similarly, owners who expect their shy or timid animals to suddenly become courageous at this age could stand a little reality therapy, too.

Dogs who enter this life stage with behavioral problems not only won't outgrow them, a very strong probability exists that these problems will become worse as the dog gets older. This occurs for two reasons. First, if the dog feels pressured to growl and snap at visitors at its physical peak, it's highly unlikely it will become *more* tolerant of strangers when normal aging changes make it feel more vulnerable. Second, it can take an inordinant amount of time and owner commitment to reverse behavioral and relationship problems in animals in this age group. Because these problems often arise because the owners didn't take the time to nail down the basics with the young pup when it required *less* time, the probability that the owner will summon *more* time to correct the now much more firmly entrenched problem seems unlikely.

From my own experience and discussions with other behaviorists and trainers, I find that a significant number of owners of problem animals in this age group go through the motions of getting professional help—put a Gentle Leader collar on for a week or two, try one or two psychotherapeutic drugs, and even make a sizable financial investment—merely to convince themselves they *tried*. That is, they consciously or subconsciously feel no desire to make the necessary changes in themselves and the dog to ensure lasting change. Then when the subject of the dog's behavior comes up, they say, "We tried everything. Even took him to a dog shrink and spent I don't know how much money. But nothing worked. It's just the way Satan is."

Anthropomorphic owners who decide to breed their dogs at this stage may discover that their babies much prefer human to canine companionship. Lenny introduces Nika to a handsome male Samoyed, and she stares at him blankly. When the dog tries to perform his masculine duty, she screams in terror and runs to Lenny for protection. Similarly, Ryan's forays into breeding make better fodder for a canine identity crisis newsletter than an article in *PlayDog*.

Other times, a female dog treated anthropomorphically will breed with few problems but then refuse to care for the pups. After all, *she's* the baby: why should she clean and nurse those squirmy little things? Some of these females will take the "You wanted them, you take care of them" approach, while others become snappy and irritable, neither of which do much for the mental stability of the litter, not to mention that of the busy owners who wanted to breed their loveable dogs.

Unfortunately, once again trying to reverse the damage caused by long-standing relationship problems can require a great deal more time than many owners will gladly spend.

Finally, dogs in this age group more commonly will attempt to move into the leadership position if no clear leader exists. At one year of age, Ryan let Libby yank him away from the front door when he menaced strangers; at two, he turns around and snaps at her when she grabs for his collar. Within multiple-dog households, an animal in this age group may decide its combination of greater physical strength but less experience give it a good shot at taking on an older, more experienced animal with a touch of arthritis. While the solution to the former situation involves getting the owner to assume a leadership position under the worst circumstances, the latter constitutes normal canine behavior that shouldn't faze good human leaders and their relationship with either dog.

Libby shakes her head in disbelief.

"How can you call it the 'Age of Fulfillment' with all those horrible things happening?"

I deliberately chose to describe first what can happen to owners who *don't* take the time to lay a solid foundation with their pets during puppyhood and adolescence to emphasize the importance of doing so. For those who do, everything they and their new dogs worked so hard to create together suddenly gels. If Lenny forgets to give a command on occasion, it doesn't matter; Nika automatically sits by the front door or won't get out of the car until he tells her to. He doesn't always need to win, either, because he and Nika both know who's in charge when it really matters. When Lenny returns home after a week's vacation, three-year-old Nika flies into his arms and joyfully slobbers all over his face, a behavior he adores now but never allowed the rambunctious, independent pup to display because of the dominant message it conveyed. Before, Lenny liked to believe he and Nika thought and worked as a unit. At this age he knows they do.

Age of Fulfillment Want List

Imagine yourself with your dream dog during the age of fulfillment. Make a list of all the things you would like to experience with your pet at that time. Do your orientation, your leadership style, and the programs you selected for your dog support that image? If not, what can you change to make them more compatible?

When Libby imagines herself taking Ryan to the summer camp where she counsels disadvantaged youngsters, she decides that the more anthropomorphic view and "best buddy" style of leadership that appear to work for her now won't prepare him for the challenges that lie ahead.

Middle-Age Mellowing

After the age of fulfillment comes the mellowing of middle age, those years around seven. As with middle-aged people, middle-aged dogs require fewer calories to maintain their optimum weight, and also as in people, some require fewer calories than others. Thus, if Libby gets into the habit of feeding Ryan four cups of food a day and feeds him that same amount throughout his life, he'll gain weight at middle age if she doesn't increase his exercise proportionately.

Unfortunately, busy owners of older animals often get caught in a vicious cycle. Ryan's weight gain makes it impossible for him to keep up with Libby when she hikes. This makes her feel so sad that she gives him a treat. When she feels guilty about leaving him at home while she goes off to climb a nearby mountain, she puts a little extra food into his bowl. When friends ask why Ryan doesn't hike with her anymore, she tells them he can't because of his "bad hips," unmindful of the fact that the excess weight put the excess strain on his hips in the first place.

Within the behavioral arena, dogs who resist yielding the leadership position in the age of fulfillment may become more amenable to change during middle age—provided their owners consciously assume the leadership position. Owners who don't will find that their dogs become increasingly edgy and intolerant as the normal physical changes associated with aging make the animal feel more vulnerable. Chubby, middle-aged Ryan doesn't bother to growl and snap at the meter reader anymore because he can't afford to give the man any warning. Instead, he just bites him.

However, for owners who take the time to develop their leadership skills and select training, exercise, feeding, and health-care programs that can evolve with their and their pets changing needs, middle age brings its own rewards. True, the fact that I'm middle-aged myself might prejudice me, but although I do enjoy the excitement and challenges offered by a young pup and the feeling of stretching the limits a good stable dog can evoke during the age of fulfillment, I particularly relish the mellowing that comes with middle age. The playful puppy prankster and two-year-old practical joker give way to a mature adult who can leave me in stitches with a look or action so subtle, it could come only from an animal who knows me intimately. Where Violet's failure to respond to the "come" command in puppyhood or the age of fulfillment hinted at all kinds of safety and leadership problems that demanded immediate attention, now when she sees me walking toward her to repeat the command, she stops what she's doing and stares right at me as if to say, "Well, geez, I found this really neat smell over here and I didn't want to leave it, but you know I wouldn't leave the yard, so there's no need to make a big deal about it, is there?"

Then I'll laugh and squat down and command in a terribly serious voice, "You get over here this instant or I'm going to give you to someone who makes you sleep on the floor and eat worms," and she flies into my arms.

Middle-Aged Dream Dog Check

To learn how much owners' orientations, lifestyle, breed, environment, and leadership style can affect middle age, look at animals in this life stage, too, when you collect your dog-related data from friends and breeders. Note the qualities that appeal to you about these animals and their relationships with their owners, and the qualities that trouble you. Compare these owners' orientations, lifestyles, environments, and leadership styles with your own. Do you need to make any fundamental changes now in order to have the dog you want in the future?

When Libby conducts this exercise she discovers two important facts. First, many of the hereditary problems that occur in purebred dogs don't show up until they get older. That bouncy pup and two-year-old becomes a seven-year-old who always requires medication for something. Second, when Libby reviews her notes about the various middle-aged dogs she visited, she realizes that the ones in stable relationships that fulfill their physical, mental, and emotional needs look and act much younger than those where the human-canine-environment balance has swung too far in one direction or the other. While the second fact shouldn't surprise us given all the information about the mind-body effect and the human-animal bond, nonetheless we often overlook this result for a very simple reason: we don't think of these dogs as middle-aged because they appear so much younger.

The Canine Senior Citizen

Like all of the other canine life stages, exactly *when* a dog becomes an "old dog" resists easy definition. In general, giant breeds such as Great Danes and Newfoundlands experience shorter life spans than smaller breeds. Consequently, an eight-year-old New-foundland might deserve senior citizen status, but we'd classify a beagle of that same age as middle-aged.

Because of this, ask the breeder and your veterinarian about the average life expectancy of your dream dog and what kinds of geriatric problems you can expect. When Lenny discovers that Samoyeds can develop skin, hip, and eye problems as they get older, he incorporates meticulous grooming and a conscientious concern for nutrition and weight control into Nika's program from day one. He also trains her using a combination of verbal and hand signals so that if she does develop vision problems, he still can communicate with her.

Of course, even with the best of care, predictable but some-times unsettling changes occur. The once incredible sense of hearing and smell begin to wane; once-crystal-clear lenses in the eyes become cloudy. When Libby stands behind the almost deaf

Ryan and shouts his name, he doesn't respond. If she maintains eye contact, however, and merely mutters the words "Let's go for a ride," the old collie races to the car.

"He can read my lips!" she exclaims proudly.

Maybe, but more likely he picked up on all the body language we owners of car-ride–loving dogs almost inevitably use to augment that simple phrase.

As Ryan's hearing declines further, Libby adds loud claps to orient her dog toward her. When the old collie becomes completely deaf and his vision starts to wane, too, Libby stamps her foot, not in anger, but because she knows Ryan will sense the vibrations and come to her.

How many of these changes an owner notices depends a great deal on lifestyle and environment. Lenny doesn't even realize that 12-year-old Nika's vision has greatly decreased because she knows her way around his home and business so well that he completely misses the fact that she uses scent cues rather than sight to find her way. However, when he takes her with him to house-sit for some friends, she refuses to leave his side.

Given the primal necessity to establish and protect a territory before she feels comfortable enough to eat or drink, we can appreciate the old dog's anxiety in a new environment. Fortunately, Lenny's benevolent leadership frees his pet of the need to assume any protective role. He also applies a lightly scented cologne to his shoes, and sprays a line of scent about a foot from the bottom and top of the stairs, and another light mist on the side of the door jambs opposite that from which the doors swing to provide reliable scent buoys to help Nika navigate the new environment. When he takes her outdoors in dim light or at night, he carries a flashlight to further help orient her, and he replaces basic hand signals with sweeping gestures that she can see more easily.

Just as more frequent at-home examinations of the young pup can produce positive behavioral benefits, increasing them from monthly to weekly can benefit older animals or those with chronic medical problems, too. As usual, though, the owner's relationship with the animal determines the success of this approach. When Libby finds a lump under 10-year-old Ryan's skin, she rushes him to the veterinary clinic.

"It's just a lipoma, a benign fatty tumor," explains the veterinarian. "Feel how smooth it is and how you can get your fingers all the way around it?"

He then uses a needle to extract a sample from the lump and shows Libby the fatty cells under the microscope.

"As long as it stays the same, I see no reason to worry about it," he assures her. "But if it gets bigger, or changes in any way, I want you to let me know."

Unfortunately, Libby succumbs to a major case of "lump-phobia," palpating the lump practically every time she pets her dog. While she thinks this will enable her to pick up any changes sooner, in fact it so confuses her that only a major change will attract her attention.

To understand how this works, imagine Libby gradually changing her hair color over a period of weeks. Unless she tells her co-workers what she's doing, most of them don't even notice because the change occurs so gradually. However, someone absent from the office during this transition notices the change immediately.

"I love your hair that color, Libby!" the returning co-worker gushes, an exclamation that causes everyone else to stare at Libby's hair as if seeing it for the first time.

The same thing happens when we palpate lumps and bumps on our dogs; we can miss subtle changes if we focus on them too much. Because the sooner we detect changes in our dogs, the more effectively we can respond, Libby should limit her checks of Ryan's lump to once a week, or however often her veterinarian recommends. If she can't do this and finds her fingers automatically straying to that area as she and Ryan sit on the couch together, then she should ask a friend to check the lump for her.

Knowing that older dogs, like older people, may develop arthritis, Lenny also pays particular attention when he raises Nika's head to look in her eyes, runs his hands over her shoulders and hips, and lifts her legs when he examines her.

"I've done that right along with her hips and rear legs because of the hip problems in the breed, but since she's gotten older I pay more attention to all her bones and joints," he explains, gently flexing the old snowball's knees. "But I have a friend with a dachshund who's paid a lot of attention to her dog's skeletal system from the beginning because that breed's so prone to slipped disks."

Geriatric veterinary consultations serve as another valuable aid at this stage of life. Although some veterinarians offer physical examinations geared to the special needs of older dogs, I'm referring to *owner* consultations that discuss what your dog's old age will mean to you as well as your pet. Consequently, you may need to tell Dr. Right exactly what kind of information you want. Don't feel shy about doing this, though, because I first learned about it from a client who asked me to provide this information about his aging Old English sheepdog, and it made such good sense that I couldn't imagine why I hadn't thought of it myself. Essentially, you meet with your veterinarian and discuss *everything and anything* that relates to your feelings about your dog's final days.

"That's horrible!" exclaims Libby angrily.

No, it isn't. Horrible is not thinking about it at all and then making a snap decision to euthanize a pet or initiate expensive treatment of a terminally ill animal that you can't afford either financially or emotionally. Horrible is living with all the regret and guilt that will plague you and obliterate all the good memories if you don't work through your feelings on this subject beforehand.

The client who taught me all this, a wonderful man I'll call Dick Glover, owned a 10-year-old dog named Fergie who was beginning to experience some geriatric changes but nothing serious. Dick and his wife, Ellie, both worked, and because he traveled a lot, he didn't want to try to deal with a canine crisis via long-distance or place the burden of making any life-or-death decisions on his wife. Although anthropomorphically oriented owners may see this as callous while chattel-oriented ones view it as totally unnecessary, I see such preparation as one of the most caring things we can do for the canine senior citizen.

Dick and Ellie met with me in my office, without their dog because they wanted to discuss these difficult subjects as objectively as possible. After we reviewed Fergie's health and behavioral record, I gave them worst-case scenarios. Could Ellie lift Fergie if the dog's hips gave out when Dick was away on a business trip? If their pet developed a treatable but terminal condition such as cancer or irreversible kidney failure, what would they want to do? I described how much I could do, and where I could refer them for more specialized care. We discussed the cost of these various options, in terms of not only money but also the time and emotional investments required. Then we discussed what kind of yield the Glovers could expect on their investment.

Over the years I've discovered that many owners initiate heroic treatment of seriously ill or injured animals prepared to face only one of two outcomes: the dog will die, or it will recover completely. However, and especially with older animals, such treatment may result in an animal who requires constant monitoring, special diets, and medication. In the worst-case scenario, the Glovers' choice to treat Fergie for cancer leads to a year filled with 100-mile trips to a specialist, surgery, radiation, and chemotherapy, not to mention all the physical, mental, and emotional side effects that can affect pet and owners alike. Far too often, what begins as an act of love deteriorates into one filled with anger, guilt, and resentment.

"What if we don't want to put her through a lot, but we don't feel we can put her down, either?" the Glovers wanted to know.

More and more veterinarians offer their clients and patients the equivalent of hospice service, complete with support teams. The animal remains in the owner's home where the owner or a member of the support team attends the dog's basic needs and administers any pain-relieving medications necessary to keep the animal comfortable. Although not for everyone, this option offers some owners and their pets the most comfort during a very difficult time.

Next, the Glovers and I discussed euthanasia, beginning with their feelings about it. Some people totally reject the notion, while others will consider it only under certain circumstances. When the Glovers indicated that they would consider it, I told them what it involved. Although many use the phrase "putting the dog to sleep" as a euphemism, in reality that accurately describes what happens. The substances normally injected into a vein on the front leg belong to the same class of drugs used for general anesthesia, but they come in much higher concentrations. Consequently, the animal *does* fall asleep first, then rapidly and painlessly dies.

"Can we stay with her when you do it?" Ellie wanted to know.

Most veterinarians will allow owners to remain with their pets if they wish. If you want to do this and Dr. Right won't permit it, find another Dr. Right. A few points to keep in mind if you stay with your pet, however. One, because of the bond effect, the more support you can offer your pet at this time, the more relaxed it will be. Whatever benefit Ellie may derive from sobbing hysterically throughout the entire process, it won't help Fergie at all. Second, whether an animal dies naturally or from euthanasia, a normal part of the dying process may include several sudden gasps (called agonal breathing) and/or emptying of the bladder and bowels, so prepare yourself for this possibility.

Three, if you want some time alone with your pet afterward, tell your veterinarian; if you desire the vet or a favorite technician to spend a few moments with you while you recover, mention that, too.

A few final points about euthanasia in general. Don't *ever* let anyone—family, friends, veterinarian—force you to put your dog down, even if their reasons sound perfectly logical to you. Owners who do this rarely thank those people. Instead, they often become angry and resentful toward them and may even come to believe they failed their pets when the animals needed them most. Given all the different treatment plus hospice options, many times you can buy yourself some time to work through your feelings. On the other hand, if you work them through now, you won't find yourself in this painfully difficult position any more than you'll allow your pet to suffer needlessly because *you're* afraid to let go. Finally, if you opt for euthanasia and don't want to stay with your pet, *don't feel guilty about it*. Loving owners can say good-by to their pets in many different ways, and what works for one person may not work for another.

Next the Glovers and I discussed disposition of the body. In the small town where they lived, they could bury her at home, but laws in more populated areas may prohibit this. Cremation (incineration of the animal's remains) with or without the return of the ashes, and burial at a pet cemetery round out the options available for most owners. However, some usually highly anthropomorphic owners who can't let go will take advantage of services that will stuff and mount, freeze-dry, or mummify the family pet.

At the conclusion of our consultation, the Glovers and I examined their relationship with Fergie within the context of their various limits. By the end of our time together, they possessed a good understanding of their options and what each of these meant for them and their dog. Then they went home and discussed it more until they felt comfortable facing this inevitable future. Considering this while Fergie was still quite healthy enabled these owners to put enough distance between themselves and the subject of death to ensure a thoughtful and objective analysis.

When we euthanized Fergie three years later, only sorrow over the passing of a dear friend and many fond memories marked the event. I never once heard the Glovers utter a word of regret before or after the fact, only their heartfelt thanks that they'd taken the time to learn about and evaluate their options before that day arrived. Like them, I didn't feel any regret, either—only gratitude to the Glovers for recognizing their limits, finding the courage to ask me to provide a wonderful service I'd never even considered before, and sharing the quality and magnitude of their love for their dog that led them to do both.

The Final Analysis

Imagine your dog as a senior citizen under the best and worst conditions. Analyze these in terms of your orientation toward dogs, your lifestyle, and your environment. How well will the training, exercise, feeding, and health-care programs you selected adapt to meet the needs of a canine senior citizen? How far can you afford to go if your dog became terminally ill? How far would you *want* to go? How do you feel about euthanasia? Treating your dog at home? What services does your veterinarian offer for the critically ill or injured animal? If you wanted more for your pet, where would you go?

Talk to people who own older animals and those whose pets have died. Many busy owners of aging animals devise all kinds of tricks and shortcuts to meet the older pet's changing needs. One thing I can guarantee: the more you learn beforehand, the less fear you'll experience during *any* problem that occurs at *any* time during your relationship with your new dog, but especially during your last years together.

Better than Gold

A sports enthusiast most likely would urge you to go for the gold when it comes to finding and keeping the perfect canine companion. However, a relationship with a new dog based on your knowledge of your orientation toward animals, your limits, your dream dog, and your environment, and the best programs to complement all this reminds me much more of silver—my mother's silver, to be exact.

When Mom died, my legacy consisted primarily of what she called the "family silver," premiums she amassed from what seemed like eight million boxes of "Mother's Oats" which she forced us to eat in her doggedly determined effort to add this bit of silver-plated elegance to our humble home.

I don't recall now whether the utensils actually came in the boxes of cereal the way towels and washcloths came in boxes of detergent back then, or whether Mom collected labels or box tops to obtain this treasure. But the memory of facing a bowlful of the dreaded glop every morning until Mom got those hundred-odd pieces of silver remains vividly clear after all these years. Then and now I truly believe that, had Mom taken the money she spent on milk, butter, raisins, brown sugar, maple syrup, and everything else we kids dumped on that oatmeal in a futile attempt to make it edible, she could have bought a set of solid sterling.

Still, Mom treasured that collection and kept it in its own special chest in the bottom drawer of the buffet for use only on special occasions. Further undermining the silver's credibility in my eyes at that age, though, was that we had to polish it, an event that loomed on the horizon of every holiday like a pasty gray blob of Wright's Silver Polish.

Perhaps because of this, I felt no desire to own any silver of my own. However, I did feel pleased when Mom's meager collection came to me, her only "silverless" offspring, and I immediately took the stainless flatware out of my kitchen drawer and installed the oatmeal collection.

"You keep your mother's silver in your kitchen drawer!" a friend squawked when I happened to mention this.

Theoretically, I could rationalize doing so by saying, "Oh, it's not expensive silver." However, I placed it there because I wanted to use it daily, to experience the weight and feel of those thousands of bowls of oatmeal and hundreds of holidays and all the other fond memories of my mom. I didn't want to keep all that tucked in a cupboard somewhere.

When we get a new dog, at first everything about it and our relationship with it seems so bright and shiny, we want that feeling to last forever. Some owners never get past this point, keeping the dog and the relationship on a shelf, as it were, never making the necessary changes and adaptations as their own and their dog's needs change.

Other, more fortunate owners become involved in a dynamic relationship that constantly molds and remolds itself as dog and owner grow, and that initial brightness slowly gives way to a special patina that only the closest examination reveals consists of all the innumerable tiny scratches that accrue in the process of living a fulfilling life. Every dog owner remembers the trauma associated with those first few scratches: that April 15th Nika chewed Lenny's completed income tax forms; the day the pup snapped at him; the time she got into the oil he forgot to put away.

Over time, however, as dog and owner begin to work more and more as a unit, the scratches take on a different quality: Nika rushing to greet customers, rolling with kids in the backyard, sitting beside Lenny every night while he reads the newspaper, wagging her tail in delight every time he mentions the word "ride."

Perhaps one of the greatest joys of dog ownership comes from the awareness that this four-legged, fur-covered creature provides us with an opportunity to learn as much about ourselves as about this member of another species willing to share itself with us. Given a solid base of knowledge and the willingness to adapt, we can celebrate the relationship with our dogs daily. We don't need to worry about it getting scratched or dinged. We don't need to coddle and baby it lest it come to harm. We don't need to apologize to others for the problems that tarnish it, or drag it out and spend hours cleaning it up before company comes.

When we recognize and accept our own needs and limits and select a dog and programs to meet them, every day becomes a holiday, and this bright new addition to our lives can only grow more precious and glowing with age.

Go for the silver!

Index